Shakespeare's Suicides

C000139776

Shakespeare's Suicides: Dead Bodies That Matter is the first study in Shakespeare criticism to examine the entirety of Shakespeare's dramatic suicides. It addresses all plays featuring suicides and near-suicides in chronological order from *Titus Andronicus* to *Antony and Cleopatra*, thus establishing that suicide becomes increasingly pronounced as a vital means of dramatic characterisation. In particular, the book approaches suicide as a gendered phenomenon. By taking into account parameters such as onstage versus offstage deaths, suicide speeches or the explicit denial of final words, as well as settings and weapons, the study scrutinises the ways in which Shakespeare appropriates the convention of suicide and subverts traditional notions of masculine versus feminine deaths. It shows to what extent a gendered approach towards suicide opens up a more nuanced understanding of the correlation between gender and Shakespeare's genres and how, eventually, through their dramatisation of suicide, the tragedies query normative gender discourse.

Marlena Tronicke is Assistant Professor of English at the University of Münster, Germany. Apart from Shakespeare and early modern drama in general, her areas of research and teaching include adaptation, Neo-Victorianism, as well as contemporary British theatre.

Routledge Studies in Shakespeare

For a full list of titles in this series, please visit www.routledge.com.

Shakespeare's Suicides
Dead Bodies That Matter

Marlena Tronicke

Routledge
Taylor & Francis Group

LONDON AND NEW YORK

First published 2018 by Routledge

2 Park Square, Milton Park, Abingdon, Oxfordshire OX14 4RN
52 Vanderbilt Avenue, New York, NY 10017

Routledge is an imprint of the Taylor & Francis Group, an informa business

First issued in paperback 2019

Copyright © 2018 Taylor & Francis

Library of Congress Cataloging-in-Publication Data
CIP data has been applied for.

ISBN: 978-0-8153-8044-3 (hbk)
ISBN: 978-0-367-89096-4 (pbk)

Typeset in Sabon
by codeMantra

Contents

Acknowledgements

During the past five years, I have learnt that writing a book is much less of a solitary experience than I expected it to be, and I am much obliged to a number of people who have been generous with their time and intellect. Since this monograph started out as a PhD thesis at the University of Münster, I first and foremost thank my supervisors Klaus Stierstorfer and Florian Kläger for their invaluable insight, guidance, as well as continued confidence in me and my work. I am furthermore greatly indebted to Franziska Quabeck, who never tired of discussing my ideas with me and without whose advice and encouragement this endeavour probably would have been less successful, but most definitely less enjoyable. To Laura Schmitz-Justen I am immensely grateful for volunteering to read and discuss the individual chapters multiple times and in various stages, and Rainer Gocke I need to thank for his meticulous proofreading. In place of the many more wonderful teachers, colleagues, and students who shared their knowledge with me and from whose suggestions I have benefitted I would also like to mention Anna Thiemann, who encouraged me not to take the easy way out on the final laps especially. Special thanks also go to the anonymous readers for their constructive and judicious comments as well as to the excellent editorial team at Routledge. Last but not least, I owe a great debt to my parents, family, and friends, without whose love and support I would not have come this far.

Individual passages of the chapter "Knitting the Cord: *Titus Andronicus*" appeared as "The Pain of Others: Silencing Lavinia in *Titus Andronicus*" in *Shakespeare Seminar Online* 13 (2015), a journal published under the auspices of the German Shakespeare Society. They are re-published here by permission.

Textual Note

Throughout, quotations from Shakespeare's works are given parenthetically. Unless indicated otherwise, all such references are to *The Arden Shakespeare Complete Works*, ed. Richard Proudfoot, Ann Thompson, and David Scott Kastan, rev. ed. (London: Arden Shakespeare, 2002). Wherever I have consulted different editions, either for editorial notes or textual differences, these are specified in a separate note.

List of Abbreviations

Ado	*Much Ado About Nothing*
AWW	*All's Well That Ends Well*
AYL	*As You Like It*
Cor.	*Coriolanus*
Cym.	*Cymbeline*
Jn.	*King John*
Luc.	*The Rape of Lucrece*
MND	*A Midsummer Night's Dream*
Oth.	*Othello*
Tim.	*Timon of Athens*
TNK	*The Two Noble Kinsmen*
Tro.	*Troilus and Cressida*

Introduction

That suicide is a pre-eminent concern of Shakespeare's tragedies hardly needs to be argued. Hamlet's "To be, or not to be" soliloquy, probably the most famous line in literature, is a speech weighing the pros and cons of committing suicide. And suicide also seals the fate of history's most iconic pair of lovers, Romeo and Juliet. In each of the tragedies, most notably in the Roman plays, the stage is virtually littered with the bodies of suicides. *Antony and Cleopatra*, for example, features no less than five onstage self-killings, and in several plays, characters die offstage, but nevertheless, their deaths are reported as suicides. In total, Shakespeare's dramatic oeuvre showcases fifteen suicides as well as several suicide attempts, a murder that is labelled suicide by the alleged victim, and a comic mock-suicide performance. Suicidal blood is only spilled in the tragedies, which, at first glance, seems understandable. Death has no place within the generic framework of comedy, and suicide even less so. In *Antony and Cleopatra*, however, Shakespeare toys with the boundaries of tragedy, not least through the play's distinctive illustrations of suicide. Moreover, *A Midsummer Night's Dream* in particular proves a striking counterpoint here.

Apart from these obvious and well-known examples, there are a number of plays in which nobody commits suicide but that address the topic nonetheless. Regardless of their specific subgenre, these plays introduce suicide as a possible option only to abandon it again immediately. Amongst others, such references include minor, playful remarks. Parolles pesters Helena by commenting "He that hangs himself is a virgin; virginity murthers itself, and should be buried in highways out of all sanctified limits, as a desperate offendress against nature" (*AWW* 1.1.139–142). To the love-sick Orlando's "Then in mine own person, I die," Rosalind-as-Ganymede mockingly responds "Troilus had his brains dashed out with a Grecian club, yet he did what he could to die before, and he is one of the patterns of love" (*AYL* 4.1.88–95). And Cressida is so annoyed by Pandarus's constant interference that she dismisses him with the words "Go hang yourself, you naughty mocking uncle" (*Tro.* 4.2.26). On the other hand, there are more serious instances. In *King John*, Constance grieves the loss of her son Arthur with the words "My reasonable part produces reason / How I may be deliver'd of these woes, / And teaches me to kill or hang myself" (3.3.54–56). And when thinking that Hubert has murdered the boy, the Bastard is quite inventive in his contempt:

> And if thou want'st a cord, the smallest thread
> That ever spider twisted from her womb
> Will serve to strangle thee; a rush will be a beam
> To hang thee on; or wouldst thou drown thyself,
> Put but a little water in a spoon,
> And it shall be as all the ocean,
> Enough to stifle such a villain up.
>
> (*Jn.* 4.3.127–133)

The Dauphin's outcry in *Henry V*, "O perdurable shame! Let's stab our-selves," (4.5.7) is a reaction to the news that the battle is lost. Tormented by his unrequited love for Desdemona, Roderigo announces that he "will incontinently drown" himself (*Oth.* 1.3.307). Last but not least, Richard manipulates Anne by crying out "bid me kill myself, and I will do it" (*R3* 1.2.190). In none of these passages is the topic explored in great detail. References to suicide here function as a means to articulate the seriousness of an emotion or a situation. Nevertheless, these instances emphasise the relevance of suicide as a concept within Shakespearean drama. But what, then, is its function in those plays that exceed the mere talking about suicide and in which actual self-inflicted deaths take place on or offstage?

Several tragedies offer relatively precise discussions of historical at-titudes towards suicide, be it in the classical, medieval, or Renaissance context. Clearly, these are never accurate historical but palimpsestu-ous representations, always infused by early modern notions towards the topic. And yet, these plays engage with what suicide meant in an-cient Rome, pre-Christian Britain, or late-medieval Denmark, general interpretive paradigms that Shakespeare's audiences would have been at least rudimentarily aware of. Most notably in this context, *Hamlet* has received extensive commentary for its illustration of contemporary ecclesiastical teachings. Thus, it is not surprising that Hamlet's iconic soliloquies, too, employ a line of argument based on religious concerns. After all, suicide was a grave sin in the eyes of the Church.

As Albert Camus has phrased it, "[t]here is but one truly serious philo-sophical problem and that is suicide."[1] He addresses the twentieth-century context, of course, and it is not until Émile Durkheim's landmark study *On Suicide* (1897) that suicide is increasingly approached as a product of society rather than the individual.[2] However, Camus's credo equally encapsulates the debate on suicide throughout the history of ideas. The following serves as an overview of the opposing forces at work in classical antiquity and the Middle Ages, leading to a somewhat fractured but also more progressive image of suicide towards the middle and late Renaissance. Inevitably, this can only be a rather curtailed account, but it should suffice to provide an understanding of the ideological background(s) against which to consider the suicides in those tragedies that presuppose a classical Roman, early-medieval, or late-medieval/Renaissance setting.

A Brief History of Suicide

Ancient Rome is renowned for its culture of suicide in particular, with illustrious examples ranging from Socrates, Plato, Cato, Seneca, Brutus, and Antony to Lucretia and Cleopatra, to name but a few. In all of these cases, the precise manner of their deaths is preserved in extensive (literary) accounts, which often describe a carefully staged spectacle. However, this sense of display and performance is not limited to these famous suicides. Rather, self-killing in classical antiquity was generally understood as a public gesture.[3] Death by falling on one's own sword came to be known as the most common form of 'Roman death', a convention Shakespeare reflects in his Roman tragedies. Characters ponder the question of how to follow this convention in an adequate way and are furthermore judged by whether they have succeeded in committing a proper Roman suicide. Nevertheless, it would be an oversimplification to state that Greek and Roman attitudes were unanimously supportive. Even though the notion of suicide as a horrifying, sinful act only developed towards late antiquity and principally the early Middle Ages, it has never been looked upon entirely positively, let alone celebrated.

Early discussions of suicide in ancient Greece are devoid of any overly positive or negative emotional connotations. Plato's *Phaedo* is usually identified as the point of origin as far as any discussion of suicide is concerned, but his account of Socrates's self-inflicted death is ambiguous at best and, as a consequence, has been used as evidence both in favour and against suicide by later commentators. The Socrates in this text considers bodily life a form of bondage, a hindrance to all wisdom and philosophical liberty; death, on the other hand, provides freedom. At the same time, Socrates makes clear that suicide is only acceptable in case one has received a divine signal.[4] According to Plato, suicide is unlawful since the taking of life is the prerogative of the gods. Still, there are certain circumstances that justify self-killing, as, for instance, a specific order by stately authorities, unbearable pain, or the attempt to avoid public humiliation. If one committed suicide for other, lesser, reasons such as fear or mundane life-weariness, it would have to be treated as a crime and punished accordingly.[5]

The philosophical school most frequently brought into context with suicide are the Stoics, even though the notion of suicide as the centre of Stoic philosophy is misleading. The Epicureans are generally thought to be opposed to suicide, and whereas suicide became a prime concern for Seneca, early Stoicism only briefly touches upon the issue. It allows suicide, but not under all circumstances and merely at the premise of having considered it rationally and carefully. Only motivations that would prevent a person from leading a virtuous life are regarded as acceptable and do not result in a rejection of one's social duties.[6] Seneca, however, saw suicide as "the ultimate justification of man's freedom, perhaps even as the only genuinely free act,"[7] thus contributing to the conception of Stoicism as a suicide cult.

As the notion of suicide as a public gesture already implies, suicide in classical antiquity was a distinctly male action. Although ancient myths recorded myriad examples of female self-killings, in reality, women's confinement to the private sphere did not allow for such actions. This is also reflected in the choice of weapon, which may sound negligible but proves significant for the Roman concept of suicide. The notion of an honourable death is closely connected to the integrity of the body because the deceased were believed to continue their afterlife in the same physical form they left this world in. For this reason, hanging and throwing oneself off a high building, potentially causing severe deformation of the body, was frowned upon and deemed a vulgar form of death. As Anton van Hoof explains, this "preoccupation with *dignitas* in living and dying is of course strongest in the elite which adheres to the values of manliness: only metal befits the representative of *virtus*."[8] Despite several mythical representations of women choosing this traditionally masculine form of Roman death, in real life, swords belonged to the public sphere, and so women, as well as slaves, had to revert to domestic weapons. Suicide by poison, on the other hand, was devalued as 'un-Roman' and too banal to be considered in philosophical debates on what makes a 'good death'.[9]

In the first place, a Roman death signified self-killing in order to preserve one's honour and to avoid public humiliation. Further motives were despair, madness, self-sacrifice, and the state of being forced into suicide. A respectable suicide out of grief could be motivated by the death of a lover, a relative, or a friend, even though grieving was considered a task reserved for women.[10] Rowland Wymer suggests that these connotations of a Roman death as a noble gesture prevailed in the collective consciousness – not least owing to the many heroic political suicides – and that these proved more influential to the Renaissance concept of suicide than any philosophical rationalisations.[11]

At the beginning of the Middle Ages, ideology hardened substantially. The Church denounced all legitimations brought forward by Greek and Roman philosophy and instead fostered reprobation of suicide as a mortal sin through religion, folk belief, and common law. When investigating the phenomenon of suicide in a medieval or early modern context, the anachronistic use of the term 'suicide' with all its modern associations proves difficult. With the Middle Ages in partic- ular, historians have to face the additional problem that the term as such does not exist. It is commonly agreed that it first occurred in Sir Thomas Browne's *Religio Medici* (1637), which is largely attributed to the fact that suicide was a taboo topic.[12] While terms for other sins and crimes already developed in the twelfth century, suicide "was ostra- cized from this great verbal colonization" because it was simply "too terrible to talk about."[13] Unlike classical antiquity, the Middle Ages saw suicide as an exclusively private act, and hence, textual documents put great emphasis on the fact that the deceased had been on their own when committing the most shameful of all actions. In case a suicide in the family was detected, relatives would have had to be prepared to face severe punishments in place of the deceased. Amongst others, this in- cluded a possible loss of property. Yet, what weighed most heavily was the stain on the family honour.[14]

The Catholic Church took an almost unanimously condemning stance towards suicide, but this was only poorly supported by the Bible itself, which provides neither moral evaluation nor outright condemnation of the act. Primarily, the Church took their legitimisation for condemning suicide from St. Augustine's *The City of God* (426), which provided a solid basis for theological writings to follow. According to St. Augustine, the mere suggestion of suicide is sinful, which may explain why until the twelfth century he had been the only one to address the topic.[15] To legitimise his crusade against suicide, he mainly builds on the Sixth Commandment. Even though the Bible remains silent in regard to how the bodies of suicides should be buried, the wide range of macabre and absurd burial rituals was as firmly grounded in religious teaching as it was in superstition. The first possible and still relatively humane option was the so-called 'non-burial', an absence of any form of religious cer- emony and consecrated gravesite. Shakespeare references this norm in 5.1 of *Hamlet*, the gravediggers' debate about whether Ophelia should receive the full burial rites. Within the English context, the specific or- der for burials as laid out in the *Book of Common Prayer*, introduced by Thomas Cranmer in 1549, is preceded by a note that "the Office ensuing is not to be used for any that die unbaptized, or excommuni- cate, or have laid violent hands upon themselves."[16] Also, there were more drastic options, such as open fields, a burial under the gallows, the carrion-pit, road junctions, riverbanks, or shores. The most shameful of these was the burial at crossroads, deliberately turned into a public spectacle as a warning to others and to shame the next of kin.[17] In the face of such practices, Brian Cummings cautions not to overestimate the role of Christian apologetics. As he suggests, theological positions were strongly influenced, if not pre-determined, by the social and especially legal condemnation of suicide.[18]

At the beginning of the early modern period, legal prosecution with its draconian punishments was still in practice. Nonetheless, in order to be found guilty of 'felonious suicide', one had to be mentally sane. As a consequence, the majority of suicides were declared lunatic, drowned, etc., and so there are no reliable figures as to how many people actually committed the act.[19] Michael MacDonald, on the other hand, asserts that madness would have counted as a mitigating factor only in theory. While the law provided the possibility of a *non compos mentis* verdict for cases such as Ophelia's, this was rarely ever put into practice.[20] Early modern thought believed suicides to be excluded from both the communities of the dead and the living. Never able to complete their passage to the afterlife, they were expected to haunt the living in the form of malevolent ghosts, and hence, the suicides' bodies had stakes driven through their hearts in order to fix them firmly to their graves.[21]

Various disciplines offered pseudo-scientific explanations for what today is often named clinical depression. Humorism established a connection to melancholy, most famously in Robert Burton's *The Anatomy of Melancholy* (1621).[22] But primarily, and in line with medieval ideology, suicide was attributed to the sin of despair. The opposite of hope as a Christian virtue, suicide was envisaged the gravest of all temptations brought about by Satan himself, an idea already inherent in the medieval concept of suicide.[23] Wymer indicates that even though despair in its original, that is, religious, connotation remains an important motif in early modern drama, the prevailing sense is that of a more generalised hopelessness resembling the modern sense of the term.[24]

Whereas the Reformation generally brought about changing attitudes towards death, this did not imply a paradigmatic shift of how to approach suicide from an ecclesiastical viewpoint. For Luther, suicidal despair was still induced by the Devil. Even though he acknowledged that humans were vulnerable to such 'satanic temptations', he fostered the established, draconian forms of punishment implemented by the Catholic Church. Simultaneously, he insisted that people who verifiably killed themselves as victims of the Devil could nevertheless receive Christian burial rites. "In this scheme of thinking," Robert Houston explains, "the Devil could be an external agent or an invited helper able to act physically."[25] Accordingly, there were only slight changes with regard to burial practices, modified solely insofar as the withholding of Christian rites was no longer considered a punishment of the dead. Instead, maimed rites were used as a method of deterrence to the bereaved.[26] More moderate views gradually began to form towards the end of the seventeenth century. During the course of the Renaissance, the notion of 'conscience' was radically re-evaluated and gained prominence, a shift that also affected the formerly dogmatic conceptualisation of suicide.

Thus, by the turn of the century, self-killing was no longer considered a crime against God's divine world order but rather a question of choice and individual conscience.[27]

At the same time, Renaissance Humanism, with its rediscovery of classical knowledge and values, promoted the more tolerant attitude towards suicide originating from before the Middle Ages. The ethics of suicide and its intricate link to sinfulness was gradually reassessed. Nonetheless, the problem was far from solved. Two of the most influential intellectual debates on suicide are provided by Michel de Montaigne and John Donne. Montaigne's complex rhetorical masterpiece "A Custom of the Isle of Cea" (1573/74) proposes a perspective that deviated from the Church's position considerably, featuring scandalous propositions such as "The fairest death is one that is most willed. Our lives depend on the will of others: our death depends on our own. [...] Living is slavery if the freedom to die is wanting."[28] Importantly, however, Montaigne argues neither in favour of nor against suicide. More precisely, his essay aims to carve out the complexity of the problem. He does not arrive at an abstract or universal conclusion but presents suicide as a solution faced by an individual in a particular, difficult situation; Georges Minois speaks of "a question of situational morality."[29] John Donne's *Biathanatos* (1608), tellingly subtitled *A Declaration of That Paradox or Thesis That Self-Homicide Is Not So Naturally Sin, That It May Never Be Otherwise*, is the first major English work challenging the sinfulness of the act. Moreover, he is the first to place himself within Christian doctrine on the subject. In the three stages of his argument, he investigates whether suicide is against the law of nature, law of reason, or law of God. Due to its paradoxical argumentative structure and style, today, *Biathanatos* is often approached as a satire rather than a treatise on suicide, and Donne is aware that he embarks on a dangerous venture. Like Montaigne's carefully veiled essay, Donne's text is traced with safeguarding remarks so as not to sound too universal and hence be responsible for possible suicides resulting from an overly positive reading.[30] Similar to Montaigne, Donne arrives at the conclusion that suicide might well be justified in some cases but not in others, and so he advances a more charitable treatment and refuses a universal condemnation.

Inevitably, such a hotly debated and controversial topic also found its way onto the early modern theatrical stage. Already throughout the Middle Ages, theological denunciation of suicide had coexisted with more favourable literary treatments, particularly in the context of the courtly love tradition. Elizabethan and Jacobean drama explored this even further because playwrights in particular became eager to explore the dramatic potential of suicide. Here, both medieval and classical influences are traceable and intermingled in the representations of suicide onstage. Notions of heroism and nobility going back to antiquity did not so much replace as add to the medieval concept of suicide as an act of despair.[31] As Jacqueline Vanhoutte points out, such a coexistence of two diverging ideologies was possible since "[t]he classical paradigm tended to select for praise those who killed themselves to preserve honor or communally held values. Thus, whereas the common suicide retreated dangerously from public responsibility, the heroic suicide in effect affirmed his or her commitment to communal life."[32] Nonetheless, the relatively favourable dramatic representation of the topic and the early modern enthusiasm for drama is not to be confused with a toleration of suicide in real life. Suicide remained controversial, which made it a tricky but simultaneously productive topic for any playwright to engage with.

Approaching Suicide in Shakespeare's Plays

Even though they are referenced in most of the tragedies included in this book, sometimes extensively so, I consider these questions of philosophical contemplation, theological denunciation, social stigma, and legal persecution mere historical background information. It is necessary to be aware of such frameworks to understand the ways in which play-inherent discussions surrounding suicide are always judgmental, either positively or negatively, but they cannot account for the more pertinent questions with regard to compelling drama or dramatic characters. Much more than by a prosaic evaluation of whether the Church might sanction suicide, audiences should be struck by the discrepancy between the deaths of Hamlet, who constantly talks about killing himself only to then defer any kind of action, and Ophelia, who, despite being marginalised into passivity by all the other characters in the play, plucks up the courage to commit suicide. And what about Macbeth's statement of not wanting to play the "Roman fool" (5.8.1), which seems an ill-fitting line in a play that could not be further apart from the moral standards of ancient Rome? Too narrow a focus on either religious or historical concerns neglects one decisive aspect: Shakespeare's suicides never simply happen out of necessity. With the exception of those cases in which Shakespeare dramatises a historical suicide – as, for instance, in the case of Brutus, Antony, and Cleopatra – self-killing is not the only way for a character to exit the play. In tragedy in particular, convention dictates that characters have to be written off at one point or another. Nonetheless, the stock of possible exits is diverse, and so the exact method and execution are to be worked out by the playwright. In this way, stage suicides are deliberate constructions imposed by the author. They necessarily carry symbolic meaning and, therefore, have to be approached as key constituents of dramatic characterisation.[33]

While it is generally problematic and often futile to discuss possible influences on Shakespeare's plays, such information may be relevant when it comes to deliberate deviations from and hence reinterpretations of the source material. With suicide, this is often the case since Shakespeare frequently imports almost everything but specifically changes the characters' deaths. Thus, it is vital to re-evaluate the myriad ways in which Shakespeare dramatises suicide in order to find out to what extent a staging, or indeed not staging, of suicide shapes the portrayal of a dramatic character. As Margaret Higonnet points out, "[t]o take one's life is to force others to read one's death. For when we categorize a death we do not record a pure fact (if any such exist). Rather, we produce a reading that depends upon the physical and subjective context: natural or unnatural death, homicide or suicide. As with all human actions, we ask questions about free will and determinism. In the case of suicide, the hermeneutic task is particularly elusive. Only when the primary evidence has been destroyed does the trace exist to be followed and interpreted."[34] Whereas some figures, such as Lady Macbeth or Portia, put an end to their life without prior announcement and die hidden away from the eyes of the audience, others add to this hermeneutic process through lengthy suicide speeches. I consider both these justifications that characters provide as their final words and the explicit denial thereof vehicles of (self)dramatisation, deliberate and carefully choreographed gestures rather than indices of resignation.

Regarding such dramaturgical concerns, the question of who dies onstage is a particularly compelling one, and it is certainly worth looking for specific patterns. Marvin Spevack does so and summarises his findings in a simple formula: "The fiendish or unrepentant tend to find a fitting end off stage: Aaron in *Tit.* and Iago, Goneril and Regan, Lady Macbeth. Sympathetic women are spared the onstage display: Portia, Ophelia, Cordelia, Lady Macduff. Dramatic pointing is apparent in the fact that the stage may be cleared of bodies to spotlight the onstage deaths of titular characters."[35] Spevack's problematic categorisation of "fiendish" and "unrepentant" aside, his argument seems flawed. Whereas for some it is a reward not having to die onstage, others deserve to be written off, he posits. What he does not consider is that in all such cases, the offstage death is a form of marginalisation, of being excluded from the central action of the play. When taking a closer look at the names he mentions, rather than a question of 'good' or 'bad', this seems to be an issue of gender. All the offstage deaths he lists are women characters, gracefully stepping aside so as not to steal the limelight from the tragic heroes.

The distinction between onstage and offstage is only one of the many parameters suggesting a gendering of suicides. For this reason, my book looks at the tragedies through a feminist lens, paying special attention to the various female suicides and their (non)staging. In *Over Her Dead Body*, Elisabeth Bronfen identifies a certain unease in looking at female bodies. Although there are a number of representations of female death, in literature as well as the visual arts, "we only see it with some difficulty."[36] For Bronfen, such discomfort speaks of culture's inability to either openly address or else fully supress the reality of death, which is why its representations tend to be localised in the feminine body, "the superlative site of alterity."[37] A differentiation between different 'kinds' of bodies, some less and some more fascinating, threatening, or important than others, similarly guides Judith Butler's *Precarious Life*. In times of war, Butler argues, the collective 'we' tends to be constructed via the politics of mourning. Whereas some lives are considered 'grievable', others are not, an understanding that both presupposes and reinforces "certain exclusionary conceptions of who is normatively human: what counts as a livable life and a grievable death?"[38] Even though the generic framework of tragedy is different from the political context Butler talks about, Shakespeare's tragedies follow similar politics of representation. Whereas male characters are supposedly dramatically superior and hence 'grievable', major female suicides – with the exception of Juliet and Cleopatra, both of whom are acknowledged in the title of their respective plays – are confined to the offstage space. Are these deaths, therefore, less 'grievable' and, by extension, less important?

What can be deduced from Butler's notion of 'grievability' is the question of whether suicides, male or female, can and should be mourned at all. This is an important concern within medieval and Renaissance theological debates, but it is equally relevant within the context of drama. As Michael Neill remarks, "[o]n the one hand, suicide can be celebrated as a sublime folding in of the self upon itself, an assertion of integrity in the very act of disintegration; on the other, it represents the extreme of paradoxical self-division."[39] For this reason, it is crucial to explore whether Shakespeare's suicides should be considered along the lines of losses and defeat or whether they should be understood in the same way many characters themselves present their deaths: as self-determined, possibly triumphant, endings and victories.

Other than implying a gendered distinction, the differentiation between onstage and offstage deaths begs a discussion of stage spaces in connection with dramatic relevance. The relationship between the onstage and offstage space has always been considered semantically charged, often contrastive. In *The Shakespearean Stage Space*, Mariko Ichikawa contextualises the relation between these locales within the concrete, early modern playhouse reality and explores how both are equally decisive in shaping the audiences' imagination. Any simplistic view of onstage/interesting versus offstage/uninteresting therefore seems naïve and dated. In the history plays, the important action equally takes place behind the scenes because staging elaborate battle scenes is simply too difficult. In the case of dying, too, this is sometimes a question of 'stageability', especially if it involves drowning or beheading.[40] However, the doubtful argument of space is still regularly invoked with regard to the significance, or rather insignificance, of (female) offstage suicides. If Shakespeare does not feel it necessary to focus on the suicides of Lady Macbeth and Goneril, why should audiences? After all, it is a matter of inclusion versus exclusion from dramatic attention. Yet, what should not be overlooked is that by telling rather than showing how a character dies, reported deaths are automatically less immediate and therefore filtered. So surely, it must be significant that this only happens with female suicides.

And yet, this ostensibly neat distribution of male and female suicides into onstage and offstage deaths does not necessarily mean that Shakespeare conforms to such an easy dichotomy. Instead, I suggest that in all of his tragedies, Shakespeare appropriates the convention of suicide, thus subverting traditional connotations of masculine versus feminine deaths. That way, such a binary is rendered obsolete, and hence, restrictive forms of gender identity are challenged. The often neglected and trivialised technicalities of suicide, too, have to be put at the centre of attention. Why, for instance, do both Horatio and Romeo seek a conventionally gentle death through poison despite holding a sword in their hand? Neither weapons nor locations are chosen arbitrarily. On the contrary, they are key parts in an intricate web of symbolic meaning, exploiting cultural contexts of suicide through both affirmation and subversion to full dramatic effect.

In *Comic Women, Tragic Men*, Linda Bamber posits a straightforward correlation between gender and genre. As her title implies, she argues that while the tragedies privilege the tragic hero and prioritise concepts of masculinity, the comedies belong to the women, not least because of the frequent instances of cross-dressing. Furthermore, she characterises the tragedies as powerfully misogynistic, a general tone and ideology she takes as indicative of Shakespeare's masculine viewpoint.[41] But her title seems a little too easy and negative as far as female agency is concerned, and subsequent feminist critics have argued accordingly. As Valerie Traub makes clear, feminist or queer approaches to Shakespeare's works do not set out to identify him as either feminist or misogynist, homosexual or homophobe. Rather, they unearth Shakespeare's infinite variety in responding "alternatively to sex, gender, and sexuality as crucial determinants of human identity and political power."[42] Such a view exceeds Bamber's categorisation and allows for a less formalist reading of gendered power relations, as I propose in this book. Phyllis Rackin, too, challenges previous Shakespearean feminist criticism for having unjustly and misleadingly overemphasised the oppression of and misogynist attitudes towards women, both on the Shakespearean stage and its early modern historical context. In her view, "the problem is that the conceptual categories that shape contemporary scholarly discourse, no less than the historical records of the past, are often man-made and shaped by men's anxieties, desires, and interests. As such, they constitute instruments of women's exclusion, and often of women's oppression."[43]

With clear distinctions between masculine versus feminine weapons and executions, suicide – Roman suicide especially – is a prime example of a man-made concept that has shaped scholarly discourse. Critical discussions of Shakespearean suicides have prioritised male over female deaths, no matter how poignant they may be, which is why the concept is worth re-examining.

My study intersects with Traub's, Rackin's, and related approaches in the way that it seeks to do away with the assumption of suicide as a sign of defeat and victimisation, an interpretation that is almost exclusively applied to female suicides in the canon. Contrary to such an opinion, I argue that Shakespeare's female suicides unanimously can be read as connoting voice, agency, and revolt against patriarchal oppression. So, if suicide is treated as one of many gendered, in other words culturally formed and sustained, conventions, this inevitably opens up a more nuanced perspective on the correlation between gender and Shakespeare's genres. More specifically, what such an approach sheds light on is that in their portrayals of suicide, the tragedies interrogate their own power structures. The often ironic, but never uncritical, representations of masculinity and suicide allow for a reading that questions rather than reaffirms patriarchal hegemony. I do not claim that Shakespeare is a feminist, and neither do I suggest that Shakespeare's tragic women are as powerful and dominant as the men. What I do, however, suggest is that through their portrayal of suicide, the tragedies query normative gender discourse more generally, certainly more strongly than is often assumed.

It is widely accepted that the normative Elizabethan and Jacobean gender discourse in question conceived of gender as "teleologically male,"[44] even though, of course, the term 'gender' did not yet exist. Next to the biblical image of creation, classical medical texts in particular proved influential, above all those by Galen and Aristotle. If certain men appeared less masculine than others, according to Humorism, such an atypical expression of gender identity could be explained by a slight imbalance of bodily humours.[45] The notion of sexual difference as operating on a continuum is also resonant in what Thomas Laqueur has named the "one-sex/one-flesh" model, the dominant paradigm of how to account for sexual difference from antiquity to the late seventeenth century. According to this model, the male body was deemed the perfect norm, whereas the female body was considered a lesser, imperfect stage. Laqueur describes this particular physiology as "a world where at least two genders correspond to but one sex, where the boundaries between male and female are of degree and not of kind."[46] The former view is certainly traceable within Shakespeare's plays, particularly in the frequently voiced fear that men have turned effeminate. However, gender is always portrayed as a flexible concept, a matter of situation and behaviour rather than essence. Thus, I believe that Shakespeare's portrayals of suicide can more adequately be explained by a Butlerian notion of gender, which famously insists that human beings are formed into men or women through gender performances, the deliberate acting out of social conventions. My book seeks to acknowledge its indebtedness to the seminal work by Butler and later critics writing in the same tradition as well as its feminist approach in its subtitle, *Dead Bodies That Matter*.

My repeated use of terms such as 'performance', 'theatricality', as well as my interest in the politics of dramaturgy begs a short note on methodology. Both the absence of significant stage directions and the fact that some characters kill themselves offstage create blank spaces as to how exactly a character dies. These gaps may prove especially problematic in performance, and so actors and directors often feel the need to decide on a suicide that seems fitting for the respective character. As such, suicide is an inherently performance-oriented topic. Whereas several suicides (e.g. Cleopatra's) are deliberate performances geared towards an onstage audience, all stage suicides still implicate an offstage audience, which raises several important questions: What does it mean to witnesses another person's death? Are the audience involved in this process? And what effect does it create if a suicide is precisely not witnessed but hidden offstage? The following analysis therefore draws on a number of performances, both on the stage and the screen. My approach is firmly situated within the field of literary studies with only minor forays into performance history, and so there is no claim whatsoever regarding temporal or geographical completeness. I refer to individual performances or adaptations wherever it proves productive. I do not analyse them as works in their own right but treat them in the same way as literary criticism, as one particular director's interpretation of Shakespeare's text.

In order to make visible how the dramatisation of suicide develops through the Shakespearean canon, my investigation addresses all tragedies that feature suicide, either on or offstage, in chronological order: *Romeo and Juliet, Julius Caesar, Hamlet, Othello, King Lear, Macbeth,* and *Antony and Cleopatra*.[47] I also take a closer look at *Titus Andronicus*, which explores a situation where liberation through suicide is physically impossible. Moreover, some of the chapters contain extended references to *Coriolanus, Timon of Athens,* and *Richard III*, none of which explicitly features a suicide. However, suicide is either implied or the dilemma at least strongly parallels that of another suicidal character, and so I include these excursions wherever I see fit.

Only if the motif is traced chronologically from *Titus Andronicus* to *Antony and Cleopatra* does it emerge fully that later plays continuously reverberate with earlier contexts or examples, thus forming one coherent line of gendered discourse. A chronological argument thus enables me to explore whether it is possible to speak of a 'suicide trajectory', whether argumentative patterns identifiable from the start – for instance, the correlation between suicide and agency, suicide as an act of honour, as well as the gendering of weapons and locations – are increasingly or decreasingly pronounced towards the later plays. The 'usual suspects' that come to mind when thinking about suicide in Shakespeare are probably Hamlet, Romeo, Brutus, Othello, and Antony. However, I begin each chapter with a focus on the women, who either tend to be neglected by criticism or at least had a problematic history of critical reception. By reading the deaths of Juliet, Portia, Ophelia, Desdemona, Lady Macbeth, Goneril, and Cleopatra in opposition to their male counterparts, I will illustrate to what extent in all of the tragedies male and female suicides are juxtaposed and traditional notions of masculinity and femininity are thus subverted.

The first chapter, "Knitting the Cord: *Titus Andronicus*," explores the ways in which Shakespeare's earliest tragedy already establishes suicide as a gesture connoting agency. By denying Lavinia the possibility to end her life in a self-determined way, I argue, the play completes her victimisation as mere by-product of a ruthlessly patriarchal world. Chapter 2, "Happy Daggers: *Romeo and Juliet*," addresses Shakespeare's most famous suicidal couple in conflict with contemporary gender conventions. I will not only discuss in what respect their suicides are pervaded by moments of distinct irony, but also how they mirror their respective gender performances throughout the play. Whereas the already suicidal Romeo's death is at least partly marked conventionally feminine, Juliet's suicide implies masculinity. As its title suggests, the third chapter, "Roman Fools: *Julius Caesar*," deals with the classical concept of suicide. I propose that the various suicides in this play undermine rather than augment the frequently evoked image of Roman death, not least since the most emphatically Roman and, hence, masculine suicide is performed by a woman. In Chapter 4, "Solid Flesh: *Hamlet*," I focus on the juxtaposition of Hamlet's suicidal inaction with Ophelia's suicidal action. By reading her death as a wilful decision rather than tragic accident, I investigate the link between her suicide, female agency, and the limits of female revolt against hegemonic power structures. Chapter 5, entitled "Before We Go: *Othello*," considers both Othello's suicide and the murder of Desdemona, which she herself re-defines as suicide. Whereas Othello's suicide completes his surrender to the (white) hegemony, I address the extent to which Desdemona's death can be understood as opposing the rigid gender norms of patriarchal Venice. My sixth chapter, "Promised Ends: *King Lear*," examines Gloucester and Goneril as representatives of an exclusively patriarchal world order on the one hand and a more progressive, inclusive one with regard to gender on the other. By contrasting Goneril's offstage suicide with Gloucester's onstage non-suicide, I suggest that it is Gloucester's, not Goneril's, tragic ending that can be read as form of punishment. Chapter 7, "Trying the Last: *Macbeth*," considers Lady Macbeth's suicide as well as Macbeth's refusal to surrender. While considering Macbeth's explicit rejection of a self-inflicted death indicative of his concept of masculinity, I suggest that Lady Macbeth's death marks her final, if fatal, attempt to undermine existing power structures. The eighth and final chapter, "Well Done: *Antony and Cleopatra*," revisits the Roman ideal of suicide and illustrates how in this play, too, notions of (Roman) masculinity are questioned. I delve into both Antony's slightly mishandled and Cleopatra's triumphant suicides as intricately choreographed performances, both fully capitalising on the communicative as well as symbolic potential of suicide. Apart from summarising my major findings, the epilogue revisits the question of genre, only briefly touched on in this introduction. By drawing a line from the tragedies to the comedies and romances, I will show that suicide in Shakespeare is not an exclusively tragic phenomenon.

Notes

1 Albert Camus, *The Myth of Sisyphus*, trans. Justin O'Brien (Harmondsworth: Penguin, 1975), 11.

2 Writing at a time when suicides were romanticised as the ultimate expression of individuality and sensibility, perverted in the numerous copy-cat suicides in the wake of Goethe's *Werther*, Durkheim established the understanding of suicide as a social phenomenon. According to his findings, psychological explanations such as mental illness could only ineffectively account for the phenomenon. Thus, he identified three forms of suicide (egoistical, altruistic, and anomic), all of which he related back to an individual's problematic integration into society. Émile Durkheim, *On Suicide*, trans. Robin Buss (1897; reprint, London: Penguin, 2006), especially 1–30; 307–325.

3 Anton J. L. Van Hooff, *From Autothanasia to Suicide: Self-Killing in Classical Antiquity* (London: Routledge, 1990), 129.

4 Catharine Edwards, *Death in Ancient Rome* (New Haven: Yale University Press, 2007), 105.

5 J. M. Rist, *Stoic Philosophy* (Cambridge: Cambridge University Press, 1969), 234–236. On Plato's larger argument, see Murray Miles, "Plato on Suicide (*Phaedo* 60C–63C)," *Phoenix* 55.3/4 (2001): 244–258.

6 Rist, *Stoic Philosophy*, 241–242.

7 Ibid., 233; Edwards, *Death in Ancient Rome*, 104–105. On Seneca's attitude towards suicide see 98–108.

8 Van Hooff, *Self-Killing in Classical Antiquity*, 77.

9 Ibid., 60.

10 Ibid., 131; 99.

11 Rowland Wymer, *Suicide and Despair in the Jacobean Drama* (Brighton: Harvester, 1986), 13.

12 Ibid., 2. According to the *Oxford English Dictionary (OED)*, 'suicide' first occurred in 1656. *The Oxford English Dictionary*, 2nd ed. (*OED Online*), accessed March 16, 2012, s.v. "suicide," def. 1a. Alexander Murray lists an even earlier example of *suicidia* for *De quatuor labyrinthos Franciae* in 1178 but points out that, surprisingly, there are no further findings between this text and Sir Thomas Browne's. Alexander Murray, *Suicide in the Middle Ages: Volume I: The Violent against Themselves* (Oxford: Oxford University Press, 1998), 38. But even in the seventeenth century, suicide was not a popular term to use, as Robert Houston clarifies. More common were reflexive expressions such as 'self-murder', 'self-slaughter', and 'self-homicide', or even

paraphrases such as 'putting down' oneself. R. A. Houston, *Punishing the Dead? Suicide, Lordship, and Community in Britain, 1500–1830* (Oxford: Oxford University Press, 2010), 23.

13 Murray, *The Violent against Themselves*, 40.

14 Ibid., 22; 29–40. On the legal persecution of suicide, notably in early modern England, see also Houston, *Punishing the Dead*, 95–181; 226–277.

15 Alexander Murray, *Suicide in the Middle Ages: Volume II: The Curse on Self-Murder* (Oxford: Oxford University Press, 2000), 102–104. Murray emphasises that, even though St. Augustine is known as the prime theologian associated with suicide, his position mirrored forces and opinions in the Church more generally rather than being his personal ideological position. On a more detailed discussion of St. Augustine's line of argument, see Murray, *The Curse on Self-Murder*, 98–121.

16 *Book of Common Prayer* (Oxford: Oxford University Press, 1965), 388.

17 Murray, *The Curse on Self-Murder*, 43–51.

18 Brian Cummings, *Mortal Thoughts: Religion, Secularity and Identity in Shakespeare and Early Modern Culture* (Oxford: Oxford University Press, 2013), 242.

19 Michael MacDonald, *Sleepless Souls: Suicide in Early Modern England* (Oxford: Clarendon, 1993), 15–16; 75.

20 Michael MacDonald, "Ophelia's Maimèd Rites," *Shakespeare Quarterly* 37.3 (1986): 313.

21 Georges Minois, *History of Suicide: Voluntary Death in Western Culture*, trans. Lydia G. Cochrane (Baltimore: Johns Hopkins University Press, 1999), 36.

22 As Burton's alter ego Democritus Junior summarises his unbearable pain in the concluding stanza of "The Author's Abstract of Melancholy": "My pain's past cure, another hell, / I may not in this torment dwell! / Now desperate I hate my life, / Lend me a halter or a knife; / All my griefs to this are jolly, / Naught so damn'd as melancholy." Robert Burton, *The Anatomy of Melancholy*, 1621, reprint (New York: New York Review Books, 2001), 13. Even though Burton's text is more a literary work *sui generis* than medical treatise, his is the first attempt to offer a (pseudo)scientific explanation for depression. He not only provides original thoughts on the topic but, in the first place, collates a wide range of perspectives by mostly classical and medieval authors across various disciplines.

23 MacDonald, *Sleepless Souls*, 36.

24 Wymer, *Suicide and Despair in the Jacobean Drama*, 24. He also suggests that the constant switching between the narrower and looser senses of the term (as, for example, found in *The Anatomy of Melancholy*) resulted in a broadening of meaning of the term 'despair'.

25 Houston, *Punishing the Dead*, 297.

26 See Vera Lind, *Selbstmord in der Frühen Neuzeit. Diskurs, Lebenswelt und Kultureller Wandel* (Göttingen: Vandenhoeck und Ruprecht, 1999), 29–31.

27 Gary B. Ferngren, "The Ethics of Suicide in the Renaissance and Reformation," in *Suicide and Euthanasia*, ed. Baruch A. Brody (Dordrecht: Springer Netherlands, 1989), 155.

28 Michel de Montaigne, "A Custom of The Isle of Cea," in *The Complete Essays*, trans. and ed. M. A. Screech (London: Penguin, 2003), 393.

29 Minois, *History of Suicide*, 91. See also Patrick Henry, "The Dialectic of Suicide in Montaigne's 'Coustume de l'Isle de Cea'," *The Modern Language Review* 79.2 (1984): 278–289. Henry emphasises that the essay is often wrongly referenced as stating Montaigne's personal stance towards suicide.

Instead, Henry insists, "this early essay is a perfect literary example of Montaigne's 'art de conferer' [...]. Montaigne argues both sides of the issue effectively and that is precisely why his essay is heterodox" (287).

30 See, for example: "I abstaynd purposely from extending this discourse to perticular *Rules*, or instances, both because I dare not professe my selfe, a Master in so curious a scyence, and because the Limmits are obscure, and steepy, and slippery, and narrow, and eurey Error deadly." John Donne, *Biathanatos*, ed. Ernest W. Sullivan II (Newark: University of Delaware Press, 1984), 145. *Biathanatos* is often (misleadingly) associated with Donne's personal suffering from melancholy and his suicidal tendencies. Still, Ernest W. Sullivan emphasises that even though Donne's personal situation might have influenced him in his defence of suicide to some extent, his argument does not build on this personal motivation but instead embarks on a rational examination of legal, philosophical, and theological viewpoints on the subject. Ernest W. Sullivan, Introduction to *Biathanatos*, by John Donne, ed. Ernest W. Sullivan (Newark: University of Delaware Press, 1984), x–xiii.

31 Wymer, *Suicide and Despair in the Jacobean Drama*, 3–4.

32 Jacqueline Vanhoutte, "Antony's 'Secret House of Death:' Suicide and Sovereignty in *Antony and Cleopatra*," *Philological Quarterly* 79 (2000): 157.

33 See also Wymer, who argues that "in a stage suicide, of course, an interplay of sincerity and theatricality may be an important part of the dramatist's conception of a character. The many connotations suicide possessed for the Renaissance meant that only lack of skill could prevent a playwright fashioning a death in every way appropriate to the character concerned, even to the extent of expressing a tendency to self-dramatisation" (9). A similar view can be found in Richard K. Sanderson, "Suicide as Message and Metadrama in English Renaissance Tragedy," *Comparative Drama* 26.3 (1992): 199–217.

34 Margaret Higonnet, "Speaking Silences: Women's Suicide," in *The Female Body in Western Culture: Contemporary Perspectives*, ed. Susan Rubin Suleiman (Cambridge, MA and London: Harvard University Press, 1985), 68.

35 Marvin Spevack, "The Art of Dying in Shakespeare," *Jahrbuch Deutsche Shakespeare-Gesellschaft West* (1989): 170–171.

36 Elisabeth Bronfen, *Over Her Dead Body: Death Femininity and the Aesthetic* (Manchester: Manchester University Press, 1992), 3.

37 Bronfen, *Over Her Dead Body*, xi.

38 Judith Butler, *Precarious Life: The Powers of Mourning and Violence* (London and New York: Verso, 2004), xiv–xv.

39 Michael Neill, *Issues of Death: Mortality and Identity in English Renaissance Tragedy* (Oxford: Clarendon, 1997), 319.

40 On 'stageability', see Mariko Ichikawa, *The Shakespearean Stage Space* (Cambridge: Cambridge University Press, 2013), 129–150, which answers the question of "What to do with onstage corpses." On the particular importance of reported scenes see, for instance, Stephen Ratcliffe, *Reading the Unseen: (Offstage) Hamlet* (Denver: Counterpath, 2010).

41 Linda Bamber, *Comic Women, Tragic Men: A Study of Gender and Genre in Shakespeare* (Stanford: Stanford University Press, 1982), 4.

42 Valerie Traub, "Gender and Sexuality in Shakespeare," in *The Cambridge Companion to Shakespeare*, ed. Margreta de Grazia and Stanley Wells (Cambridge: Cambridge University Press, 2001), 129.

43 Phyllis Rackin, *Shakespeare and Women* (Oxford: Oxford University Press, 2005), 15–16.

44 Stephen Greenblatt, *Shakespearean Negotiations: The Circulation of Social Energy in Renaissance England* (Oxford: Clarendon, 1988), 88.

45 See Laura Gowing, *Gender Relations in Early Modern England* (London and New York: Routledge, 2014), 7–8.

46 Thomas Laqueur, *Making Sex: Body and Gender from the Greeks to Freud* (Cambridge, MA and London: Harvard University Press, 1992), 25. On a contrastive and more nuanced view, cf. Valerie Traub, M. Lindsay Kaplan, and Dympna Callaghan, who argue, "the subject is always, although not essentially, gendered at any given historical moment. Because of its provisional and contradictory nature, gender itself continually must be reproduced. Through this expenditure of cultural energy, the terms of gender change over time. We thus reject the now prevalent argument, based on the theory of physiological homology between the sexes that there existed only one gender in early modern culture. Rather, gender exists as a term of definition even when it is not specifically articulated; it operates according to the exigencies of various discursive domains, and relates to and interacts with other axes of social formation." Valerie Traub, M. Lindsay Kaplan, and Dympna Callaghan, Introduction to *Feminist Readings of Early Modern Culture: Emerging Subjects*, ed. Valerie Traub, et al. (Cambridge: Cambridge University Press, 1996), 4.

47 According to Stanley Wells and Gary Taylor, *William Shakespeare: A Textual Companion* (Oxford: Clarendon, 1987), 69–109.

1   Knitting the Cord
Titus Andronicus

In *Titus Andronicus*, nobody commits suicide. Thus, at first glance, this might appear an unlikely choice to begin an analysis of suicide in Shakespeare. Yet Lavinia, often discounted as mere collateral damage in a play in which the bodies keep piling up, allows for one of the most interesting discussions of the topic in all of the tragedies. Whereas *Hamlet* reinforces suicide as the only possible way out of the tragic hero's dilemma, *Titus Andronicus* reverses this scenario. Lavinia never talks about killing herself because she has lost her tongue, and the play repeatedly announces that of all the possible solutions to end her pain, suicide is the only one that is not available.

While suicide is the one violent action that does not happen, there is not exactly a lack of violent spectacle. Whereas for a long time *Titus Andronicus* had been discounted as artistically immature and impossible to stage, more recently, directors and audiences alike have come to re-evaluate and appreciate the play.[1] A particularly striking example in this context is Lucy Bailey's popular but also controversial staging at Shakespeare's Globe (2006/2014), suggestively advertised as "brutality of the highest order." *Telegraph* critic Charles Spencer described the production as marked by graphic violence and gleeful cruelty, exerting "a dramatic power that makes the stomach churn and the hands sweat."[2] Considering today's ever-increasing familiarity with depictions of violence, such a gory staging seems a timely twenty-first-century approach to a text which has often been accused of gratuitous violence.[3] As productions such as Bailey's have shown, *Titus Andronicus* is not impossible to stage at all. Conversely, it seems that it can only be understood fully in performance. It is vital that the audience see Lavinia suffer, physically and emotionally, before their eyes. The more she suffers, the more their discomfort increases, and eventually, they want her to commit suicide in order to put an end to her agony. That the play withholds this relief is not mere sadism. Rather, it is a structural necessity.

Taking feminist criticism's concern with an investment in the female voice as its point of departure, the chapter at hand argues that the play defines suicide as a means of expressing such a voice and exerting agency; somewhat peculiarly, this is a definition *ex negativo*. *Titus Andronicus* is a Roman play, and within the classical context, suicide is conceptualised as an act of agency per se, a means of safeguarding reputation and honour. Lavinia seems to be denied this agency. As all the other characters indicate, her physical inability to commit suicide constitutes an extreme form of lacking agency. However, I argue that this defeatist notion, as far as female agency is concerned, only holds true within the realm of the play. From the point of view of an audience, the play's successive attempts at either victimising Lavinia or else insisting that she is a victim make her the focal point of attention, thus exposing the perversity of the play's aggressively masculine ideology and rhetoric.

"If Thou Hadst Hands": Withholding Suicide as Torture

When Lavinia re-enters the stage raped and mutilated, she has turned into a spectacle, bleeding from her mouth and the stumps of her hands. The stage tableau is contrasted with Chiron and Demetrius's mocking comments. To Chiron's "An 'twere my cause, I should go hang myself," Demetrius replies "If thou hadst hands to help thee knit the cord" (2.3.9–10). These words not only heighten the pain for both Lavinia and the audience, but also, with perverse poignancy, sum up the hopelessness of her situation. Through rape and dismemberment, she literally loses her voice. She is stripped of all forms of agency, which is epitomised in her inability even to kill herself. The play repeatedly addresses suicide as a possible option only to then negate it, thus defining its denial as a form of torture.

If something is denied, the implication is that this something must also be wished for, but it should not be taken for granted that Lavinia wants to die. Providing a more optimistic view on Lavinia's self-determination and interpreting her as co-author of her own narrative, Bethany Packard raises the question of why the Andronicus family fails to acknowledge that Lavinia deliberately stays alive when she could just as well kill herself.[4] As far as sheer logistics are concerned, this is a valid point. As the canon of Shakespearean suicides illustrates, there are a number of ways even a handless Lavinia could kill herself, as for example drowning or jumping from up high. But what is more important than this quibble of whether she is truly unable to kill herself, within the discourse of the play, she is denied taking control over her own body. She does not kill herself because she cannot, a fact the play reiterates. In addition, and this is an essential distinction, whereas everyone else seems to believe her to be suicidal, she herself never gives any such hints. Her speechlessness renders her an enigma impossible to crack, even if the play all too willingly suggests that she must want to die. Lavinia's case raises questions concerning the degree of a suicide's self-ownership as well as control over one's own death narrative, which is why she proves the ideal starting point for a discussion of suicide in Shakespeare.

The denial of voice and control over her own body is predetermined on a structural level. To begin with, the text seems uninterested in giving Lavinia a voice. She only has fifteen speeches, an equivalent of 2 per cent of the entire text; only Young Lucius speaks less.[5] Her lack of agency is not only exemplified by her name, which according to Virgil's account casts her as the chaste and passive mother of Rome, but also by the play's hypotexts, Ovid's accounts of Philomel, as well as Lucrece. Yet, these hypotexts do not merely function as a faintly recognisable palimpsest but rather provide for active intertextual communication with the play. All the characters seem to have read the *Metamorphoses* and, hence, know what will happen to Lavinia. Her fate is pre-written by the classical texts, and so she is denied any form of agency on a meta-level. The two hypotexts are defined by their sexual violence against their female protagonists, but Lavinia has to suffer worse than both Philomel and Lucrece. Ovid's Tereus first rapes Philomel and then cuts her tongue out. Lavinia's tormentors, by contrast, know better. They, too, have read the *Metamorphoses* and, therefore, Lavinia has to lose her hands as well.

Whereas Philomel survives and regains her voice through her metamorphosis into a nightingale, Lucrece puts an end to her suffering and commits suicide. Shakespeare revisits this story in *The Rape of Lucrece*, in which the heroine gets an elaborate and moving suicide scene:

> Even here she sheathed in her harmless breast
> A harmful knife, that thence her soul unsheathed;
> That blow did bail it from the deep unrest
> Of that polluted prison where it breathed.
> Her contrite sighs unto the clouds bequeathed
> Her winged sprite, and through her wounds doth fly
> Life's lasting date from cancell'd destiny.
> [...]
> And bubbling from her breast, it doth divide
> In two slow rivers, that the crimson blood
> Circles her body on every side,
> Who like a late-sack'd island vastly stood
> Bare and unpeopled in this fearful flood.
>
> (*Luc.* 1723–1741)

In addition to describing her suicide in an elaborate and captivating manner, the text fetishises the image of the bleeding body and aestheticises her wounds in a manner similar to Marcus's monologue about the bleeding Lavinia in 2.3. But at the same time, Lucrece's suicide is presented as a scene of triumph, which releases her from her "cancelled destiny."[6] In repeatedly pitying Lavinia for not being able to kill herself, *Titus Andronicus* similarly defines suicide as an act that may bring release, with emphasis on the limitation that Lavinia is denied this freedom.

This chapter's argument of how Lavinia is denied such release through suicide is embedded in the play's overall strategy of silencing her – of denying her a voice of her own. Already the opening scene identifies her as a trophy for the future emperor and tosses her around between Bassianus and Saturninus, both of who claim her as their future wife. Her objectification already shows in the first mention of the term 'rape', a slippery signifier in the play, and here used in the sense of 'theft' or 'abduction': when Saturninus likens Bassianus's seizing of Lavinia to rape, the latter replies "'Rape' call you it, my lord, to seize my own, / My true betrothed love, and now my wife" (1.1.410–411).[7] Even the actual rape is not directed at her personally but happens as *quid pro quo* in response to Titus tearing off the limbs of Tamora's son Alarbus. Therefore, even when she suffers most cruelly, Lavinia only serves as a means to an end. As soon as Aaron announces "Lucrece was not more chaste than this Lavinia" (1.1.110), it is evident what will happen. Emily Detmer-Goebel notices that, unlike in other early modern rape scenes, Chiron and Demetrius never address Lavinia directly or seek to make her consent to the act.[8] Even though she is present onstage, they cheerfully discuss their cruel intentions and ignore her as an individual. Once she realises what they are planning, she begs Tamora to kill her instead: "O Tamora, be called a gentle queen / And with thine own hands kill me in this place" (2.2.168–169). Whereas Ovid's Philomel verbally tries to defend herself against Tereus before he rapes her and also speaks before her tongue is cut out, Lavinia is silenced mid-sentence (2.2.182–184). As Detmer-Goebel suggests, "Shakespeare undoubtedly makes Lavinia's verbal defence against rape less persuasive (emotionally moving)" than Lucrece's defence against Tarquinius, which indicates "the limitations of authority vested in Lavinia's voice."[9] It is only in performance that the dimensions of such a lack of investment in her voice show fully and silencing materialises as a physical reality.

Using Lavinia's striking bodily presence, the play creates a tension that justifies its own need to dispose of her, which makes suicide, or the denial thereof, such a relevant topic. Judith Butler's work on mutilated and gendered bodies refers to non-heteronormative and specifically intersex bodies. What these have in common with Lavinia is that they do not conform to hegemonic discourse. Butler posits the question of whether discursive constructions of sexual difference might also produce "a domain of unthinkable, abject, unlivable bodies? This latter domain is not the opposite of the former, for oppositions are, after all, part of intelligibility; the latter is the excluded and illegible domain that haunts the former domain as the spectre of its own impossibility, the very limit to intelligibility, its constitutive outside."[10] After the rape,

Lavinia transforms into such an unthinkable, abject, unlivable body. Only the play reverses the scenario Butler advocates, for it is Lavinia's unviolated and, therefore, intelligible body that haunts the play as a spectre; it would not do so if suicide were possible and Lavinia indeed wanted to kill herself. Butler's words also reference Julia Kristeva's concept of the 'abject', which can be loosely translated as 'execrable'. As developed in *Powers of Horror*, the abject is a waste product resulting from the development of the 'I', displacing the subject into a liminal, taboo space neither inside nor outside the body. Thus, it "is radically excluded and draws [...] toward the place where meaning collapses."[11] The abject refers to that which "disturbs identity, system, order. What does not respect borders, positions, rules."[12] A powerful female voice would disturb homosocial Rome, which, therefore, violently rejects her. In turn, she begins to subvert the social order. According to Kristeva, the confrontation with the abject is a traumatic, repulsive experience, often caused by the encounter of wounds or corpses.[13] Lavinia's body, which never fully stops bleeding, elicits a similarly repulsive reaction.

Her transformation into the abject culminates in Lavinia's loss of voice. On the diegetic level, the question of why Shakespeare silences her is rhetorical. She needs to remain silent so as not to be able to reveal the crime. But simultaneously, her silence renders her helpless against all male attempts of patronising her, which in turn ideologically sustains the male supremacy. Strikingly, Lavinia's silence enhances her status in the play, not only because from now on, everything leads towards Titus's revenge. Although passive, she sits at the centre of attention, a position she has never held before. As Alexander Leggatt notes, "[i]n silencing her [Chiron and Demetrius] have inadvertently made her the most powerful character in the play. What the rape means for them is straightforward: an expression of power. What it means for her is beyond language, beyond imagining. That is what her silence conveys to us, and from this point on that silence haunts the play."[14] It is indicative of the play's gender politics that a woman needs to be violated in the most brutal way in order to be able to arrest her fellow characters' as well as the audiences' attention.

The new importance that Lavinia has gained shows in one of the most disturbing moments, a scene so odd that it is often shortened in performance or even cut entirely.[15] Cutting this passage, however, reduces Lavinia's dramatic impact because this scene provides the key to her function within the play. When Marcus discovers his bleeding niece in 2.3, instead of helping her, he erupts into forty-seven lines of beautiful poetry, arguably the most lyrical lines in the play. First of all, his speech is painful to hear because it is unrealistic, exceeding any credibility of theatrical representation. A grotesque eroticisation that can be deemed typically Ovidian,[16] Marcus's rhetorical flourish runs counter to the stage tableau, and his words create stasis at a moment that would require action. Bate supposes that Marcus needs this pause in order to realise the extremity of what has happened, to allow himself a moment to suffer.[17] Yet, the prime function of this deliberately stylised scene is another, as Pascale Aebischer makes clear: "while the incisions in [Lavinia's] body open her up to the spectators' voyeuristic gazes, her obscene on-stage presence renders outside observation (whether visual or verbal) obscene."[18] Seemingly unrelated in the context of Shakespearean drama but illuminating in this case, the notion of the voyeuristic gaze with regard to injured or dismembered bodies is reminiscent of Susan Sontag's *Regarding the Pain of Others*, her seminal essay on war photography. Sontag traces the iconography of suffering and addresses the rather unsettling but visceral attraction to watching others in agony, provided it is from a safe distance. She speaks of a "prurient interest" in both the display of and looking at mutilated bodies, be they imaginary or real. As she underlines, "[a]ll images that display the violation of an attractive body are, to a certain degree, pornographic."[19] Lavinia's maimed body keeps reappearing on the stage until the final scene, and it is integral to the play's sadism that neither the other characters nor the audience can avert their eyes. They are trapped within their position as voyeurs and have to keep staring.

The audience inevitably adopt Marcus's point of view, whose poetic language is inadequate to grasp the horrific sight in front of him but instead turns it into an ekphrastic scene. Rather grotesquely, the vivid image created by Marcus epitomises the Elizabethan notion of *ut pictura poesis*. Horace's dictum, going back to his theory of mimesis in *Ars Poetica*, originally conceptualised painting and poetry as closely related art forms. Following Sidney's translation as 'a speaking picture', it referred to the "sensory impression necessary both to delight and affect the reader" and, therefore, emphasised that Elizabethan poetry, like painting, is a visual art form.[20] Marcus's decision to stare at his helpless niece rather than attend to her wounds anticipates Gertrude's elaborate description of the floating Ophelia. The latter image is less sensational and violent than that of the butchered Lavinia, but both Marcus and Gertrude remain inert bystanders. Marcus aestheticises Lavinia's bleeding body, enacting a perverted version of the blazon with reference to the "crimson river of warm blood" (2.3.22) and cheeks as "red as Titan's face" (2.3.31). Even in its traditional form, the blazon objectifies and colonises the female body.[21] Marcus, albeit unwittingly, repeats this offense. His speech re-creates a version of Lavinia's body that is no longer there, and so he verbally constructs a spectral body of the kind that Butler refers to. Christina Wald argues in another direction, suggesting that Marcus's blazon conjures up an Ovidian metamorphosis by means of which Lavinia transforms into nature. For Wald, these "counter-images of the transformed Lavinia [...] will make audiences hope for a process of reverse ekphrasis, of the word made flesh."[22] The certainty that this reverse *ekphrasis* will not happen only increases the audiences' discomfort. The scene is almost unbearable to endure.

Although Marcus's explicit reference to Tereus indicates that he understands what has happened (2.3.26), the family continues firing questions at Lavinia, which highlights her silence: "Speak, Lavinia, what accursed hand / Hath made thee handless in thy father's sight?" (3.1.67–68). As Farah Karim-Cooper observes, the word 'hand' and related puns appear much more frequently after Lavinia's dismemberment. In addition to providing black comedy, Karim-Cooper suggests, Shakespeare thereby physically involves the audience and makes them aware of their own hands.[23] Richard Brucher discusses the grisly comic undertones that permeate the entire play, foregrounding the fine line between tragedy and farce. As he points out, this combination of violence and the grotesque is crucial to the audiences' reaction towards the play: "The comic heightening of the brutality helps to reveal a world in which the malevolence is too witty, the violence too extreme, and the sense of order too illusory, to sustain the redemptive tragic emotions of pity and fear."[24] Put differently, the mixture of the grotesque and violence is alienating as per Brecht. It estranges audiences rather than capturing their imaginations. The punning on non-existent hands continues in the second passage that explicitly discusses Lavinia's physical inability to commit suicide:

TITUS: Thou map of woe, that thus dost talk in signs,
When thy poor heart beats with outrageous beating,
Thou canst not strike it thus to make it still.
Wound it with sighing, girl, kill it with groans,
Or get some little knife between thy teeth
And just against thy heart make thou a hole,
That all the tears that thy poor eyes let fall
May run into that sink and, soaking in,
Drown the lamenting fool in sea-salt tears.

MARCUS: Fie, brother, fie! Teach her not thus to lay
Such violent hands upon her tender life.

TITUS: How now, has sorrow made thee dote already?
Why, Marcus, no man should be mad but I.
What violent hands can she lay on her life?

(3.2.12–25)

Titus and Marcus give voice to her inner conflict, but gratuitously so. As if it were not enough for everyone onstage and in the audience to see that Lavinia has lost her hands and hence cannot kill herself, at least not easily, the two additionally verbalise this repeatedly. For Titus, this is a straightforward situation: Lavinia must want to commit suicide; the possibility of her wanting to stay alive is not even implied. It would be a logical consequence of this dialogue if at this moment, one of the two characters decided to release her from what they believe to be intense pain. Instead, the play prolongs Lavinia's suffering.

Lavinia's suffering is further increased by her inability to communicate properly and especially the other characters' refusal to understand what she tries to express. Presupposing that the body itself is a culturally and politically fabricated surface, Butler raises the question of what means are left to read and decode this corporeal enactment.[25] In the case of Lavinia, this is even more difficult because hers is a mutilated, illegible body, and she can communicate through neither words nor gestures. Still, Titus proclaims "I can interpret all her martyred signs" (3.2.36) and takes over her voice, believing that his daughter communicates through him and that he acts on her behalf. In a further bizarre image of the rape and mutilation, Lavinia caries his severed hand in her mouth, which Titus enacts as a symbolic transfer of power onto her (3.1.283). Katherine Rowe correctly remarks that this scene subverts the symbolism of the hand as a means of action because Titus does not act on behalf of his daughter at all. Rather, this gesture attests to a mere emblematic quality, an instrumentality in her father's plan of revenge.[26] The passage, thus, foreshadows the killing of Lavinia, more specifically Titus's belief that he must act as the hand Lavinia does not have and cannot use against herself.

Ironically, Lavinia reveals the exact circumstances of the rape through a copy of Ovid's *Metamorphoses* that she opens at the story of Philomel. For the first time since the rape, Lavinia is able to communicate information herself. She writes *stuprum* instead of the more common *raptus* with its associations of theft and women as male property. That way, she identifies the rape as something that has happened to her personally rather than a public offence against her father, which Packard reads as an attempt to co-author her own story.[27] Nonetheless, Lavinia cannot do this in a language of her own but has to borrow another's, namely Ovid's, voice. This depersonalises her suffering even further, as Leggatt explains: "Like Caesar's '*Et tu, Brute*' at the moment of his death, this fixes and formalizes the accusation as a literary tag, weighting her personal voice with the voice of a whole culture."[28] Even if Lavinia's choice of words intentionally reinterprets the rape and mutilation as a personal offence, this goes unnoticed by her father, who continues to read Lavinia's suffering as a public offence against Rome: "I will go get a leaf of brass / And with a gad of steel will write these words" (4.1.102–103). Inevitably, the words Titus intends to write could never represent Lavinia's own voice. Unlike her transitory writing in sand, Titus's version is the one destined to survive.

Up to this moment, the text, hence, repeatedly establishes that Lavinia is victimised on all possible levels. She no longer has a voice to raise and no hands to kill herself with – an action, the other characters are convinced, she must want to commit. By defining this ostensible lack of agency as something that needs to be remedied, the play, thus, constructs a justification to take over her voice fully and kill her on her own behalf.

"A Pattern, Precedent, and Lively Warrant": The Need to Kill Lavinia

Having revealed the identity of her rapists, Lavinia has served her purpose and needs to be killed off somehow. By this point, it has been sufficiently established that she cannot do this herself; someone else must knit the cord for her. Nevertheless, the text does not offer such closure and relief. Instead of leaving room for these loose ends to be tied up and poetic justice to be established, the final moments of Act V are overloaded with action, culminating in the gory banquet hosted by Titus. The sensationalism and spectacle of the scene diverts the attention away from Lavinia and instead builds up towards Tamora feasting on her own sons, a moment that – in the eyes of the audience – is revolting and rewarding in equal measure.

For Lavinia's death, the play draws on another hypotext, this time taken from the Roman historian Livy.[29] Titus casts himself in the role of the avenging father but feels it necessary to establish that killing Lavinia would be an act of justice or his moral obligation:

TITUS:	Was it well done of rash Virginius
	To slay his daughter with his own right hand,
	Because she was enforced, stained and deflowered?
SATURNINUS:	It was, Andronicus.
TITUS:	Your reason, mighty lord?
SATURNINUS:	Because the girl should not survive her shame,
	And by her presence still renew his sorrows.
TITUS:	A reason mighty, strong, and effectual;
	A pattern, precedent, and lively warrant
	For me, most wretched, to perform the like.
	[*Unveils Lavinia.*]
	Die, die, Lavinia, and thy shame with thee,
	And with thy shame thy father's sorrow die.
	[*He kills her.*]

(5.3.36–46)

Even though Titus's question may sound rhetorical or ironic, it is indicative of the shame culture predominant in ancient Rome. Vis-à-vis guilt cultures, which focus on the victim's lack of consent and in which the victim is able to vindicate her honour by making the offence public, in shame cultures, lack of consent is irrelevant. After the rape, the woman looms as a threat to her family's reputation and, thus, has to be killed in order to re-establish the status quo.[30] Although Titus's reasoning appears inacceptable to a twenty-first-century audience, the play makes audiences complicit with his line of argument. Derek Cohen rightly observes that "[w]hen Lavinia is alive, we are repelled by her deformities; when she is dead, we are consoled by our pity for them."[31] Thus, no matter how ideologically questionable, at this point, the audience may welcome Lavinia's death, not only because of empathy, but primarily because it would provide release from the voyeuristic position of having to see her suffer.

The first of a sequence of bodies, the killing of Lavinia appears unexpected and bathetic, lacking ceremony, and poses another directorial challenge. As the stage directions suggest, she remains faceless throughout most of the scene. The veil over her face not only denies her all means of communication that she has left, but also suggests that her body is too disturbing and obscene, something that must be covered. When the veil is lifted, there is no time to process this revelation since Titus already kills her within the next two lines of speech. Describing the murder, Cohen euphemistically speaks of an "almost iconic simplicity,"[32] which fails to grasp the perversity of Titus's action. Anticlimactic and shocking in its banality, this is not the ending the audience had wanted and which they had been prepared for. Moreover, it is impossible to contemplate the image of Lavinia's dead body. Within only nineteen lines of speech, the stage tableau also piles up the corpses of Tamora, Titus, and Saturninus. Suddenly, Lavinia is only one of the many casualties claimed by the play. She had begged Tamora to kill her as an act of mercy earlier, which implies that she would welcome death to put an end to her shame. After the rape, Lavinia never expresses the wish to die, but even if she wanted to, she could not communicate this anymore. Thus, the question arises as to whether her killing really can be read as "a substitute for the suicide she cannot manage alone,"[33] as Carolyn Williams suggests.

Aebischer criticises previous commentators for brushing over the scene's misogynist undercurrents, in terms of not only Titus's words, but also what happens onstage. Rightfully deemed questionable, these include views such as Maurice Charney's, who feels that "[t]he murder is shown as an act of love to which Lavinia gives her tacit consent."[34] Adding to those interpretations, Cohen writes that Lavinia "passively and unresistingly collaborates in her own killing."[35] Even more emphatically positive, Nicola M. Imbracsio states that "Lavinia actively participates in the revenge of her rape and mutilation and Titus wields the knife, both effectively reconstituting the disabled body as the capable body."[36] These comments, at least implicitly, take Titus's self-proclaimed act of mercy at face value, which inevitably results in taking over Lavinia's voice. At this point in particular, when Lavinia is about to be killed, such a reading is deeply problematic.

The critical tendency of considering Lavinia complicit in her death – of her being wilfully slaughtered by her loving and tormented father – has equally found its way into stage and screen productions. Aebischer identifies Peter Brook's iconic production in 1955 as the starting point of this interpretative blueprint that was subsequently adopted by most other directors. Under Brook's direction, Vivien Leigh's Lavinia stood up from the table as if to announce her willingness to die. Upon this ostensibly previously agreed-on signal, Titus moved towards her, kissed her, and then killed her.[37] In Julie Taymor's 1999 adaptation *Titus*, Laura Fraser's Lavinia seems oddly excited when entering the kitchen where the banquet takes place. As soon as Titus lifts her veil, she exhibits a trance-like expression, smiling even as Titus breaks her neck. All of these productions paint the picture of a Lavinia who is grateful for being killed, thereby reinforcing a relentlessly patriarchal ideology. Bailey's 2006/2014 production, by contrast, offered a different take. This Lavinia was not fully veiled but bandaged from top to toe. In a grotesque form of dance, Titus led her across the stage and pulled her onto his knee. Rather than signalling an eager involvement in Titus's plan, Lavinia looked distracted and turned away her face. When she buried her head in his neck, ashamed and looking for shelter, Titus strangled her, at first unnoticed by the guests of his banquet. Rather than dying immediately, as realised by those productions in which Titus stabs her or slashes her throat, Lavinia struggled to stay alive for more than thirty seconds, accentuated by the unpleasant sound of a musical saw. As soon as Saturninus and Tamora noticed what was happening, they left the table in shock. Like the production at large, the banquet scene was played as darkly comic, and the audience still cheered and laughed when Tamora swallowed her first spoonful of pie. The killing of Lavinia, however, marked a drastic shift of tone, taking audience members by surprise and silencing all previous amusement. In doing so, Bailey's production emphasised the moment's uncomfortable double edge: while shocking yet finally cathartic for the audience, for Lavinia herself, her death means that she loses her struggle against male silencing and suppression.

Titus's final lines before he kills his daughter are cryptic. On the one hand, he re-emphasises both her status as an object and his own authority. On the other, they open up a different but no less troubling dimension. As Heather James writes, "Titus knows that if his sorrows die with his daughter's shame, it is only because his revenge guarantees his own death. By killing Lavinia, he can commit suicide by proxy; by appropriating her rape as an outrage committed on him [...] he can assume the role of Lucrece."[38] In other words, even the moment he kills Lavinia, Titus manages to cast himself as both victim and martyr while Lavinia is denied any control over her death or the interpretation thereof. What is more, Titus even allocates her the role of the perpetrator. If she is the source of his sorrow, she must die. Yet by killing her, his argument goes, he also kills a part of himself. Simultaneously, it is clear that he will die for this murder in return, a consequence he faces gladly. Titus, thus, enforces a reading of his eventual death as suicide, a suicide he does not even have to commit himself. Again, his self-stylisation runs counter to what happens onstage because killing his daughter is anything but a noble, self-sacrificial gesture.

Lavinia remains an extension of her father even in death, as Lucius proclaims "My father and Lavinia shall forthwith / Be closed in our household's monument" (5.3.192–193). Even though presented as the ultimate honour, Lucius's announcement takes on a negative connotation. It appears to be a punishment rather than reconciliation or honour. Against the background of the later plays, this image additionally evokes associations of similar Shakespearean burials, namely that of Romeo and Juliet or Antony and Cleopatra. Other than supporting the play's latent Freudian subtext, such parallels provide an absurdly romanticised notion that undermines the brutality and distinct masculinity of the ending, a mere celebration of Rome's patriarchal authorities. Both of these pairs of tragic lovers commit suicide. They choose death as a means of liberation. In all four cases, this is turned into elaborate suicide scenes, and their joint burials serve to reunite them in death. Lavinia, by contrast, is not given this freedom of choice, and, furthermore, she is reunited with what she has sought to escape from. Throughout, the play has identified her as her father's property, and so she has to remain with him forever.

For all its unmasking juxtaposition between the 'noble' Romans and the 'barbaric' Goths, *Titus Andronicus* is a decidedly unheroic play. As Coppélia Kahn points out, it builds up this antithesis only to shatter it again; "the real enemy lies within Rome, in its extreme, rigid conception of manly virtue, personified in Titus."[39] Together with a lack of lyricism, this is certainly one of the reasons why generations of critics and audiences have disapproved. The assumption of it being simply too violent, however, is a misunderstanding. Through its extreme cruelty, the play guides the audiences' investment towards Lavinia; she emerges as the linchpin against which everything and everyone else is measured. *Titus Andronicus* is Shakespeare's earliest play featuring a discussion about suicide, and so it automatically serves as a foil for similar concerns in the later plays. Lavinia's death raises several questions that resurface in the later tragedies, albeit in different contexts and often with different undertones: honour, shame, mercy, and, most importantly, gender.

Against this early composition date, it is surprising that this less popular play provides one of the most poignant discussions of suicide. The audience witness how Lavinia is systematically stripped of all her agency until relief through suicide seems to be impossible. If seen in production, this may be even to the extent of physical repulsion. In line with the Roman concept, the play clearly presents suicide as a positive, self-determined action – a way of liberation. As the text suggests, denying Lavinia this freedom is the ultimate form of cruelty. The problem is that, unlike in *Hamlet*, the question of "To be, or not to be" can never be (audibly) raised by Lavinia herself. The audiences' insight into her psyche is blocked, and any contemplation of suicide is taken over by the men in the play. While it remains speculation as to whether the play indeed denies her the possibility of exerting agency through suicide, what Lavinia is unarguably denied is control over her own death narrative. Instead, the task of interpreting her tragic ending shifts towards the audience. Considering the uncomfortable ways in which the play makes them complicit – however reluctantly – with its masculinist ideology, this is an ungrateful role.

Notes

1 Although since the second half of the twentieth century there has been a major shift in acknowledging the play's importance within the canon, not all of the more recent commentators have judged kindly. In *Shakespeare: The Invention of the Human* (London: Fourth Estate, 1999), Harold Bloom still insists that "[w]ithout Aaron, *Titus Andronicus* would be unendurable" (82). Moreover, editors of the play have introduced it on an oddly apologetic note. J. C. Maxwell, amongst others, criticises that "[t]here is admittedly lack of skill and uncertainty of purpose here, but surely not of a kind surprising in an inexperienced dramatist." Introduction to *Titus Andronicus*, by William Shakespeare, ed. J. C. Maxwell, The Arden Shakespeare Second Series (London: Arden Shakespeare, 1953), xxxviii–xxxviv. On a more extensive overview of the play's critical reception, especially the more favourable approaches since the late twentieth century, see Philip C. Kolin, "*Titus Andronicus* and the Critical Legacy," in *Titus Andronicus: Critical Essays*, ed. Philip C. Kolin (New York and London: Garland, 1995), 3–55.
2 Charles Spencer, "A Dramatic Power that Makes the Stomach Churn and the Hands Sweat," review of *Titus Andronicus*, by William Shakespeare, directed by Lucy Bailey, Shakespeare's Globe, London, *The Telegraph*, May 2, 2014, accessed April 27, 2017, www.telegraph.co.uk/culture/theatre/theatre-reviews/10803436/Titus-Andronicus-review-a-dramatic-power-that-makes-the-stomach-churn-and-the-hands-sweat.html.
3 R. A. Foakes's *Shakespeare and Violence* (Cambridge: Cambridge University Press, 2003) describes the Shakespearean canon as tracing "a trajectory that begins with a delight in representing violence for entertainment" (2). On opposing stances that show violence to be an integral and meaningful feature of the play, cf. Brian Vickers, *Shakespeare, Co-Author: A Historical Study of Five Collaborative Plays* (Oxford: Oxford University Press, 2002), 150; Stanley Wells, "The Integration of Violent Action in *Titus Andronicus*," in *Shakespearean Continuities. Essay in Honour of E. A. J. Honigmann*, ed. John Batchelor et al. (Basingstoke and London: Macmillan, 1997), 206–200.
4 Bethany Packard, "Lavinia as Coauthor of Shakespeare's *Titus Andronicus*," *SEL* 50.2 (2010): 288.
5 William Shakespeare, *William Shakespeare: Complete Works*, ed. Jonathan Bate and Eric Rasmussen (London: Palgrave Macmillan, 2008), 1619.

6 On the poem's particular use of *ekphrasis*, see Christopher Johnson, "Appropriating Troy: Ekphrasis in Shakespeare's 'The Rape of Lucrece'," in *Fantasies of Troy: Classical Tales and the Social Imaginary in Medieval and Early Modern Europe*, ed. Alan Shepard and Stephen D. Powell (Toronto: CRRS, 2004), 193–214. On the depiction of Lucrece's suicide more generally, see Margaret Rice Vasileiou, "Violence, Visual Metaphor, and the 'True' Lucrece," *SEL* 51.1 (2011): 47–63.

7 On the early modern definition of 'rape', see Carolyn D. Williams, "'Silence, Like a Lucrece Knife': Shakespeare and the Meaning of Rape," *The Yearbook of English Studies* 23 (1993): 99–102.

8 Emily Detmer-Goebel, "The Need for Lavinia's Voice: *Titus Andronicus* and the Telling of Rape," *Shakespeare Studies* 29 (2001): 79.

9 Ibid., 80. Ovid's passage reads as follows: "Helpless, she screamed in vain for her father, she screamed / for her sister, and called above all on the gods to come to her rescue. [...] 'You cruel barbarian! How could you / do such a dreadful deed? [...] I'll tell the world of your crime myself. If I'm given the chance, / I'll cry it aloud in the marketplace; and if you still hold me / prisoner deep in the forest, my words will ring through the trees; / the rocks will know and be moved to pity by what I have suffered; / the sky will listen and so will the gods, if any exist there'." *Metamorphoses* (London: Penguin, 2004), book 6, 525–548.

10 Judith Butler, *Bodies That Matter: On the Discursive Limits of 'Sex'* (London and New York: Routledge, 1993), x.

11 Julia Kristeva, *Powers of Horror: An Essay on Abjection* (New York: Columbia University Press, 1982) 1–2.

12 Ibid., 4. Kristeva and Butler use the term differently, though: for instance, whereas Kristeva describes the abject as a 'non-object', Butler situates the abject within discourse, comparing it to a 'non-subject'. Similar to Kristeva, the Butlerian abject subverts discourse, yet this happens from within. Through adopting the terms of hegemonic discourse, Butler argues, its artificiality can first be exposed and eventually challenged (cf. *Bodies that Matter*, 3).

13 Kristeva, *Powers of Horror*, 3.

14 Alexander Leggatt, *Shakespeare's Tragedies: Violation and Identity* (Cambridge: Cambridge University Press, 2005), 8.

15 For an overview of several realisations of this scene in performance, see Christina Wald, "'But of Course the Stage Has Certain Limits'? The Adaptation of Ovid's *Metamorphoses* in Shakespeare's Plays," *Anglia* 127.3 (2010): 442–447.

16 On Shakespeare's appropriation of Ovid, see A. B. Taylor, "Animals in 'Manly Shape As Too the Outward Showe': Moralizing and Metamorphosis in *Titus Andronicus*," in *Shakespeare's Ovid: The Metamorphoses in the Plays and Poems*, ed. A. B. Taylor (Cambridge: Cambridge University Press, 2000), 66–80; Grace Starry West, "Going by the Book: Classical Allusions in Shakespeare's *Titus Andronicus*," *Studies in Philology* 79.1 (1982): 62–77.

17 Jonathan Bate, Introduction to *Titus Andronicus*, by William Shakespeare, ed. Jonathan Bate, The Arden Shakespeare Third Series (London: Arden Shakespeare, 1995), 62.

18 Pascale Aebischer, *Shakespeare's Violated Bodies: Stage and Screen Performance* (Cambridge: Cambridge University Press, 2004), 30–31.

19 Susan Sontag, *Regarding the Pain of Others* (New York and London: Penguin, 2003), 85.

20 A. Leigh DeNeef, "Poetics, Elizabethan," in *The Spenser Encyclopedia*, ed. Albert Charles Hamilton (Toronto: Toronto University Press, 1990), 552.

21 On Shakespeare's reinterpretation of the blazon tradition in this play, see Mary Laughlin Fawcett, "Arms/Words/Tears: Language and the Body in *Titus Andronicus*," *ELH* 50.2 (1983): 261–277; Lisa S. Starks-Estes, "Transforming Ovid: Images of Violence, Vulnerability, and Sexuality in Shakespeare's *Titus Andronicus*," in *Staging the Blazon in Early Modern English Theatre*, ed. Deborah Uman and Sara Morrison (Farnham and Burlington: Ashgate, 2013), 53–66.

22 Wald, "'But of Course the Stage Has Certain Limits'," 447.

23 Farah Karim-Cooper, *The Hand on the Shakespearean Stage: Gesture, Touch and the Spectacle of Dismemberment* (London and New York: Arden Shakespeare, 2016), 222.

24 Richard T. Brucher, "'Tragedy, Laugh On': Comic Violence in *Titus Andronicus*," *Renaissance Drama* 10.1 (1979): 91.

25 Judith Butler, *Gender Trouble: Feminism and the Subversion of Identity* (London and New York: Routledge, 1990), 189.

26 Katherine A. Rowe, "Dismembering and Forgetting in *Titus Andronicus*," *Shakespeare Quarterly* 45.3 (1994): 296.

27 Packard, "Lavinia as Coauthor," 293.

28 Leggatt, *Shakespeare's Tragedies*, 22.

29 See Bate's note to 5.3.36 in *Titus Andronicus*, ed. Jonathan Bate, The Arden Shakespeare Third Series (London: Arden Shakespeare, 1995). According to Livy, the centurion Virginius killed his daughter Virginia after she had been raped. As Bate explains, in some editions, Virginius kills his daughter to prevent her from being raped while in others he does so after the rape.

30 Williams, "'Silence, Like a Lucrece Knife'," 94–95.

31 Derek Cohen, *Searching Shakespeare: Studies in Culture and Authority* (Toronto: University of Toronto Press, 2003), 173.

32 Derek Cohen, *Shakespeare's Culture of Violence* (Ipswich and New York: St. Martin's, 1993), 80.

33 Williams, "'Silence, Like a Lucrece Knife'," 107.

34 Maurice Charney, *Titus Andronicus* (London: Harvester Wheatsheaf, 1990), 118.

35 Cohen, *Shakespeare's Culture of Violence*, 80.

36 Nicola M. Imbracsio "Stage Hands: *Titus Andronicus* and the Agency of the Disabled Body in Text and Performance," in *Titus Out of Joint: Reading the Fragmented Titus Andronicus*, ed. Liberty Stanavage and Paxton Hehmeyer (Cambridge: Cambridge Scholars, 2012), 119.

37 Aebischer provides a detailed and nuanced overview of directorial choices concerning Lavinia's death. She discusses a number of productions that followed the interpretive model suggested by Brook and only lists those by Deborah Warner (1987/88) and Gregory Doran (1995) as notable exceptions (*Shakespeare's Violated Bodies*, 56–63); see also Alan C. Dessen, *Shakespeare in Performance: Titus Andronicus* (Manchester: Manchester University Press, 1989), 94–97.

38 Heather James, "Cultural Disintegration in *Titus Andronicus*: Mutilating Titus, Vergil, and Rome," *Violence in Drama, Themes in Drama* 13 (1991): 134–135.

39 Coppélia Kahn, "Shakespeare's Classical Tragedies," in *The Cambridge Companion to Shakespearean Tragedy*, ed. Claire McEachern (Cambridge: Cambridge University Press, 2002), 210.

2   Happy Daggers
Romeo and Juliet

It is a truth universally acknowledged that *Romeo and Juliet* is the greatest love tragedy of all time – after all, their immortal love culminates in a love suicide. Unlike *Hamlet*, Shakespeare's other play set in a Christian context in which suicide plays a major role, *Romeo and Juliet* does not engage with religious damnation of self-slaughter. Given that its Veronese setting is distinctly Catholic, this may seem surprising. Perhaps also surprisingly, already the Prologue prepares the audience for the couple's eventual suicides. Despite tragedy's teleological formula, such a detailed narrative prolepsis is unusual. Nevertheless, it anticipates the play's peculiar quality of "pre-scriptedness," its overall theme of haste and prematurity.[1]

The reputation of the quintessential love tragedy is perpetuated by popular culture as well as scholars who, like Harold Bloom, describe the lovers' relationship as "as healthy and normative a passion as Western literature affords us. It concludes in mutual suicide, but not because either of the lovers lusts for death, or mingles hatred with desire."[2] Bloom's view may be contested because Romeo can indeed be read as lusting for death, and furthermore, his picture of Romeo and Juliet's love is much less critical than that painted by the text. On the one hand, their relationship is idealised, described through stylised rhetoric. On the other, as Stanley Wells has shown, this is one of the bawdiest of all the plays, saturated with sexual puns and innuendo.[3] What also speaks against any idealising notion is that from the first lines of the Prologue onwards, love resembles a destructive force. The couple "take their life" (Prologue 6) from the "fatal loins" (Prologue 5) of their parents' rival houses, which is an ambiguous phrase. If it means 'derive their live', the prologue merely offers a chronological order of events. But if understood as 'deprive themselves of life', it merges beginning and conclusion of the story, presenting their suicides as an inevitable result of the familial feud.[4] Furthermore, and following both these alternative readings, Romeo and Juliet are associated with sexuality rather than romantic love. The *Liebestod* convention the text invokes from the beginning, thus, forms a powerful narrative, but one that needs to be scrutinised rather than adopted without further reflection.

In the following, I will, therefore, consider the ways in which the portrayal of Romeo's and Juliet's suicides works against the play's self-constructed ethos of undying, romantic love. As will be shown, their love is described in ambivalent terms. Moreover, Romeo's love for Juliet is presented in a different way than Juliet's love for Romeo, and in both cases, traditionally masculine and feminine roles are turned upside down. This reversal of roles continues, or rather culminates in, their joint suicide. *Romeo and Juliet* features the only joint suicide scene in the canon and, hence, the only case in which a male and a female death are immediately juxtaposed. Elsewhere in the tragedies, male and female deaths are equally defined in opposition to one another but split into separate scenes – the contrast is not as (visually) graspable. The manner in which Shakespeare choreographs Romeo and Juliet's death scene toys with tragedy's generic boundaries, and again, I argue, this is because gendered expectations regarding traditionally masculine and feminine deaths are reversed.

"These Violent Delights": Romeo's and Juliet's Suicidal Aspirations

Even before her suicide, Juliet appears the stronger of the two, not least because Shakespeare develops her more fully and gives her an unusual amount of backstory. He makes her even younger than she is in Arthur Brooke's text, and so the contrast between her young age and mature presence in the play is striking. Similar to Brabantio's misrepresentation of Desdemona, Capulet describes Juliet as a naïve and innocent creature who is "yet a stranger in the world" (1.2.8). Within her defiance of parental authority, however, Juliet is much more daring than Romeo. She takes the initiative in advancing their relationship and is aware of her physicality, with an eagerness to act on her desire for sexual experiences. As Catherine Belsey points out, on the spectrum between masculinity and femininity, so diametrically opposed in *Titus Andronicus*, Romeo and Juliet find themselves in roughly the same position. He is not more masculine than her, and Juliet is just about as feminine as Romeo.[5] Until the end, their relationship follows the generic formula of romantic love, and, therefore, Juliet never fully leaves her conventional female role. Nonetheless, her unconventionally dominant behaviour conflicts with Renaissance gender norms and patriarchal discourses that require her to be silent and submissive.

It is obvious that Juliet's attitude towards suicide, which fully materialises in the suicide scene, is different from Romeo's. Juliet is desperate after hearing about his banishment, but unlike Romeo, she decides to ask for advice first: "If all else fail, myself have power to die" (3.5.242). She explicitly considers suicide an option, but her reaction is rational rather than impulsive. Her choice of the term "power" associates suicide with strength. In case the Friar cannot provide any help, she says, "'Twixt my extremes and me this bloody knife / Shall play the umpire" (4.1.62–63). She even makes it clear that she is ready to die: "I long to die, / If what thou speak'st speak not of remedy" (4.1.66–67). Still, the latter part of her line is important; taking her own life would only be the last resort. Despite her grave words, she appears to be in control of her emotions and able to speak rationally. Her desperation has not clouded her judgement, and this determination enhances the brutality of her words. As follows, the Friar counters:

> If, rather than to marry County Paris,
> Thou hast the strength of will to slay thyself,
> Then is it likely thou wilt undertake
> A thing like death to chide away this shame,
> That cop'st with death himself to scape from it.
> And if thou dar'st, I'll give thee remedy.
>
> (4.1.71–76)

Surprisingly, Friar Laurence does not reprimand Juliet for her suicidal intentions. What is more, he interprets her relative calmness and control of emotions as signs of strength, if not daring.

In order to stress her conviction further, Juliet provides a list of various possible forms of suicide. Rather than marry Paris, she would prefer to jump "off the battlements of any tower," "lurk / Where serpents are," be chained "with roaring bears," buried alive "with dead men's rattling bones," or "a dead man in his shroud" (4.1.71–85). Juliet's enumeration resembles a catalogue of all Shakespearean deaths. What these rather inventive methods have in common is that they are drastic, violent, and dreadful; they speak of strength and determination. Nevertheless, the Friar's seemingly well-devised fake suicide plan frightens her, however safe he claims his plan to be:

> How if, when I am laid into the tomb,
> I wake before the time that Romeo
> Come to redeem me? There's a fearful point!
> Shall I not then be stifled in the vault,
> To whose foul mouth no healthsome air breathes in,
> And there die strangled ere my Romeo comes?
>
> (4.3.30–35)

Juliet anticipates the monument she later dies in as a place of Gothic horror. As the stage direction following 4.3.23 indicates, she even lays down a knife to prepare for this worst-case scenario. A few lines earlier, she has told the Friar that she would accept such a death "without fear or doubt" (4.1.87). But in this previous scene, she had merely spoken in theory. Now, this option becomes real, and her language in the above passage reinforces how she sees death: as a means of escaping possible shame, not a goal in itself. Juliet does not embrace death. No matter how bravely she tries to act, the prospect of death horrifies her. Her monologue ends with a triad of Romeo's name, in which Alexander Leggatt senses a growing estrangement from her lover who continues to romanticise their fate and brushes aside its potential horror.[6] As will be discussed in more detail, this sense of detachment and alienation between the two is equally tangible throughout the suicide scene itself. If all these indicators are taken together, Juliet cannot be deemed suicidal. She is willing to embrace death if need be, but she does not seem to be longing or even lusting for death.

Contrary to Juliet, Shakespeare builds up Romeo as suicidal from the start. Even before he appears onstage, Montague introduces him as suffering heavily from his unrequited love for Rosaline and reports that he "private in his chamber pens himself, / Shuts up his windows, locks fair daylight out" (1.1.138–139). Montague lists symptoms that, according to Renaissance Humorism, indicate a surplus of the black humour melancholy. Renaissance pseudo-medical records recognised love as a disease, an understanding that is equally topical in Renaissance drama.[7] At his first entrance, Romeo likens his feelings to "A madness most discreet, / A choking gall, and a preserving sweet" before concluding "I have lost myself, I am not here" (1.1.193–194; 197). He echoes Benvolio's earlier metaphor of love as disease (1.2.45–50), and his choice of words suggest an identity crisis. At the same time, Romeo reveals a self-deprecating delight in his pain, which translates into stylised, hyperbolic, and melancholic language. In other words, this is a performance of the Petrarchan lover.

In its foremost late sixteenth-century English form, Petrarchism presupposes the subject position of a male speaker who expresses his desire for an extraordinarily beautiful yet unreachable woman. Among the key features of Petrarchan poetry is its paradoxical nature, which envisions love as a desired but simultaneously painful experience – the lover's masochistic delight in his lady's cold indifference. Gary Waller stresses that the lady's "[a]bsence is a seeming necessity; presence is not conducive to poetry."[8] As can be inferred from this definition, Juliet is an unlikely Petrarchan mistress. She is not absent but present. Unlike with Rosaline, Romeo's affections are not declined but requited, which causes problems with Romeo's self-concept of the Petrarchan lover. Juliet herself and her feelings only play a minor role because by definition, the focus is on the speaker; the elaborate praise of the beloved's beauty only serves to give voice to his dilemma. Accordingly, Romeo, as a Petrarchan stereotype, has lost all rights to exist after the first kiss in 1.5. Yet, as will be further elaborated, he remains trapped within this convention until the end.

It is important to note that Petrarchism is a gendered convention, not only in the way that the subject position is mostly, though not exclusively, male. Discussions of what it means to be a man and of what constitutes early modern masculinity are at the heart of the courtly love tradition.[9] Negotiations of masculinity – debates on what makes a man – operate on a more general level as well. From the start, the text challenges Romeo's masculinity, in the voice of others as well as himself. His excessive emotions make him 'unmanly'. Like Antony, who will later blame all his lapses on Cleopatra, Romeo holds Juliet responsible: "Thy beauty hath made me effeminate / And in my temper soften'd valour's steel!" (3.1.115–116). Apart from the fact that it cannot be reconciled with his self-image, this ostensible weakness complicates Romeo's social role. Shakespeare's Verona is a masculine world, full of performances of masculine aggression and testosterone. The play, however, exclusively shows Romeo as the Petrarchan cliché; wallowing in emotions, lovesick, and pitying himself.

From the beginning, Romeo senses impending disaster. As Robin Headlam Wells comments, "[t]hat Romeo, as an aspiring Petrarchist, should have premonitions of 'untimely death' cutting short a 'despised life' [...] is only to be expected; it goes with the role."[10] In particular, Romeo reveals hot-headedness when he considers suicide. He not only talks about suicide early on in the play, but also tries to kill himself before the actual suicide scene, which is why Marilyn L. Williamson believes him to be "more faithful to his commitment to death than he is to any living woman – Rosaline or Juliet."[11] Upon learning about his banishment, he – unlike Juliet – reacts impulsively: "In what vile part of this anatomy / Doth my name lodge? Tell me that I may sack / The hateful mansion" (3.3.106–108). Whereas neither the Folio nor Q2–Q4 provide any stage directions here, Q1 indicates that after speaking this line, Romeo offers to stab himself, but the Nurse snatches away the dagger at the last moment.[12] The latter suggestion seems particularly appropriate since Friar Laurence criticises:

> Hold thy desperate hand.
> Art thou a man? Thy form cries thou art.
> Thy tears are womanish, thy wild acts denote
> The unreasonable fury of a beast.
> Unseemly woman in a seeming man,
> And ill-beseeming beast in seeming both!
>
> (3.3.108–113)

Whereas Friar Laurence does not reprimand Juliet for her readiness to die and even praises her daringness, Romeo's suicidal intentions are considered a weakness of character, an emotional overreaction. For Juliet, the stakes are much higher, of course. Whereas she faces both the prospect of being married to a man she does not love and the resulting shame of being married twice, Romeo is merely absorbed by his performance of the tragic lover. In keeping with the Friar's argument, irratio. equals femininity. Furthermore, Romeo's irrational behaviour no emasculates him, but also dehumanises him. The notion of gendei a.... even a fixed concept of sex originate later than the Renaissance, but contemporary gender discourse nevertheless perpetuates a male teleology.[13] Within the understanding that all humans begin their life cycle as females, masculinity signals advancement from femininity. Stephen Orgel explains that the particular threat of such male teleology lies within its potential reversal, by which men were imagined to be turned (or turned back) into women, thus relapsing into what was considered a lower evolutionary stage.[14] Within the Friar's cultural horizon, Romeo's behaviour appears potentially alarming. Romeo's conventionally feminine gender performance in combination with a male body collapses normative gender constructions.

Closely related to the debate of what Romeo's precipitate suicide attempt communicates is the question of his motivation for suicide. In Melvyn Donald Faber's view, Romeo's suicide attempt is "prompted by a mixture of thwarted love and guilt."[15] What Faber overlooks is that although guilt would seem a plausible reason for such suicidal despair, Romeo does not talk about guilt. More importantly, initially, he rather seems to be troubled by the prospect that "[t]here is no world without Verona walls" (3.3.17); the first reference to Juliet follows thirteen lines later. He decides on actual suicide just as quickly as he previously offers to kill himself, which also speaks in favour of a general life-weariness rather than an immediate response to the prospect that he will have to live without Juliet. After Balthasar tells him about Juliet's alleged death, Romeo's reply is fatalistic: "Is it e'en so? Then I defy you, stars!" Yet, Balthasar's "I do beseech you sir, have patience. / Your looks are pale and wild and do import / Some misadventure" again suggests an emotional overreaction on Romeo's part. He then concludes "Well Juliet, I will lie with thee tonight. / Let's see for means" (5.1.24–35). The swiftness with which he comes to this decision as well as the coldness of his words support the reading that his mind is firmly set on death. No wonder that Juliet's intuition when misinterpreting the news about Tybalt's death is to ask whether Romeo has killed himself (3.2.45); considering the vehement reiteration of his readiness to die, he might just as well have done so.

Romeo's following search for a weapon is peculiar since he takes pains to make this as complicated as possible. The obvious choice in his situation would have been the sword he carries with him throughout the entire play – the sword with which he has fought against the Capulets and killed Tybalt. Nonetheless, he decides on poisoning himself, and already buying the poison is difficult. As the Apothecary, whom Romeo describes as the archetypal criminal in order to stress the illegality of the act, warns, this could mean death for both of them (5.1.66–74). Still, Romeo insists on

A dram of poison, such soon-speeding gear
As will disperse itself through all the veins,
That the life-weary taker may fall dead,
And that the trunk may be discharg'd of breath
As violently as hasty powder fir'd
Doth hurry from the fatal cannon's womb.

(5.1.60–65)

Again, he reinforces his urge to die, and almost every word he uses connotes extreme violence. Tanya Pollard remarks that his comparison of poison and gunpowder furthermore "conveys an eroticized urgency, likening death to an explosive sexual consummation. [...] In evoking this earlier reference, Romeo's words appropriate the scale and force of a cannon for his own humbler means of death; they also serve to identify his suicidal frenzy with the passion that spawned it."[16] Suitably, it seems, the Apothecary offers him a liquid that will kill him quickly and even "if [he] had the strength / of twenty men it would dispatch [him] straight" (5.1.78–79). Despite these strong words, poison is a conventionally gentle and, ever since the classical concept of suicide, a rather profane weapon. It is 'un-Roman' and, by extension, unmanly. The only other male character who intends to poison himself is Horatio. Horatio's attempt to kill himself by drinking from the poisoned cup not only appears unduly dramatic and out of place, but also allows for a reading that finds him effeminate, potentially also romantically attached to Hamlet. If Romeo had stabbed himself, he would have died a violent, conventionally and symbolically masculine death.

As far as the gendering of weapons is concerned, Romeo conveys an altogether different impression when he arrives at the Capulets' tomb, armed with an axe and wrenching iron; within the image of the tomb as Juliet's bedchamber, this is a troubling resurgence of masculine forcefulness. This is one of the many passages in which Shakespeare draws on *topoi* from the *danse macabre* tradition, which is rooted in religious iconography and would have been identifiable to a Renaissance audience: the 'marriage with Death' and 'life in Death'.[17] The former, in particular, is a prevalent motif since Juliet voices a belief that her "grave is like to be [her] wedding bed" (1.5.135). Romeo is similarly violent when he kills Paris. The officially chosen husband for Juliet, Paris, has been a rival to Romeo all along. Now, he even metaphorically intrudes into Juliet's bedchamber, thus becoming a direct threat to Romeo. Through violence, Romeo seeks to secure his position as Juliet's lover. Simultaneously, this is an attempt to (re)assert his masculinity. In both contexts, it can only be deemed ironic that not Romeo but Paris is the one who last kisses Juliet while she is still alive. Hence, the performance Romeo gives when entering the monument and especially the tools he uses stand in stark opposition to the connotations of frailty and femininity communicated by his weapon of choice for suicide.

"Misadventured Overthrows": The Comic Structures of a Tragic Ending

Prima facie, Romeo and Juliet's suicides are the epitome of a love death with all its conventional associations. They are denied a happy life as husband and wife, and, thus, only suicide can bring them together. It is their only way out of eternal separation. As W. H. Auden clarifies, it is part of romantic love's literary formula that "the obstacle that the lovers ideally require must be insurmountable. That is to say, their union must be possible only through their deaths. This is the secret, the religious mystery, of Romantic Love, the mystery that is represented by the suicides of Romeo and Juliet."[18] One can already sense a pinch of sarcasm in Auden's words, and this undertone is traceable in Shakespeare's text as well. To begin with, the Capulets' tomb by definition is a place of death, but it is symbolic on a different level. As the place of Juliet's second wedding night with Romeo, the tomb still suggests a romanticised notion of dying for love and with the beloved, but its ultimate implications are destructive. Filled with the bodies of Juliet's ancestors, all of who will have contributed their share to the families' feud, the tomb not only proves an unpleasant, but also a highly ambivalent setting for a love suicide. In the same manner as Juliet, Romeo experiences it as a place of horror: "Thou detestable maw, thou womb of death, / Gorg'd with the dearest morsel of the earth" (5.3.45–46). The setting, thus, conjures death with all its destructive force.

Ruth Nevo argues that Romeo "hastens disaster by his very conviction of it,"[19] a tendency that shows when he enters the monument. Romeo already expects Juliet to be dead. The illusion of her dead body only confirms his assumptions and, therefore, renews his decision to commit suicide. His first reaction to finding her in the tomb is not one of shock, excessive grief, or despair. Quite the opposite, he praises the beauty of death: "her beauty makes / This vault a feasting presence full of light. / Death lie there, by a dead man interred" (5.3.85–87). Reconsidering Romeo's Petrarchan role, this presents the ideal condition for the role to perpetuate itself. Death has taken Juliet, and so his desire will ultimately remain unfulfilled. Again, he associates himself with death, emotionally and soon also physically. In *Death, Desire and Loss in Western Culture*, Jonathan Dollimore lays out Western culture's long-standing fascination with the relationship between desire and death. Within this paradox, Dollimore explains, "desire comes to seem destructively insatiable, a permanent lack whose attempted fulfilment is at once the destiny of the self and what destroys it."[20] Romeo harbours such an inexorably self-destructive desire for death, as can be taken from the way he aestheticises and eroticises the dead Juliet: "Death that hath sucked the honey of thy breath / Hath no power yet upon thy beauty. / Thou art not conquered" (5.3.91–94). Of course, her beauty remains untouched because she is not actually dead. In conjunction with Romeo's hyperbolic and artificial language, this aestheticisation of Juliet's body has the potential of creating detachment on the part of the audience. It complicates sympathy with Romeo because he merely quotes a (literary) convention.

In Tom McAlindon's view, upon "[h]earing of Juliet's death, Romeo stoically defies the stars and decides to join her; his conduct here contrasts vividly with the adolescent and indeed bestial frenzy of his first reaction to bad news, and marks his attainment of manhood."[21] This description, however, conflicts with Romeo's suicide soliloquy, which, like his previous speeches, is conventional in its tone as well as imagery:

> Here, here will I remain
> With worms that are thy chambermaids. O here
> Will I set up my everlasting rest
> And shake the yoke of inauspicious stars
> From this world-wearied flesh. Eyes, look your last.
> Arms, take your last embrace! And lips, O you
> The doors of breath, seal with a righteous kiss
> A dateless bargain to engrossing Death.
> Come, bitter conduct, come unsavoury guide.
> Thou desperate pilot now at once run on
> The dashing rocks thy seasick weary bark.
> Here's to my love. [*He drinks.*] O true apothecary,
> Thy drugs are quick. Thus with a kiss I die.
> [*He falls.*]

(5.3.108–120)

Rather than characterising Romeo's words as stoical, it is more accurate to say that he still speaks in a Petrarchan voice. He uses a variety of different images, which enhances the tragic dimension of his words but at the same time heightens the effect of alienation. First, he fashions himself as a victim of fate. Second, he lays emphasis on the physicality of him as a lover, which culminates in a last kiss as the ultimate romantic gesture. The fact that this is also Romeo's final line in the play highlights this action even further, but this is mainly due to dramatic convention; the kiss is verbalised rather than simply acted out. Furthermore, he compares his parting kiss to sealing a bargain and, in doing so, draws on a legal context.[22] Against the backdrop of his emotional words, this initially appears odd, but it emphasises that his decision is irrevocable. He has signed a contract with death and is now past the point of return. His kissing Juliet identifies her as the reason for making this contract and simultaneously serves as a means of confirming it. Also, Romeo makes use of a maritime metaphor, describing himself as a ship that has lost its course and, thereby, expresses his weariness of life. Even though he knows the poison to be distasteful, he relies on it for guidance out of his despair. René Weis references a pun on the word 'quick', which can also be understood as 'alive'.[23] This acutely captures the paradox of his suicide: the deadly poison kills Romeo and, yet, his expectation to be reunited with his beloved in death revitalises him.

It is noteworthy that all the images of despair refer to him. In the preceding lines of this soliloquy, he has extensively described Juliet's beauty in the moment of death, but in his dying moment, he does not talk about her any longer. In true Petrarchan fashion, the speech is primarily about him and his emotional suffering. Williamson thus goes so far as to say that "Romeo's suicide fulfils a pattern to which Juliet is both necessary and accidental: if she had not been the inspiration, there would have been some other."[24] In accordance with the *Liebestod*-cliché, Romeo kills himself on Juliet's body. In ancient Greece, this way of committing suicide on top of the beloved's body was such a commonplace that it could be described by a distinct word: *epi(kata)sphattein heauton*.[25] Romeo's suicide next to or even on top of Juliet's body is the ultimate Petrarchan gesture, united with, yet at the same time eternally separated from, his beloved. This is how he defines himself and fashions his last image.

Throughout, Nevo points out, "Juliet's suffering is finely discriminated from Romeo's as is her suicide and indeed her experience of love."[26] Juliet's suicide soliloquy is telling in this respect:

> What's here? A cup clos'd in my true love's hand?
> Poison, I see, hath been his timeless end.
> O churl. Drunk all, and left no friendly drop
> To help me after? I will kiss thy lips.
> Haply some poison yet doth hang on them
> To make me die with a restorative. [*She kisses him.*]
>
> (5.3.161–166)

Compared to Romeo's final lines, hers is a straightforward speech. It is considerably shorter, and there is less melodrama. Not a single word refers to her suffering and despair. Romeo delights in his suffering, but Juliet does not. Her language appears so inornate and almost matter-of-fact that one can sense a bitter undertone. She simultaneously addresses Romeo as her true love and "churl," which suggests an emotional conflict of loving him and at the same time hating him as Tybalt's killer. The way she phrases it, she kisses Romeo as a means to an end. Her kiss is not a dramatic gesture of expressing their undying love but an attempt to retrieve the remaining poison. However, her language does not entirely separate her from Romeo, which can be taken from her naming the poison a "restorative." This mirrors Romeo's earlier reference to the poison as lethal, but also "friendly" and revitalising. Both exhibit a belief in a reunion in the afterlife, even though this is only hinted at rather vaguely.

While *Antony and Cleopatra* consistently portrays suicide as a transcendental act and celebrates the belief in a reunion in death, *Romeo and Juliet* remains indecisive about the matter.

According to Faber, Juliet's decision for suicide is as quick and impulsive as Romeo's: "Once again reflection becomes superfluous. Once again impulse and ardour hold sway."[27] But apart from the fact that Romeo's decision to kill himself is far from sudden, for Juliet, further reflection is not superfluous but altogether impossible; it is her option once she is out of options. As also exemplified by Ophelia, death is clearly more desirable than life in a convent, the alternative offered by the Friar. Juliet needs to die quickly, and so there is simply no time and occasion to ponder the question of what would be an appropriate weapon. However, her choice of weapon is no less symbolic than Romeo's. To start with, her attempt to poison herself with the remaining drops on Romeo's lips fits the love suicide perfectly well. Like Romeo, she intends to die on a kiss, an endeavour that ironically remains unsuccessful. If one recalls the Apothecary's words, the poison is strong enough to kill twenty men within an instant. Still, it does not seem to be strong enough to kill her. The reason is, of course, that there is not enough poison left. Yet, figuratively speaking, the gentler weapon poison may kill the weak Romeo but is not strong enough to kill the stronger Juliet.

Against this backdrop, it is not surprising that she, without hesitation, draws a dagger when she hears the others approaching: "Yea, noise? Then I'll be brief. O happy dagger. / This is thy sheath. There rust, and let me die" (5.3.168–169). 'Happy' is an ambivalent term that, in addition to its basic denotation of 'fortunately available', both emphasises Juliet's desire to die and bolsters a reading of her suicide as substitute for the sexual act.[28] Particularly with the latter part of this interpretation, the question arises as to whose dagger Juliet uses. At first glance, this may seem a trivial question. Weis suggests that it is Romeo's, which is also what Capulet assumes (5.3.203–204) and what seems to be the general consensus in criticism.[29] The text itself remains inconclusive on the matter, and as a result, this is largely for an individual production's director to decide. Katherine Duncan-Jones argues against it being Romeo's dagger because such symbolism would convey a sense of unity or harmony entirely at odds with the couple's increasing estrangement.[30] What also speaks in favour of her reading is that Juliet taking Romeo's weapon undercuts the notion of autonomy and agency in choosing death. By stabbing herself, Juliet chooses a masculine weapon, in terms of both its Roman connotation and the play's inherent Freudian symbolism. As Clayton G. MacKenzie puts it, "in this final, resolute act she upturns that very masculine typification of Death as the marital predator, selecting and ravishing his victim."[31] On the other hand, the eagerness with which she awaits the dagger resembles her anticipation of the wedding night. If Romeo cannot penetrate her any more, his dagger is the next best thing. This obvious Freudian reading is too poignant to be discarded and provides a fitting counterpoint to the conventionalised rhetoric and imagery surrounding their suicides.

While Juliet's suicide appears more reasonably thought-out and resolute than Romeo's, she nevertheless believes it to be unavoidable, which begs the question of how self-determined a choice she makes. Paul Kottman comments on the misery of Juliet's choice between a marriage to Paris and suicide because both options forever imprison her within the family, the latter in the form of a body in the family tomb. As follows, he feels that suicide would be "a sad necessity, an act demonstrating her absolute loss of freedom."[32] If Juliet can only assert her freedom by killing herself, it is indeed a sad necessity. Yet, what should not be overlooked is that she herself considers suicide a way out; within the realm of the play, choosing death provides a way to assert her freedom. Juliet's is a limited freedom, but she has a choice nonetheless.

Emphasising the significance of the feminine when it comes to tragic endings, Dympna Callaghan writes that "the most important characteristics of the body upon which denouement focuses are that it is silent, dead and female. I contend that major female characters become 'dead centres' of tragic consummation. [...] Female corpses are constructed as focal points for ocular inspection by other characters in a way that male bodies are not. A dead man onstage swiftly becomes part of the stage furniture, and even in the death of the tragic hero, we glance at him only momentarily before the curtain falls and the lights go out."[33] Dead female bodies in particular matter, and the same is true for Juliet. As already the title suggests, Juliet is surely integral to both the play's overall tragic dimension and the hero's tragic downfall. Both their bodies are displayed together, but the seemingly dead Juliet for a much longer period. In production, Juliet would most likely even be elevated from the stage. Her body is the tragic image the audience can contemplate most fully. Following Callaghan's argument, Juliet, not Romeo, is the tragic centre.

If Juliet is a strong, if not stronger, contender for the tragic centre, this also poses a question with regard to the play's genre. When in John Madden's *Shakespeare in Love* (1998) Philip Henslowe is pressed for money, he promises his creditor a new comedy by William Shakespeare: "Romeo and Ethel, the Pirates Daughter," a real crowd-tickler including mistaken identities, shipwreck, and a dog. However, halfway through the writing process, Joseph Fiennes's Shakespeare abandons the catchy title and opts for tragedy instead. Obviously, this fictional anecdote hints at the question of the play's generic transformation. There is only a fine line between comedy and tragedy. The danger of tragedy tripping into farce is always lurking beneath, and in Shakespeare in particular, comic elements are an inherent part of tragedy. They function as a contrastive tool, as a means of irony, and as what Tom McAlindon calls "a safety valve forestalling the kind of inappropriate laughter" that high tragedy potentially provokes.[34] *Romeo and Juliet* is not only likely to provoke such inappropriate laughter, but also stands out from the canon for its peculiar bi-partite structure. As Susan Snyder has shown, the play "becomes, rather than is, tragic."[35] This trajectory of comedy gradually developing into tragedy is widely acknowledged: in the first half, young lovers overcome their parental blocking figures with the help of confidant sidekicks. The couples' love is celebrated in a marriage that promises hope for generations to come; in other words, the prototypical Shakespearean comic ending. After Mercutio's death, the world of the play turns darker, finite, and inevitably geared towards death.[36] Despite these generic shifts, Petrarchan Romeo, another comic stock character, does not disappear; neither do the comic undertones, and not only in the generic sense of the term.

Martha Tuck Rozett scrutinises the play's comic structures with its parallels to *Antony and Cleopatra*. What in her opinion distinguishes both these plays from Shakespeare's other tragedies is the way the protagonists exist and die not as individual characters but as tragic couples; their deaths are linked to and defined by one another.[37] Accordingly, although Juliet's and Cleopatra's motivations to fake their own deaths could not be more different, in both these plays, the heroes' deaths are triggered by the 'false death' *topos*. Traditionally, this is a comic device, and here, as elsewhere in comedy, timing is vital. Unfortunately, within the underlying atmosphere of haste, timing is amiss. The suicide scene is constructed through several such accidents of timing, which Rozett poignantly refers to as "reminiscent of the comic near misses in *A Comedy of Errors*."[38] The audience know that Juliet is not actually dead, and the feeling of wanting to stop Romeo from drinking the poison makes them cringe. The impression of an accident rather than inevitable tragedy prevails. This is developed further when, directly after Romeo drops dead, Friar Laurence enters the scene. Juliet rises on cue, just about a minute too late. Immediately after Juliet's suicide, other characters enter the tomb, this time merely a few seconds too late to prevent her from killing herself. This is particularly relevant because Shakespeare deviates from his sources here. In Brooke's text, "An howre too late fayre Iuliet awaked out of slepe."[39] By reducing this period until her awakening so drastically, Shakespeare not only increases dramatic tension and pace, but also, and above all, heightens the almost slapstick-esque effect of bad luck.

That timing is key shows even more clearly when taking a look at one of the further possible source text for the play, the Italian author Matteo Bandello's novella *Giulietta e Romeo*. In Bandello's text, Juliet wakes before Romeo dies, and so the two are given the chance to say their goodbyes. Several directors, notably David Garrick, have re-written Shakespeare's text accordingly, assuming that Shakespeare denied the lovers their parting scene only because of a mistake in the translation of Bandello.[40] Speculation about the playwright's use of his sources is, of course, generally problematic, and moreover, such an emendation makes a substantial difference. Weis remains divided on the issue. While he does not ultimately dismiss Garrick's argument, he still believes that "Juliet has so far outgrown Romeo by the end of the play that it seems entirely right that her final act of courage, a 'Roman' suicide unlike his gentler poisoning, should linger in our minds' eyes rather than a maudlin, however heart-wrenching, leave-taking of the two."[41] Leggatt opposes a re-written ending for the two. For him, the text subtly but effectively subverts this maudlin and heart-wrenching parting of the lovers and instead ends on a conflicting note, separating rather than uniting the lovers.[42] As argued above, the way Shakespeare wrote it, Romeo and Juliet's joint suicide runs counter to the image of tragic, star-crossed love. There is a deliberate friction in Shakespeare's text. Baz Luhrmann highlights this dissonance in his blockbuster adaptation *Romeo + Juliet* (1996) starring Leonardo DiCaprio and Claire Danes. Luhrmann, too, changes the suicide scene, only to an entirely different effect than Garrick. In the film, Juliet awakes, but Romeo notices this only after he has already swallowed the liquid. Both recognise their fatal mistake and start to panic. That way, Luhrmann underlines the sense of accident – of these being unnecessary rather than inevitable deaths.

Many productions end with Juliet's suicide, resting on the dramatically powerful image onstage. But even if the final scene is not cut, there are significant differences with regard to its interpretation. Barbara Hodgdon identifies two contrastive paradigms of concluding the play in performance: one a conservative nineteenth-century interpretation of a glorified and romanticised *Liebestod*, the other a more radical approach that is rooted in Brechtian aesthetics.[43] Whereas the former model follows the play's self-generated myth, the second much more adequately captures the undertones of the final scene. After Juliet's suicide, the stage crowds quickly. Paris's page, several watchmen, the Friar, Montague, Capulet, Capulet's wife, the Prince, and Balthasar all enter the scene and divert from the peaceful, tragic image of the two lifeless bodies in the tomb, which could be read as parody of the ritualistic guiding the newly married couple into their bed chamber.[44] In addition, news arrives that Montague's wife has died of grief for Romeo's banishment and, thus, rivals the tragedy that has just happened onstage. The revelatory nature of the final act as well as its atmosphere of forgiveness are much more typical of comedy or romance than of tragedy.[45]

The final scene is anticipated by the analogous 'lamentations scene' 4.5, which is often discussed for its excessive and stylised rhetoric. Through exaggerated emotional reactions, the characters pity themselves rather than the dead Juliet, thereby highlighting the artifice of the situation. The audience are reminded of the fact that this is solely "a thing like death," and so Pollard dubs the scene "a parody of death announcement."[46] In the final scene, by contrast, there is no hysterical crying and hyperbolic self-pity. Rather oddly, everybody is so calm and reserved that Friar Laurence can offer a lengthy account of what has happened. Even though he promises "I will be brief" (5.3.229), his retelling of the events runs on for forty-one lines without a single interruption. In presenting Romeo's and Juliet's death as direct results of the feud, the Friar's speech serves as reproach and appeal to both families. However, it fails to do so convincingly. What is intended as a solemn conclusion remains preachy, stale, and anticlimactic.

The feud between the rival houses ends surprisingly quickly. Echoing the Prologue, Capulet's eulogy presents the lovers as "Poor sacrifices of [their] enmity" (5.3.304). Juliette Marie Cunico comments on the lack of criticism on moral or religious grounds and, thus, questions the presentation of the two suicides as martyrs that have died for a greater cause.[47] Within the context of *Hamlet*, which addresses religious and legal impediments against suicide, this would be an odd lacuna. But religious debate is absent from *Romeo and Juliet*. The sudden air of reverence is, however, striking insofar as it appears misplaced, and the plan to set up a monument in remembrance of the two only reinforces this incongruity. Romeo and Juliet never consider themselves as uniting forces between the two rival houses; this reading is exclusively inscribed on them by their parents. Furthermore, the installing of a statue would provide a form of resurrection from the dead and, similar to the monument of Antony and Cleopatra, serve as a visual reminder of their eternal love. It is telling that such a work of art(ifice) forms the last visual image of Romeo and Juliet, even if it is verbally created. Rather than concluding on the symbolically powerful scene of their suicide, the play, therefore, prioritises a stylised and idealised recreation of the protagonists' love.

In the text, the focus is drawn even further away from the individuals and directed towards a sense of moral. Twice removed from the couple's suicides, the Prince draws the myth of Romeo and Juliet to a close and returns to the Prologue's level of a symbolic tale. This is the greatest tragedy of all time. There "never was a story of more woe" (5.3.309). Duly, he advises both the characters onstage and the audience to "have more talk of these sad things" (5.3.307) and, thus, develop this myth further through retelling. Clifford Leech comments on the notion of dying twice, first the actual physical death and second the moment one is no longer remembered and talked about by others. In Romeo and Juliet's case, this loss of remembrance will never come, which is why Leech concludes that "[c]ertainly this is a sad affair [...]. But we may ask, is it tragic?"[48] Thus, the play ends on a conflicting note similar to the one it begins on.

From the Prologue onwards, its incongruous portrayal of suicide works against the play's compelling myth of tragic love. Compared to Juliet, Romeo appears to be in love with death itself. As the play turns into tragedy, he stays put within the comic stereotype, which is reflected in the way he dies. Staged as an intricate moment of (mis)timing that can almost be deemed comic, the contrast between the two deaths becomes all the more evident. Everything in this play happens too quickly – too much in haste – Romeo's suicide conspicuously so. He accepts the – in his case merely proverbial – dagger all too happily, dying not in a reinforcement of masculinity but emotional excess. Juliet's suicide, unembellished and rationally motivated by comparison, challenges Romeo's suicide in terms of resolution and underpins her status as the tragic hero's equal, as far as power structures are concerned. Through this gendered juxtaposition of the two suicides, the play, thus, not only interrogates the convention of Petrarchism, but also, by extension, tragic power structures that equate 'feminine versus masculine' with 'weak versus strong'.

One step ahead from *Titus Andronicus*, here, too, suicide is defined as means of agency by which characters can control their fate. Unlike Lavinia, Juliet is not only able to kill herself but even does so onstage. However, though not as gladly as Romeo, she does so dutifully, thus subjecting herself to the grand *Liebestod* narrative reserved for her. As will be discussed, her female successors commit suicide not in order to follow obligations but to rebel against them, which shows that in this early tragedy the subversive potential of (female) suicides is not yet fully exploited.

Notes

1 Emma Smith discusses this quality in *"Romeo and Juliet," University of Oxford Podcasts: Approaching Shakespeare*, May 5, 2015, accessed May 3, 2017, https://podcasts.ox.ac.uk/romeo-and-juliet.
2 Harold Bloom, *Shakespeare: The Invention of the Human* (London: Fourth Estate, 1999), 93. On a contrary view cf., W. H. Auden, who believes that "Romeo and Juliet don't know each other, but when one dies, the other can't go on living. Behind their passionate suicides, as well as their reactions to Romeo's banishment, is finally a lack of feeling, a fear that the relationship cannot be sustained and that, out of pride, it should be stopped now, in death." *Lectures on Shakespeare*, ed. Arthur Kirsch (Princeton, NJ: Princeton University Press, 2000), 48.
3 Stanley Wells, *Shakespeare, Sex, and Love* (Oxford: Oxford University Press, 2010), 148–167.
4 William Shakespeare, *Romeo and Juliet*, ed. Jill L. Levenson, The Oxford Shakespeare (Oxford: Oxford University Press, 2000), textual note to line 6 of the Prologue.
5 Catherine Belsey, "Gender and Family," in *The Cambridge Companion to Shakespearean Tragedy*, ed. Claire McEachern (Cambridge: Cambridge University Press, 2002) 130.
6 Alexander Leggatt, *Shakespeare's Tragedies: Violation and Identity* (Cambridge: Cambridge University Press, 2005), 50.

7 Ivo Kamps, "'I Love You Madly, I Love You to Death:' Erotomania and Liebestod in *Romeo and Juliet*," in *Approaches to Teaching Shakespeare's Romeo and Juliet*, ed. Maurice Hunt (New York: MLA, 2000), 38. Amongst others, Robert Burton extensively discusses contemporary views on love-sickness and love-melancholy in the third partition of *The Anatomy of Melancholy* (1621, reprint; New York: The New York Review of Books Classics, 2001), 3–259.

8 Gary Waller, *English Poetry of the Sixteenth Century*, 2nd ed. (London and New York: Longman, 1993), 76.

9 On the question of Petrarchism and masculinity, see Ibid., 61–65. Natasha Distiller cautions that to speak of Petrarchism as a male convention inevitably accounts for a presentist reading, applying our own rather than the early modern concept of gender. In her view, a dichotomy of male oppressor versus female victim is too easy. Instead, she argues, these dynamics have to be placed within the context of early modern gender hierarchies, which Petrarchism reacted to. *Desire and Gender in the Sonnet Tradition* (Basingstoke and New York: Palgrave, 2008), 43–46.

10 Robin Headlam Wells, "Neo-Petrarchan Kitsch in *Romeo and Juliet*," *Modern Language Review* 93.4 (1998): 916.

11 Marilyn L. Williamson, "Romeo and Death," *Shakespeare Studies* 14 (1981): 129.

12 William Shakespeare, *Romeo and Juliet*, ed. René Weis, The Arden Shakespeare Third Series (London: Arden Shakespeare, 2012), critical apparatus to 3.3.107.

13 Stephen Greenblatt, *Shakespearean Negotiations: The Circulation of Social Energy in Renaissance England* (Oxford: Clarendon, 1988), 88.

14 Stephen Orgel, *Impersonations: The Performance of Gender in Shakespeare's England* (Cambridge: Cambridge University Press, 1996), 25.

15 Melvyn Donald Faber, "Suicide in Shakespeare" (PhD diss., University of California, 1963), 261.

16 Tanya Pollard, "'A Thing Like Death:' Sleeping Potions and Poisons in *Romeo and Juliet* and *Antony and Cleopatra*," *Renaissance Drama* 32 (2003): 103.

17 Clayton G. MacKenzie, "Love, Sex and Death in *Romeo and Juliet*," *English Studies* 88.1 (2007): 30–31. On the *danse macabre* tradition more generally see MacKenzie, *Emblem and Icon in John Donne's Poetry and Prose* (New York: Peter Lang, 2001), 24–35.

18 Auden, *Lectures on Shakespeare*, 48.

19 Ruth Nevo, "Tragic Form in *Romeo and Juliet*," *SEL* 9 (1969): 248.

20 Jonathan Dollimore, *Death, Desire and Loss in Western Culture* (New York: Taylor & Francis, 2001), xvii.

21 Tom McAlindon, "What is a Shakespearean Tragedy?" in *The Cambridge Companion to Shakespearean Tragedy*, ed. Claire McEachern (Cambridge: Cambridge University Press, 2002), 15.

22 See Levenson's note to 5.3.113–115 in the Oxford Shakespeare: "The legal metaphor is straightforward, and the idea behind it commonplace in Shakespeare: lips = seal; kiss = imprint of the seal on a contract; sealing a bargain = confirming an agreement [...]. The term and second party make this agreement less conventional: dateless means 'having no limit'; engrossing identifies death as a figure that observes legal protocol while monopolizing his trade."

23 See Weis's note to 5.3.120 in the Arden Third Series.

24 Williamson, "Romeo and Death," 132.

25 Anton J. L. van Hooff, *From Autothanasia to Suicide: Self-Killing in Classical Antiquity* (London and New York: Routledge, 1990), 48.

26 Nevo, "Tragic Form in *Romeo and Juliet*," 255.

27 Faber, "Suicide in Shakespeare," 204.

28 Stanley Wells, *Shakespeare, Sex, and Love*, 167.

29 See Weis's note to line 5.3.169 in the Arden Third Series. The SD reads "Takes Romeo's dagger" and the note to l. 170 says "[t]he dagger is probably Romeo's." As points of reference, Weis mentions Capulet's reaction as well as Brooke's source story. For an overview of the debate, see Katherine Duncan-Jones, "'O Happy Dagger:' The Autonomy of Shakespeare's Juliet," *Notes and Queries* 45.3 (1998): 314.

30 Duncan-Jones, "O Happy Dagger," 315.

31 MacKenzie, "Love, Sex and Death in *Romeo and* Juliet," 33.

32 Paul A. Kottman, "Defying the Stars: Tragic Love as the Struggle for Freedom in *Romeo and Juliet*," *Shakespeare Quarterly* 63.1 (2012): 30. On an opposing view, similar to my own, cf. MacKenzie, "Love, Sex and Death in *Romeo and Juliet*," 33.

33 Dympna Callaghan, *Woman and Gender in Renaissance Tragedy: A Study of King Lear, Othello, The Duchess of Malfi and The White Devil* (New York: Harvester Wheatsheaf, 1989), 90.

34 McAlindon, "What is a Shakespearean Tragedy," 5–6.

35 Susan Snyder, "*Romeo and Juliet*: Comedy into Tragedy," *Essays in Criticism* 20 (1970): 391.

36 On a more detailed discussion of the play's generic transformation, see Snyder, "Comedy into Tragedy," 391–402; Clifford Leech, "The Moral Tragedy of *Romeo and Juliet*," in *Critical Essays on Shakespeare's Romeo and Juliet*, ed. Joseph A. Porter (New York: Hall, 1997), 7–22.

37 Martha Tuck Rozett, "The Comic Structures of Tragic Endings: The Suicide Scenes in *Romeo and Juliet* and *Antony and Cleopatra*," *Shakespeare Quarterly* 36.2 (1985): 153.

38 Ibid., 155.

39 Arthur Brooke, "Romeus and Juliet," in *Romeo and Juliet*, ed. G. Blakemore Evans (Cambridge: Cambridge University Press, 2003), l. 2706.

40 René Weis, Introduction to *Romeo and Juliet*, by William Shakespeare, ed. René Weis, The Arden Shakespeare Third Series (London: Arden Shakespeare, 2012), 61. Garrick inserted the new parting scene in his textual version of 1748, revised in 1750. See also George C. Branam, "The Genesis of David Garrick's *Romeo and Juliet*," *Shakespeare Quarterly* 35 (1984): 170–179. This change to the scene is found in several earlier versions of the Romeo and Juliet story. See A. H. Diverres, "The Pyramus and Thisbe Story and its Contributions to the Romeo and Juliet Legend," *The Classical Tradition in French Literature*, ed. H. T Barnwell et al. (London: Grant & Cutler, 1977), 9–22.

41 Weis, Introduction to *Romeo and Juliet*, 61.

42 Leggatt, *Shakespeare's Tragedies*, 53.

43 Barbara Hodgdon, "Absent Bodies, Present Voices: Performance Work and the Close of *Romeo and Juliet*'s Golden Story," *Theatre Journal* 41.3 (1989): 343.

44 Leggatt, *Shakespeare's Tragedies*, 53.

45 Rozett, "The Comic Structures of Tragic Endings," 158.

46 Pollard, "'A Thing Like Death'," 99. For a more detailed analysis see Thomas Moisan, "Rhetoric and the Rehearsal of Death: The 'Lamentations' Scene in *Romeo and Juliet*," *Shakespeare Quarterly* 34.4 (1983): 389–404.

47 Juliette Marie Cunico, "Audience Attitudes toward Suicide in Shakespeare's Tragedies" (PhD diss., University of New Mexico, 1991), 146.

48 Leech, "The Moral Tragedy of *Romeo and Juliet*," 15–16.

3   Roman Fools

Julius Caesar

Julius Caesar features three suicides and one suicide by proxy. After *Antony and Cleopatra*, these amount to the second highest suicide count in Shakespeare's oeuvre; unsurprisingly perhaps, given that both are Roman tragedies. Characters frequently announce and comment on the gesture of Roman death, and in its philosophical discussion of the topic, *Julius Caesar* is more explicit than any other text in the canon. By the late Elizabethan and early Jacobean period, the concepts of 'Romanness' and suicide were inextricably linked. Thus, apart from creating verisimilitude with regard to historical accuracy, the repeated and varied references to suicide as a Roman convention – in *Julius Caesar* as well as in other Roman contexts – function as meta-drama. Shakespeare toys with the expectations of his audiences, for whom suicide was a prime constituent of what makes a Roman.[1]

'Romanness' and masculinity are similarly related concepts. Ancient Rome upheld a strict demarcation of gender, most visibly through the separation between the private *domus* as opposed to the public sphere, exclusively assigned to women and men respectively. "For almost four centuries," Coppélia Kahn writes, "both the scholarly community and the general public have taken Shakespeare's Roman works to represent Romanness – reading them *within the terms of this ideology.* Thus the degree to which Romanness is virtually identical with an ideology of masculinity has gone unnoticed, and it has been generally assumed that Shakespeare didn't notice it either."[2] Contrary to such previous assumptions, it seems that Shakespeare not only noticed but also utilised the ideological connection between 'Romanness' and masculinity to great effect.

If all these related concepts – 'Romanness', suicide, and masculinity – are taken into consideration, any portrayal of Roman death inevitably engages with negotiations of masculinity. Even though the play's most prominent, in the sense of both visible and critically discussed, suicides are committed by male characters, this chapter begins with Portia's offstage death. Throughout, Portia challenges her submissive female role, suicide being the logical culmination of her struggle. Even though the male suicides take place centre stage, I argue that it is her reported suicide, structurally excluded from dramatic attention, that steals the show with regard to both 'Romanness' and masculine virtue. Setting the play's portrayal and staging of female and male suicide side by side, I suggest that Shakespeare's Romans simultaneously reinforce and undermine notions of what makes a Roman death, thus eventually interrogating 'Romanness' as an exclusively masculine concept.

"A Man's Mind, But a Woman's Might": Portia's Suicide as Voice

Portia's death is documented in Plutarch's *Lives*, but while Shakespeare otherwise follows North's translation of Plutarch closely, her death marks a departure. According to Plutarch, Portia faints on the day of the assassination, which leads to a false report of her death that Brutus initially mistakes for the truth.[3] Whereas there her self-wounding as well as her grief when Brutus leaves Rome cause her illness and subsequent death, in Shakespeare's play, her suicide comes rather unexpectedly.[4] Unlike in the cases of Ophelia and Lady Macbeth, both of whom the audience witness descending into madness, there are no such indications with Portia. Precisely because her suicide is reported only, critical reception tends to downplay its importance. And many of those who do discuss her death in more detail blame it on her gradual separation from Brutus. Margaret Higonnet reads Portia's death within the mythical tradition of female suicides that are committed for either defeated love or protection of chastity. Whereas "Brutus commits suicide for the nation," she writes, "Portia commits suicide in order not to live without Brutus."[5] For Jan Blits, it primarily explores "the limits of sharing within a Roman marriage. It marks the unattainability of the intimacy she desires from a virtuous marriage."[6] Although such readings may be sustained by the text, they attribute Portia's suicide to an exclusively private, rather than political, motivation.

The habit of dismissing her suicide as the desperate act of a deserted wife goes hand in hand with a general neglect of her character in scholarly discussions, many of which dismiss her as minor.[7] Even though quantitatively Portia is a rather thin presence – according to Bate and Rasmussen, she merely speaks 4 per cent of the lines and is present in two scenes only – this critical neglect appears to be based on a misconception.[8] Without doubt, ancient Rome is a man's world. As Alison Sharrock puts it, "[i]t is very difficult to come to a sense of Roman constructions of femininity that do not tell us more about masculine attitudes to the 'Other' (female, slave, foreigner) than they do about real Roman women." Simultaneously, she notes, the "category 'Woman' is crucially important, and perhaps at first sight simple, since you just need to look at the opposite of the ideal Man (start with 'soft, passive, and silent')."[9] Women, thus, primarily functioned as foils against which to measure masculinity, which in turn rendered them vital to the construction of Rome itself. Whereas this claim denies women an importance in their own right, Portia has much more than a mere symbolic function. She belies the simplified dichotomy of masculinity versus femininity. Like that of the Macbeths, her marriage to Brutus is portrayed as a union between equal partners, conspicuously juxtaposed to Caesar and his wife Calphurnia. As Cato's daughter, Portia enjoys a high social status, but, comparable to Lady Macbeth, she is troubled by the discrepancy between what she aspires to and its socio-political reality. As she says herself, she has "a man's mind, but a woman's might" (2.3.8), which resembles a less disturbing and drastic version of Lady Macbeth's "Unsex me here."

Portia's first appearance is telling in this respect. To Brutus's reprimand "It is not for your health thus to commit / Your weak condition to the raw cold morning," she replies "Nor for yours neither" (2.1.234–236). Portia's illness is only introduced later on, so the question arises as to what "condition" Brutus refers to. Whereas David Daniell explains that in performance this term commonly hints towards pregnancy,[10] Gail Kern Paster reads Brutus's line as a remark not on Portia's illness but her gender identity. For Paster, Portia's response undermines the notion of difference that Brutus inscribes onto her, indicating that there is no logical reason as to why she as a woman should be in bed at night while the men wander about.[11] Since Brutus's conflict is a political one, there is no room for female voices. Her place is in the *domus*, not the public sphere. Portia's language acknowledges this distinction as well. She speaks in a formal, oratory way, identifiable as the masculine language of the Forum.[12] In addition to the formal quality of her language, Portia strategically defines herself through powerful men, Brutus on the one hand and Cato on the other: "Think you I am no stronger than my sex / Being so fathered and so husbanded?" (2.1.295–296). Their integrity and masculine virtue, she argues, is transferred onto her via the bond between husband and wife as well as father and daughter. Although she does not rank her as such, Portia can thus be labelled what Marianne Novy understands as the concept of 'outsiders as insiders'. Novy re-imagines the status of being an outsider, a category that is often used to classify those that are marked 'Other', be it for questions of gender, race, class, age, or illegitimate birth. She emphasises the empowering quality of being such an outsider and suggests that, though not always to the same degree, women are "the kind of outsider who provides a fresh perspective, the kind whose protest about exclusion arouses assent, or she can be, to a greater extent or lesser extent, an insider."[13] In this case, it is Portia's rebellion against her insufficient recognition as a politically minded individual that stands out, thus accentuating the play's (and Rome's) masculinist gender politics.

In *Roman Shakespeare: Warriors, Wounds, and Women*, Kahn examines the correlation between Shakespeare's Roman plays and the wound, "the most problematic, self-cancelling figuration of masculinity in the Roman works. [...] In an obvious sense, wounds mark a kind of vulnerability easily associated with women: they show the flesh to be penetrable, they show it can bleed, they make apertures in the body. But through the discursive operations of *virtus*, wounds become central to the signification of masculine virtue, and thus to the construction of the Roman hero."[14] This is equally relevant in the context of *Julius Caesar*; only here, it is a woman who evokes these discursive operations of Roman virtue. Through her self-inflicted wound in the thigh, Portia seeks to provide "strong proof of [her] constancy" (2.1.298) and demonstrate that she can bear pain just as much as a man. Melvyn Donald Faber considers this pathological, self-destructive behaviour. For him, both Plutarch's and Shakespeare's Portias are unstable characters, and her "anger and frustration are ultimately rooted in an exaggerated dependence upon her spouse."[15] Contrary to Faber's view, though, Portia's self-harm is commonly seen in a more positive light and identified as Stoic elevation of the mind over the body, a Roman ideal many (men) aspired to.[16]

In addition to its masculine connotation, i.e. its display of masculine *virtus*, Portia's wound can be read in another way. Paster stresses the ideological connection between gender and bodily intactness, comparing Portia's bleeding body to that of Lavinia. Whereas Lavinia's body bleeds uncontrollably and is furthermore captured and reproduced by the male voice, Portia's wound is "not the involuntary wound of the leaking female body but the honorifically gendered, purgative, voluntary wound of the male."[17] In other words, Portia's wound is not that of a woman but a warrior. Cynthia Marshall, for whom Portia performs a double role, also picks up this connotation: "the will (topologically masculine) attacks and conquers the body (correspondingly female). As both wielder and victim of the knife/phallus, Portia momentarily brings gender opposition into equilibrium – but at the cost of violence to herself."[18] That way, the gender performance she gives is difficult to decipher; it connotes both masculinity and femininity. A violent, masculine action, Portia's self-inflicted wound, therefore, connotes 'Romanness' and prefigures her suicide, an even more distinctly Roman gesture.

The close association of wounds with masculine *virtus* becomes even more apparent if compared to another Roman tragedy. More than any other Shakespearean play, *Coriolanus* establishes the wound as the pre-eminent symbol of manhood, thus interrogating contemporary Renaissance as well as classical discourses of masculinity and the male body.[19] Clearly, Coriolanus is a man of action rather than words. He lets his deeds, or rather his wounds, speak for themselves, and the entire play is saturated with references to his bleeding body as well as rather specific stage directions in the manner of "*Enter* MARTIUS, *bleeding, assaulted by the enemy*" (following 1.4.61). That wounds are touchstones of masculine valour, achievements that should be celebrated and displayed, is mostly explicitly voiced by Volumnia, a champion of both Rome's masculinist ideology and her son's embodiment of it.[20] When Martius returns from the battle at Corioles, she anxiously awaits his appearance:

VOLUMNIA: Oh, he is wounded; I thank the gods for't.
MENENIUS: So do I too, if it be not too much. Brings a victory in his pocket? The wounds become him.

(Cor. 2.1.120–122)

These wounds, Menenius indicates, mark Coriolanus as 'manly'; they are proof of his heroism. At the same time, they function as a strong persuasive tool when he tries to get the peoples' votes, as reflected in Volumnia's relief that "there will be large cicatrices to show the people when he shall stand for his place" (*Cor.* 2.1.147–149). Similar to Portia's wound in the thigh, Coriolanus's wounds and scars acquire a fetish-like quality, as Kahn emphasises: "he must mention them, but only to prevent mention of them. Even as they evoke the female aperture, they deny it, or only sword-wielding men are enabled to seek wounds, whereas women are born with them."[21] Thus here, like in the case of Portia, it is the voluntariness of the wound that makes the difference and functions as a marker of masculinity.

The play's Roman context, as well as its emphasis on the significance of wounds, begs the question of suicide, but *Coriolanus* contains none. In fact, it only shows one death, namely that of the eponymous hero. However, Coriolanus seems to deliver himself on a platter. His "Cut me to piesces, Volsces, men and lads, / Stain all your edges on me" (*Cor.* 5.6.111–112) at least suggests a certain recklessness, although it is not entirely clears as to whether he is driven by rage, the desire to provoke, or indeed suicidal intentions. Lisa S. Starks-Estes opts for the latter, arguing that his "final 'bring it on!' shout reveals his underlying death wish to be savagely emblazoned – to be slaughtered brutally like Actaeon, torn to bits by the Volscians over whom he has been both a scourge of death and a domineering commander."[22] In performance, too, Coriolanus's death is frequently portrayed as suicide. In Dominic Dromgoole's staging at Shakespeare's Globe in 2006, for instance, Coriolanus stage-dived into the arms of the Volscian soldiers in the yard. Gregory Doran's 2007 production with the RSC even took this interpretation a step further in that Coriolanus first laid down his sword, inviting the conspirators to kill him. Subsequently, he stabbed himself with Aufidius's sword, which then prompted the Volscians to finish the task.[23] Moreover, another line suggesting suicide is uttered by Menenius, who, in the face of the approaching attack on Rome, proclaims "He that hath a will to die by himself, fears it not from another" (*Cor.* 5.2.102–103). And although in the text Menenius does not kill himself either, Ralph Fiennes's film adaptation shows the character on a riverbank as he first throws his watch into the water and then slices his wrist with a tiny knife he carries. Thus, even though the text itself does not have it that way, it seems that for both characters, suicide could well be a fitting ending. *Coriolanus* is concerned with raw action, contempt, and a tragic hero who tries to dissociate himself from the political system. For this reason, it is not surprising that none of the characters philosophises about the question of a proper Roman death or feels compelled to commit suicide by convention. The parallel to *Julius Caesar*, nevertheless, shines light on the act of self-wounding as a gesture of 'Romanness' and bravery, something that separates men from women and, hence, reinforces gender binaries.

Portia, by contrast, does not leave it at the self-inflicted wound, but similarly to Ophelia, Lady Macbeth, and Goneril, she kills herself offstage. Her death is announced by Brutus, presumably quite some time after he has received this information himself:

BRUTUS: No man bears sorrow better. Portia is dead.
CASSIUS: Ha? Portia?
BRUTUS: She is dead.
CASSIUS: How scaped I killing when I crossed you so?
    O insupportable and touching loss!
    Upon what sickness?
BRUTUS: Impatient of my absence,
    And grief that young Octavius with Mark Antony
    Have made themselves so strong – for with her death
    That tidings came – with this she fell distract,
    And, her attendants absent, swallowed fire.

                  (4.3.145–154)

This strange dialogue has sparked several scholarly controversies. First, Brutus's calm reserve and laconic presentation of such a shocking event seem surprising against the background of their affectionate marriage. To explain this incongruity, Alexander Leggatt argues that Brutus uses the announcement of Portia's death to fashion himself as a man of Stoic integrity who can bear even the strongest pain.[24] Second, Brutus's self-congratulatory and, furthermore, self-involved remark appears inappropriate to begin such a conversation. As E. A. J. Honigmann comments, "it wins less than total sympathy, focusing as it does upon the loser not the loss."[25] For all this incompatible information, Daniell raises the question of why Shakespeare includes the news of Portia's death at all, and why here of all places. Plutarch gives no hint as to the specific time of her death, and in addition, there is no dramatic need for this announcement. Unlike, for instance, Ophelia's suicide, Portia's death does not prompt any action. Daniell's explanation is that through Portia's death, Shakespeare introduces a different emotional quality to the scene; it completes the destruction Brutus faces.[26] What all of these concerns have in common is a gender bias, treating Portia's suicide as insignificant in its own right. The only reason one should be concerned with or surprised by her death, the argument goes, is because it sheds an ambivalent and, thus, dramatically problematic light on the (male) tragic hero.

What is more, Portia's death is not only strange in the emotional tone it is communicated in, but also in the way that it is reported twice within the same scene. When Messala asks him whether he received any letters from or news about Portia, Brutus lies to him twice and then continues:

BRUTUS: Why ask you? Hear you aught of her in yours?
MESSALA: No, my lord.
BRUTUS: Now, as you are a Roman, tell me true.
MESSALA: Then like a Roman bear the truth I tell,
           For certain she is dead, and by strange manner.
BRUTUS: Why, farewell, Portia: we must die,
MESSALA: With meditating that she must die once
           I have the patience to endure it now.

                                                   (4.3.182–189)

If the first death announcement were not enough, the second paints a confusing picture of Brutus. Either Brutus's behaviour remains entirely implausible, or it makes him appear unlikeable. Either alternative poses a problem for both the text and the play in production, and so this inconsistency is often deemed a textual error. It must be, Leggatt argues, "if not – particularly in view of Brutus' pretence that he is hearing the news for the first time – it takes his display of self-command to the point of caricature."[27] Such readiness to blame the textual tradition neatly resolves all implausibility and, furthermore, protects the view of Brutus as a noble Roman, as the grand tragic hero the audience can sympathise with without any reservations.

Among those who oppose this view, Stirling says the double announcement is exactly right where it is because Brutus's reply serves to "elevate Brutus to stoical sainthood with no accompanying taint of priggishness."[28] Warren Smith, on the other hand, draws attention to matters of inconsistency in North's translation of Plutarch, which includes the false report that Portia is dying earlier on. This, he speculates, might have led Shakespeare to introduce a notion of hope that here, too, the report is mistaken and that Portia is still alive. As this is false hope, however, it is as if Portia dies twice, which again, renders Brutus's self-composure all the more admirable.[29] Both Stirling's and Smith's positions consider Portia's suicide a necessary means to characterise Brutus. The double announcement is deliberate, they argue, but merely for the sake of glorifying the tragic hero even further. Portia herself functions as a mere object, a prop in Shakespeare's design to extol Brutus. Daniell argues in another, more convincing direction. For him, the second announcement by an official messenger stresses that she has died in the outer, public world.[30] It is perfectly justified to maintain that the two announcements are deliberate, and what Brutus's reactions also document is how much he has been destroyed and absorbed by his mission. It seems that nothing else matters anymore. By this point, Portia, and by extension all women, has turned into collateral damage of the glorious mission.

Apart from the way it is announced, Portia's suicide is striking in itself. First of all, unlike in the case of Ophelia, whose death is often interpreted as a tragic accident by both other characters and critics, there is not the shadow of a doubt that she has killed herself on purpose. Of course, it is infinitely more difficult to accidentally swallow burning coals than to accidentally fall into a river, so nobody even tries to question the news of suicide. While Cassius, for instance, seems shocked that she is dead, he does not comment on the fact that it was a suicide. In other words, Portia is considered capable of such a forceful deed. Still, Wymer feels that this is an ill-fitting end for Portia, "not a rational act but the result of being overwhelmed by grief and impatience."[31] What Wymer describes in slightly derogatory terms is the shock value of her death. Portia swallows fire and, thus, kills herself in the most brutal way of all of Shakespeare's suicides, male or female. In all likelihood, such a way of killing oneself would be physically impossible, even though there are records of suicides by asphyxiation with carbon monoxide resulting from fumes from charcoal fires.[32] In this respect, it is perhaps no wonder that it happens offstage; such a death would be both difficult to stage and unpleasant to watch. It is unprecedented even by Senecan theatre, whose plays are not only particularly gruelling, but also the first to feature suicides on the stage, real or implied.[33]

Given that there is so much dramatised mutilation on the Shakespearean stage, its drastic nature alone cannot be a convincing enough reason for not staging Portia's suicide. At this point, it is worth reconsidering the general pattern of Shakespearean suicides: men kill themselves onstage, and female suicides tend to be reported. This, of course, mirrors tragedy's tendency towards marginalising the female voice. All things that are considered minor and unimportant are simply pushed off the stage; some – like Lady Macbeth and Ophelia – additionally acquire the labels 'demon' and/or 'madwoman' to justify their exclusion. Yet, in *Julius Caesar*, this principle does not work. Portia's suicide is neither uninteresting, and, hence, less deserving of dramatic attention, nor is it portrayed as weaker or less of a Roman gesture than the male suicides; as will be shown, the opposite is the case. Moreover, her suicide does not even stay confined to the offstage space. The description of her swallowing fire, so quickly passed over by the guard, creates a striking image of abject horror, much more captivating than any of the male deaths.

Since it is hidden from the eyes of the audience, one could argue that Portia's suicide is a private, that is, 'un-Roman', and, hence, feminine act. A glance at Plutarch's text, from which Shakespeare takes the description of Portia's death, helps shed light on this issue:

> And for Porcia, Brutus' wife, Nicolaus the Philosopher and Valerius Maximus do write, that she determining to kill herself (her parents and friends carefully looking to her to keep her from it) took hot burning coals, and cast them into her mouth, and kept her mouth so close that she chocked herself.[34]

If compared to Shakespeare's account, there is a notable difference: Plutarch's detailed, prosaic description is translated into that she "fell distract" and then, rather poetically, "swallowed fire." Commenting on these textual differences, Kahn reads the death of Shakespeare's Portia as emphatically feminine, a subversion of her 'unfeminine' agency and re-inscription of 'Otherness'. In her opinion, Shakespeare deprives Portia "of the agency and dignity that she has in Plutarch. Her crazed, bizarre act of self-destruction reinserts her firmly into the feminine, while Brutus's suicide signifies his *virtus*."[35] In a similar vein, Lloyd Davis compares Portia's suicide to that of Lucrece, to whom he ascribes a much greater sense of agency, even after the rape.[36] However, the reverse seems to be the case. Whereas Plutarch's image is domestic – the coals she swallows are supposedly those from the kitchen fire, and the surrounding friends are necessarily female – Shakespeare, in true Roman fashion, transforms her suicide into a public gesture. It is announced by a public official and connotes masculinity rather than femininity. As Leggatt points out, the masculine image of fire reminds of "the fires that sweep through Rome after Caesar's death. [...] Far from establishing a centre of private value, Portia symbolically involves herself with the public world, using its key images, sword and fire."[37] Similarly, R.A. Foakes draws attention to the play's circular movement, interpreting Portia's gesture as a reference to and extinction of the figurative fire started by the conspirators.[38] Undoubtedly, the lasting image Portia creates of herself is one of strength. By thus questioning traditional dichotomies of male/strong/major versus female/weak/minor, Portia's suicide challenges the idea of Roman suicide as a masculine concept. Even though it takes place offstage, her suicide does not marginalise her; rather, it makes her voice heard. In doing so, it ultimately questions the distribution of dramatic interest and, thus, dramatic power structures as such.

"Honourable Men": Performing 'Romanness'

Portia's reported suicide stands in opposition to the play's male suicides, all of which happen onstage with lengthy announcements and preparations. Other than this, what Brutus's, Cassius's, and Titinius's deaths have in common is a shared goal: to reclaim a lost sense of honour and, thereby, reaffirm their 'Romanness'. The play's point of origin, the question of whether to kill Caesar, revolves around the concept of honour. However, unlike with other tragedies following the *de casibus* structure, here, the moral problem is remarkably opaque.[39] Within the context of a gendered reading of the play's suicides, it should be noted that the Roman ideals of honour and the public good are unmistakably gendered concepts. Roman masculinity always encompasses civic responsibility, and so Shakespeare's Roman heroes are exclusively public rather than private figures.[40]

Unlike other Roman heroes such as Titus, Antony, and Coriolanus, Brutus is not a war hero. Although the play shows him as military commander at Philippi, there are no accounts of him gloriously winning battles or praising his raw masculinity; he is a strategist rather than a warrior. Nevertheless, he embodies a certain ideal of Renaissance masculinity. With his calm reserve and contemplation, he conforms to the humanist ideal of the 'man of moderation' as described by Roger Ascham in his educational treatise *The Schoolmaster* (1570). Bruce Smith describes Brutus's masculine qualities as a "tempering of masculine traits, an equanimity of spirit that enables him to face wisely and confidently whatever challenges the world brings his way."[41] For this reason, Cassius's appeal to Brutus's sense of public duty directly addresses his masculinity. Similarly, Brutus's initial scruples against taking action, a masculine concept per se, signal conventionally female passivity. This potentially compromised masculinity is especially problematic when Portia seeks to interfere. Set in the *hortus conclusus*, a private space sheltered against the outside world, the conversation between Portia and Brutus in 2.1 is formally introduced as a personal matter.[42] Yet, since the secret Brutus bears is a political one, Portia's adamant "I should know this secret" (2.1.290) marks a transgression from the private into the political. She describes the changes in Brutus's behaviour, as for instance his sleeplessness and impatience, making both himself and the audience realise how much his conscience troubles him. But since Portia addresses Brutus as her husband and reiterates that, as such, he has to confide in her, he is able to reject her worries as motivated by her love for him only. At the same time, Portia repeatedly emphasises that she could bear his sorrow, thereby suggesting that the capacity to stand firm in moments of crisis requires masculine strength. If Brutus confided in her, this would be a quality he lacks. He would be admitting to weakness – to being weaker than an exceptionally strong woman. What she intends to be an encouragement to confide in her, then, challenges Brutus as both a good husband and a proper man.

Since honour, ascribed to Brutus by himself as well as others, appears to be his defining characteristic, the option of a Roman death to preserve this honour resonates early on. The audience learn that Brutus thinks about suicide and is aware of what others might expect of him should the conspiracy fail. Other characters, likewise, raise the debate of whether and when to kill themselves. Antony and Cleopatra, too, encounter this dilemma. By contrast, Brutus's reasoning explicitly draws on philosophical positions towards suicide:

> Even by the rule of that philosophy
> By which I did blame Cato for the death
> Which he did give himself – I know not how,
> But I do find it cowardly and vile,
> For fear of what might fall, so to prevent
> The time of life – arming myself with patience
> To stay the providence of some high powers
> That govern us below.
>
> (5.1.98–105)

It seems that Brutus opposes suicide, condemning it as the cowardly opposite of heroic endurance. Critics have sought to pinpoint what exactly he means by "that philosophy," and most identify him as a Stoic.[43] Since suicide is such an important concern of Roman, especially Stoic, philosophy, these arguments underline the relative precision with which Shakespeare depicts the historical context of suicide. For this reason, it may be tempting to focus on the question of whether Brutus subscribes to any philosophical school in particular. Yet, given that *Julius Caesar* offers as much a Roman version of Renaissance values as vice versa, this is a somewhat futile debate to enter. Historical or philosophical accuracy is simply not the point, neither here nor in any of the other plays featuring suicide.

The inconstancy of Brutus's stance provides further evidence that the philosophical context of suicide only plays a minor role. Eventually, Brutus does kill himself, and he even argues in favour of it a mere two lines succeeding the above passage. When Cassius asks him if he could bear the humiliation of being paraded through the streets of Rome, Brutus replies "No, Cassius, no: think not, thou noble Roman, / That ever Brutus will go bound to Rome. / He bears too great a mind" (5.1.108–110). At this point, suicide is the only possible way of avoiding the shame of surrender, captivity, or defeat. In order to account for this sudden, ostensibly contradictory change of mind, critics often quote a possible mistranslation by North.[44] In the first place, this line of argument speaks of an apparent wish for unity and logic in dramatic characters much more than it helps to solve the problem. When Brutus eventually kills himself, he considers this a graceful moment: "I shall have glory by this losing day / More than Octavius and Mark Antony / By this vile conquest shall attain unto" (5.5.34–36). His self-inflicted death is not defeat but victory, Brutus makes clear. In Brutus's last words, "Caesar, now be still. / I killed not thee with half so good a will" (5.5.49–50), Stephen Greenblatt detects "a quality of epic self-regard and a capacity to envision himself as the savior of Rome that link him to the megalomaniac he has murdered."[45] Greenblatt is right in commenting on the uncomfortable undertones in this final, grand gesture. These last words carry an air of the self-delusional and self-important, which fits Brutus's characterisation throughout the play. Franziska Quabeck offers an interpretation that is more favourable towards Brutus. For her, "[h]is suicide [...] represents his faith in justice and morality, which makes him sacrifice himself in the same manner that he sacrifices Caesar. This is why he receives a eulogy that praises his honourable intentions."[46] She correctly points out the achieved effect because eventually, through suicide, Brutus reaches his goal of dying nobly. Antony's and Octavius's praises, not Brutus's own words, are the play's final verdict on him.

Despite these reverential eulogies, Anne Paolucci dismisses Brutus's suicide as functional and anti-climactic, maintaining that its exact circumstances are irrelevant because he would have killed himself no matter the battle's outcome.[47] But the circumstances of his death are far from unimportant. It is true, though, that Brutus's death appears anti-climactic in that it is longed for neither by himself nor the audience. Unlike *Macbeth*, *Julius Caesar* does not build up towards the destruction of the tragic hero/villain. Its actual climax, the assassination of Caesar, passes midway through. Instead, Brutus's suicide marks the peak of his nobility, or so his eulogies confirm. Antony concedes that "This was the noblest Roman of them all" (5.5.68). Interestingly, this praise coincides with a gendered verdict: "This was a man!" (5.5.75). Brutus's masculinity, challenged by his earlier scruples and lack of masculine resolve, is officially reinstated. Yet simultaneously, Antony seems to qualify his praise. Brutus no longer is, but was, a man; his masculinity is a glory of the past. Eventually, though, through the order to bury Brutus "Most like a soldier, ordered honourably" (5.5.79), Octavius re-instates the shattered monument. That way, the heroic and, furthermore, indisputably masculine Brutus is the one the play ultimately perpetuates.

In addition to the effect it creates, the exact manner of Brutus's suicide deserves scrutiny. Notwithstanding the final reconciliation, Brutus's suicide is surrounded by a number of dissonant undertones that seem to stand in opposition to his laurels. First, he does not commit suicide right away but asks several followers and servants to take this burden from him. While Dardanius, Clitus, and Volumnius decline, Strato feels compelled to if not kill him then at least to hold Brutus's sword while he runs into it. With reference to the BBC's 1979 adaptation (dir. Herbert Wise), Andrew James Hartley describes the scene as contributing to "a sense of anticlimax that reaches maddening proportions."[48] This episode is missing from Plutarch's text, which paints a less uncomfortable picture than Shakespeare does:

> Having said so, he prayed every man to shift for themselves, and then he went a little aside with two or three only, among the which Strato was one, with whom he came first acquainted by the study of rhetoric. He came as near to him as he could, and taking his sword by the hilts with both his hands, and falling down upon the point of it, ran himself through. Others say that, not he, but Strato (at his request) held the sword in his hand, and turned his head aside, and that Brutus fell himself down upon it: and so ran himself through, and died presently.[49]

Plutarch's text, too, acknowledges what Lois Potter names the "[b]iggest problems involved in dying like a Roman: the fact that it's hard to do without help."[50] So, there is nothing inherently degrading in running against a sword held by someone else because it follows the Roman tradition. But why, furthermore, add Brutus's several pleas for help if not to stress that, firstly, he makes these requests and, secondly, that they are declined repeatedly? Brutus's claim that "in all my life / I found no man but he was true to me" (5.5.33–34) is particularly puzzling; in the face of the previous unsuccessful searches for a friend who relieves him, this is a peculiar thing to say. Brutus's death, thus, shows him curiously out of touch with the reality around him. As Wymer remarks, these notions of sorrow, defeat, and most importantly tragic error are unusual for a Roman death.[51] He is right in characterising Brutus's suicide as an unsatisfactory death that not only fails to resolve the remaining tension but also raises further question marks. As Mary Beth Rose argues, suicide in the Roman plays functions as an attempt at re-defining ostensible loss as profit. While successful in *Antony and Cleopatra*, in *Julius Caesar*, this endeavour fails. At first glance, Antony's eulogy of Brutus seems nothing but reverential, yet Rose takes a closer look: "The irrefutable historical irony of hindsight reveals what Antony cannot know: that the assassination of Julius Caesar, meant to restore the Roman Republic, in fact hastened the beginnings of empire, introducing decades of tyrannical Caesarism. Sympathetically evoking Brutus's honourable character, Antony's epitaph – so dignified in tone, and so beautiful – manages to deprive Brutus's suicide of any possibility of triumphant meaning."[52] Hence, despite their adamant eulogies for Brutus, the feeling remains that Antony and Octavius are too exuberant. Inadvertently, Antony re-writes Brutus's self-proclaimed victory as a final defeat. Thus, in addition to enhancing Brutus's nobility, his suicide also makes him look slightly foolish, not only since his mission has failed, but also because it does not entirely conform to the standards of what makes a perfect Roman death.

In the same way as the two characters are juxtaposed, Brutus's death is contrasted with that of Cassius. If Brutus is the strongest candidate for the tragic hero, Cassius is the obvious antagonist. He openly admits to manipulating Brutus into joining the conspiracy, but unlike a self-confident villain in the manner of Iago, Cassius never admits to doing this for egoistic reasons. And yet, he, like Iago, seems to be driven by a hunger for power and feelings of unregarded merit. As Antony says in Brutus's eulogy, Cassius acts out of "envy of great Caesar" (5.5.70). For Cassius, too, honour is a decisive concept; but for him, it is defined by rank and prestige rather than personal integrity and public duty. Like Romeo, Cassius threatens to kill himself several times, for the first time as early as 1.3:

> I know where I will wear this dagger then:
> Cassius from bondage will deliver Cassius.
> Therein, ye gods, ye make the weak most strong;
> Therein, ye gods, you tyrants do defeat.
> Nor stony tower, nor walls of beaten brass,
> Nor airless dungeon, nor strong links of iron,
> Can be retentive to the strength of spirit:
> But life being weary of these worldly bars
> Never lacks power to dismiss itself.
>
> (1.3.89–97)

Cassius presents suicide as the more favourable alternative to living "in bondage," should Caesar be crowned. The images he uses – beaten brass, iron links, and dungeons – all present insurmountable barriers, but none of them, he proclaims, would be strong enough to prevent him from killing himself. Later, he desperately pleads to Brutus: "what shall be done? If this be known, / Cassius or Caesar shall never turn back, / For I will slay myself" (3.1.20–22). This time, however, it is the fear that their conspiracy might be discovered that prompts his suicidal thoughts.

Ironically, Cassius's suicide is the result of a misunderstanding. "Alas, thou hast misconstrued everything" (5.3.82), is Pindarus's reaction to finding Cassius's dead body. Rather than an honourable Roman gesture, it sounds like a tragic accident, and the rashness and irrationality with which Cassius kills himself furthermore falls short of the standards of Roman masculinity. In 5.3, Brutus makes clear that he will not endure captivity, yet, since it is Cassius who raises this question, it appears that he shares Brutus's position. Besides, when he is misinformed that Pindarus and Titinius have been captured by Antony's legions, Cassius cries out "O, coward that I am, to live so long, / To see my best friend ta'en before my face" (5.3.32–33), thus equating the avoidance or postponing of suicide with cowardice. Cowardice also signals lack of manliness. Instead of killing himself, which would be the logical consequence of all his previous musings, he asks Pindarus to do this for him: "Come now, keep thine oath. / Now be a free man, and with this good sword / That ran through Caesar's bowels, search this bosom" (5.3.38–40). Anticipating Antony's plea to Eros, Cassius appeals to Pindarus's sense of duty – the loyalty of a servant to his master. Unlike Eros, however, Pindarus feels compelled to follow his order, sparing Cassius the embarrassment that Shakespeare saves for Antony. Despite this dignified exit, Honigmann is disappointed by Cassius's death: "In the first act we must resist the temptation to simplify Cassius; in the last, Shakespeare himself seems to simplify him, chiefly in his suicide. Such an efficient way to go, after all his big talk of suicide and fine flourishes!"[53] Honigmann's description of Cassius's quasi-suicide as a moment of bathos seems apt, especially since his death is triggered by a misinterpretation of the situation.

What distinguishes Cassius's death from Brutus's is not only that the former's plea for help falls on sympathetic ears immediately, but also that it prompts another suicide. Titinius, who like everyone else is desperate because their venture has failed, kills himself out of loyalty to Cassius: "see how I regarded Caius Cassius. / By your leave, gods. This is a Roman's part. / Come, Cassius' sword, and find Titinius' heart" (5.3.86–88). It is telling that such a decisive line is given to one of the minor figures, one that has not made a significant appearance before. Compared to Brutus and Cassius, who either barely or not at all manage a proper Roman death, Titinius is the one who performs the "Roman's part" as it should be done. He is, thus, given a "graver ending" than in Plutarch's text, in which he dies cursing himself.[54] Furthermore, Titinius's loyalty redeems his master to some extent, offering a glimpse into Cassius's character never given before. Nevertheless, Cassius's inability to take the consequences and kill himself gracefully leaves a sour note. As Davis comments, if these three male deaths are looked at in combination, "[t]he pattern of suicides verges on the mock-heroic, suggesting contradictions in the aristocratic code of valour and honour [...]. The paradox of the suicides is that they render the male body its own self-defeating site."[55] If, as Davis argues, these suicides can be considered mock-heroic, then, by extension, they are also mock-masculine. In true Roman fashion, Brutus's and Cassius's deaths are public gestures, both in the sense that they happen in the presence of others and that they are explicitly marked as related to public duty. At the same time, however, they suggest a mostly rhetorical, troubled performance of masculinity, particularly when compared to the play's portrayal of female suicide.

In summary, then, the play offers four rather conflicting depictions of suicide. Brutus struggles with the ideal of Roman masculinity. His suicide only partly conforms to Roman standards and makes him appear less heroic than his eulogies suggest. By comparison, Cassius's performance of 'Romanness' is almost entirely unsuccessful. Titinius's act of loyalty, however, alleviates such an interpretation and rehabilitates Cassius the Roman. Both Brutus's and Cassius's somewhat inadequate performances of masculinity are finally countered by Portia's suicide, whose swallowing of burning coals is both a literal and symbolic extinction of the female voice. She dies offstage; but from the moment it is announced, the image of her radical and, furthermore, political gesture continues to haunt the play. That way, her suicide becomes an outcry against female silencing, both within and outside the world of the play. Portia's suicide follows her father Cato's example, whose suicide in the face of defeat by Julius Caesar is known by history as an equally honourable gesture. Both provide models for Brutus to follow, Alison Findlay suggests,[56] killing themselves in line with Roman suicide protocol: determinedly, as a political statement, and without involving others. Given his initial wavering rather than steadfast resolution and plea for assistance, Brutus follows these models to a limited extent only; even though he uses a sword, his suicide is less of a Roman gesture than either of these two deaths. As a result, in *Julius Caesar*, it is a woman who defines the standards of 'Romanness' and, thus, also of masculinity.

In *Macbeth*, which in so many ways bears similarities to the play at hand, the eponymous hero distances himself from the Roman concept of suicide by proclaiming that he is no "Roman fool." Although not intended for comic effect, Shakespeare's portrayal of Roman death in *Julius Caesar* suggests that this is not an altogether unfair assessment of the noble Romans as they present themselves here. Kahn has illustrated the ways in which Renaissance Humanism consolidated 'Romanness' as a touchstone of masculinity, which lead to a conflation of Roman and early modern cultural contexts.[57] In this respect, any critique or interrogation of 'Romanness' and its masculine virtue is necessarily a critique of gender ideologies, both Roman and Elizabethan.

Notes

1 Rowland Wymer, *Suicide and Despair in the Jacobean Drama* (Brighton: Harvester, 1986), 134.

2 Coppélia Kahn, *Roman Shakespeare: Warriors, Wounds, and Women* (London and New York: Routledge, 1997), 2.

3 Plutarch, *Shakespeare's Plutarch*, trans. Thomas North, ed. C. F. Tucker Brooke, vol. I, containing the main sources of *Julius Caesar* (New York: Duffield and Company, 1909), 130.

4 "There was a letter of Brutus found written to his friends, complaining of their negligence, that his wife being sick, they would not help her, but

suffered her to kill herself, choosing to die, rather than to languish in pain. Thus it appeareth that Nicolaus knew not well that time, sith the letter (at the least if it were Brutus' letter) doth plainly declare the disease and love of this Lady, and also the manner of her death." (Plutarch, *Shakespeare's Plutarch*, vol. I, 191).

5 Margaret Higonnet, "Speaking Silences: Women's Suicide," in *The Female Body in Western Culture: Contemporary Perspectives*, ed. Susan Rubin Suleiman (Cambridge, MA and London: Harvard University Press, 1985), 73.

6 Jan H. Blits, "Manliness and Friendship in *Julius Caesar*," in *William Shakespeare's Julius Caesar*, ed. and intro. Harold Bloom (New York: Infobase, 2010), 38.

7 In "Social Role and the Making of Identity in *Julius Caesar*," *SEL* 33.2 (1993): 305, Sharon O'Dair likens Portia to a servant figure who dutifully keeps Brutus company in the same way as his boy Lucius; in *Shakespeare's Women* (Newton Abbot: David & Charles, 1981), Angela Pitt sees her as a prime example of 'the good wife', a stereotype she identifies within the history and Roman plays (163).

8 *William Shakespeare: Complete Works*, ed. Jonathan Bate and Eric Rasmussen (London: Palgrave Macmillan, 2008), 1804.

9 Alison Sharrock, "Gender and Sexuality," in *The Cambridge Companion to Ovid*, ed. Philip Hardie (Cambridge: Cambridge University Press, 2002), 96.

10 William Shakespeare, *Julius Caesar*, ed. David Daniell, The Arden Shakespeare Third Series (London: Arden Shakespeare, 1998), note to 2.1.235. Also, Daniell's note states that "Plutarch tells later [...] of Portia's constitutional weakness; a hint, like Ligarius' ague, of an effect of conspiracy on ordinary life in Rome."

11 Gail Kern Paster, "'In the Spirit of Men There Is No Blood': Blood as Trope of Gender in *Julius Caesar*," *Shakespeare Quarterly* 40.3 (1989): 293.

12 See David Daniell, Introduction to *Julius Caesar*, by William Shakespeare, ed. David Daniell, The Arden Shakespeare Third Series (London: Arden Shakespeare, 1998), 66–67.

13 Marianne Novy, *Shakespeare and Outsiders* (Oxford: Oxford University Press, 2013), 70.

14 Kahn, *Roman Shakespeare*, 17.

15 Melvyn Donald Faber, "Lord Brutus' Wife: A Modern View," *Psychoanalytic Review* 52.4 (1965): 450.

16 See Wymer, *Suicide and Despair in the Jacobean Drama*, 153; Coppélia Kahn, "Shakespeare's Classical Tragedies," in *The Cambridge Companion to Shakespearean Tragedy*, ed. Claire McEachern (Cambridge: Cambridge University Press, 2002), 214–215.

17 Paster, "'In the Spirit of Men There Is No Blood'," 294.

18 Cynthia Marshall, "Portia's Wound, Calphurnia's Dream: Reading Character in *Julius Caesar*," *English Literary Renaissance* 24.2 (1994): 476.

19 In Lisa S. Starks-Estes's view, *Coriolanus* examines the underlying dangers inherent in extreme, martial *virtus* as well as neo-Stoicism. Further, she argues that here, "Shakespeare examines the cultural trauma that results from the clash between the newly bounded body and that of the earlier Galenic model. Shakespeare addresses these traumatic changes in notions of the self and the importance of them in ideals of masculinity by staging the emblazoned male body as a martyr on display." *Violence, Trauma, and Virtus in Shakespeare's Roman Poems and Plays: Transforming Ovid* (Basingstoke: Palgrave, 2014), 58.

20 On the relationship between Coriolanus and his mother, specifically regarding the intricate relation between motherhood and masculinity, see Kahn, *Roman Shakespeare*, 144–159.

21 Ibid., 153.

22 Starks-Estes, *Violence, Trauma, and Virtus*, 158.

23 Lois Potter, "Assisted Suicides: *Antony and Cleopatra* and *Coriolanus* in 2006–7," *Shakespeare Quarterly* 58.4 (2007): 520–529.

24 Alexander Leggatt, *Shakespeare's Political Drama: The History Plays and the Roman Plays* (London and New York: Routledge, 1988), 148.

25 E. A. J. Honigmann, *Shakespeare: Seven Tragedies: A Dramatist's Manipulation of Response* (London: Macmillan, 1976), 50.

26 Daniell, Introduction to *Julius Caesar*, 139–142.

27 Leggatt, *Shakespeare's Political Drama*, 148. On the question of whether this is a textual error, see Thomas Clayton, "'Should Brutus Never Taste of Portia's Death but Once?' Text and Performance in *Julius Caesar*," *SEL* 23.2 (1983): 239–240; Daniell, Introduction to *Julius Caesar*, 137.

28 Brents Stirling, "Brutus and the Death of Portia," *Shakespeare Quarterly* 10.2 (1959): 211.

29 Warren D. Smith, "The Duplicate Revelation of Portia's Death," *Shakespeare Quarterly* 4.2 (1953): 154–155.

30 Daniell, Introduction to *Julius Caesar*, 143.

31 Wymer, *Suicide and Despair in the Jacobean Drama*, 153.

32 J. Madison Davis and A. Daniel Frankforter, *The Shakespeare Name Dictionary* (Abingdon and New York: Routledge, 1995), 396.

33 James Ker, *The Deaths of Seneca* (Oxford: Oxford University Press, 2009), 125.

34 Plutarch, *Shakespeare's Plutarch*, vol. I, 191.

35 Kahn, *Roman Shakespeare*, 103.

36 Lloyd Davis, "Embodied Masculinity in Shakespeare's *Julius Caesar*," *Entertext* 3.1 (2003): 173, accessed April 12, 2017, www.brunel.ac.uk/__data/assets/pdf_file/0008/111023/Lloyd-Davis,-Embodied-Masculinity-in-Shakespeares-Julius-Caesar.pdf.

37 Leggatt, *Shakespeare's Political Drama*, 148.

38 R. A. Foakes, "An Approach to *Julius Caesar*," *Shakespeare Quarterly* 5.3 (1954): 262.

39 See Camille Slights, "Murder, Suicide and Conscience: The Case of Brutus and Hamlet," in *Familiar Colloquy: Essays Presented to Arthur Edward Barker*, ed. Patricia Bruckmann and Jane Couchman (Ottawa: Oberon, 1978), 114. On the tyrannicide debate in both Plutarch and Shakespeare, see Daniell, Introduction to *Julius Caesar*, 29–38; John Roe, "'Character' in Plutarch and Shakespeare: Brutus, Julius Caesar, and Mark Antony," in *Shakespeare and the Classics*, ed. Charles Martindale and A. B. Taylor (Cambridge: Cambridge University Press, 2004), 173–178.

40 See Erik Gunderson, *Staging Masculinity: The Rhetoric of Performance in the Roman World* (Ann Arbor: University of Michigan Press, 2000), 7–9.

41 Bruce R. Smith, *Shakespeare and Masculinity* (Oxford: Oxford University Press, 2000), 49.

42 On the setting's implications regarding the political and private dimensions of the conversation, see Mariko Ichikawa, *The Shakespearean Stage Space* (Cambridge: Cambridge University Press, 2013), 125–128.

43 See Anne Paolucci, "The Tragic Hero in *Julius Caesar*," *Shakespeare Quarterly* 11.3 (1960): 331; Marvin L. Vawter, "'Division 'Tween Our Souls': Shakespeare's Stoic Brutus," *Shakespeare Studies* 7 (1974): 177; Patrick

Gray, "The Compassionate Stoic: Brutus as Accidental Hero," *Shakespeare Jahrbuch* 152 (2016): 30. Mark Sacharoff challenges this recurring position because he considers Brutus's stance too incoherent. For him, Brutus's stance could be rooted in a wide range of philosophical schools or viewpoints that share a general opposition to suicide. Mark Sacharoff, "Suicide and Brutus' Philosophy in *Julius Caesar*," *Journal of the History of Ideas* 33.1 (1972): 119.

44 In North's translation of Plutarch, the passage reads as follows: "'Being yet but a young man, and not over greatly experienced in the world, I trust (I know not how) a certain rule of Philosophy, by the which I did greatly blame and reprove Cato for killing of himself, as being no lawful nor godly act, touching the gods, nor, concerning men, valiant; not to give place and yield to divine providence, and not constantly and patiently to take whatsoever it pleaseth him to send us, but to draw back and fly: but, being now in the midst of the danger, I am of a contrary mind" (Plutarch, *Shakespeare's Plutarch*, vol. I, 170). Mungo MacCallum attempts to reconstruct the process of translation and suggests it is likely that North confused past and present here, using 'trust' in the first sentence as a synonym for 'trusted', which Shakespeare then considered present tense. *Shakespeare's Roman Plays and Their Background* (1910; reprint; London and Melbourne: Macmillan, 1967), 185. In his note to 5.1.110 in the Arden Third Series, Daniell simply states that "Brutus' contradiction, implying suicide, necessitates a distinction between killing oneself when faced with assumed dangers from a political enemy (as Cato did) and not suffering captivity."

45 Stephen Greenblatt, *Hamlet in Purgatory*, rev. ed. (2001, reprint; Princeton and Oxford: Princeton University Press, 2013), 183–184.

46 Franziska Quabeck, *Just and Unjust Wars in Shakespeare* (Berlin: de Gruyter, 2013), 151.

47 Paolucci, "The Tragic Hero in *Julius Caesar*," 332.

48 Andrew James Hartley, *Julius Caesar in Performance* (Manchester: Manchester University Press, 2014), 130.

49 Plutarch, *Shakespeare's Plutarch*, vol. I, 190.

50 Potter, "Assisted Suicides," 509.

51 Wymer, *Suicide and Despair in the Jacobean Drama*, 154.

52 Mary Beth Rose, "Suicide as Profit or Loss," in *Shakespeare in Our Time: A Shakespeare Association of America Collection*, ed. Dympna Callaghan and Suzanne Gossett (London and New York: Arden Shakespeare, 2016), 74.

53 Honigmann, *Seven Tragedies*, 52.

54 Daniell's note to 5.3.89 in the Arden Third Series.

55 Lloyd Davis, "Embodied Masculinity," 174.

56 Alison Findlay, *Women in Shakespeare: A Dictionary* (London and New York: Continuum, 2010), 327.

57 Kahn, *Roman Shakespeare*, 19–20.

4 Solid Flesh
Hamlet

According to critical history, *Hamlet* is Shakespeare's quintessential play about suicide. After all, "To be, or not to be," the most famous of all speeches, apparently ponders the question of whether suicide is acceptable. For centuries, scholars have discussed the play's perspective on religion, which Stephen Greenblatt has so succinctly boiled down to the formula that "a young man from Wittenberg, with a distinctly Protestant temperament, is haunted by a distinctly Catholic ghost."[1] Accordingly, a plethora of scholarly research has focused on the religious debates surrounding suicide. If this were the end of the discussion, it would be perfectly justified to conclude that Hamlet alone conditions critical interest in suicide in *Hamlet*. Yet, the more interesting character to look at when investigating this topic is Ophelia, unjustly degraded by critics who often suggest that she gains momentum only by her madness.[2] While herein scholars have reaffirmed, or rather complicated, the ways in which the play itself silences and ostracises her, the connection between her suicide and the play's gender ideology has so far remained understudied.

This chapter shifts the focus of discussion towards Ophelia, illustrating to what extent an understanding of her death as suicide rather than tragic accident re-attributes some of the agency the character is so often considered to lack. I suggest that previous discussions have overemphasised Hamlet's suicidal musings without paying attention to the striking contrast between Hamlet's continuous (onstage) inaction and Ophelia's drastic (offstage) action. Read in juxtaposition, I argue, these two contrastive depictions of suicide unlock what is at the heart of the debate on suicide in the play: the 'genderdness' of suicide as an act of agency as well as the nature of that agency, specifically within a patriarchal world inimical to everything female.

"Her Death Was Doubtful": Ophelia's Resistance to Interpretation

As the final scene proves, *Hamlet* does not shy away from exhibiting bodies. And still, Ophelia dies offstage; she simply disappears from the play. This not only increases her marginalisation, but also denies closure. It seems that she is simply too weak a figure to either take part in the dramatic finale or too unimportant to be given a visible, and, therefore, potentially moving, death scene. In this context, it is worth reconsidering Dympna Callaghan's concept of the dead female body as the "dead centre" of tragic consummation.[3] Juliet's body is displayed and elevated. Ophelia's body, on the other hand, remains concealed, hidden from the audiences' – and everyone else's – eyes. That way, Shakespeare denies her a part in the play's denouement, a key role in the play's tragic consummation. At the same time, Ophelia's offstage death is one of the most memorable deaths Shakespeare wrote, so much so that one tends to forget the scene is merely reported.

In Kaara Peterson's words, "we have become anaesthetized to the oddness attending the speech only because it has been augmented by a substantial catalogue of representations of a primarily visual nature [...]. For us, Ophelia's drowning scene has become a 'seen' playing through our collective memory."[4] Two examples of such visual augmentations are Laurence Olivier's (1948) and Franco Zeffirelli's (1990) film adaptations, both of which feature Ophelia's death scene. Olivier's adaptation shows it as a flashback, accompanied by Gertrude's voice-over. Here, the floating Ophelia is an obvious re-creation of Millais's painting. In Zefirelli's version, Helena Bonham Carter's Ophelia suggestively stares into the water, followed by a cut to Gertrude bringing the news of her death. The next scene shows that Ophelia has drowned; the moment of her fall or jump, however, is missing. Kenneth Branagh's film (1996), by contrast, follows the text in presenting the scene as reported. Kate Winslet is a rebellious Ophelia – an impression aided by Branagh's large-scale textual and scenic additions – and one that takes an active part in bringing about her own death. In the scenes preceding her drowning, Winslet's performance channels anger rather than distraction, and her last appearance while Ophelia is still alive shows her in a torture-like situation, splashed with cold water in a cell. After the guard has left, she pulls the key to the door out of her mouth; the look on her face suggests grave determination. When at the end of Gertrude's speech the camera captures the floating Ophelia's face, again exhibiting a sense of determination and accompanied by solemn music, it is implied that she drowned herself on purpose.

Whether critics interpret Ophelia's death as suicide or accident usually depends on how strong, or rather how weak, a character they find her. In "Representing Ophelia: Women, Madness, and the Responsibilities of Feminist Criticism" (1985), Elaine Showalter traces Ophelia's history of representation. She explains that Ophelia has evolved into an iconic figure who functions as an ideological blank canvas, mirroring a culture's values and attitudes towards gender and the role of feminism.[5] In the first place, this paradoxical dual identity of silenced voice on the one hand and cultural icon on the other emanates from her representation in the text. Ophelia embodies the whole trajectory of stereotypical female roles, from beautiful young lady and dutiful daughter to madwoman and drowned, innocent victim. In each case, she appears an emblem rather than a character in her own right. These emblematic representations prove problematic because they are difficult to read, and so Martha Ronk rightly considers Ophelia's "picture-like existence" a matter of epistemology.[6] Ophelia's status in the play raises epistemological questions because throughout, others attempt to mould her into an easily decoded image. The most obvious example is the conversation between Laertes, Polonius, and Ophelia, in which both men urge her not to give in to Hamlet's sexual advances and safeguard her chastity instead. Ophelia's reactions to this advice are two lines of seeming submission, a few words that she is often reduced to: "I do not know, my Lord, what I should think" (1.3.104) and, finally, "I shall obey, my lord" (1.3.136). For Gabrielle Dane, Ophelia stays within the role of a mere object, an "asset to Polonius, a commodity to be disposed of, ideally at the greatest profit to himself."[7] Coppélia Kahn opts for a more progressive interpretation and suggests that Ophelia "is cagily fending off her father's intrusive queries by using disavowal as a defense, to protect her own thoughts from his intimidating scrutiny. Ophelia has not yet given in; as this scene demonstrates, she can think for herself."[8] Against the backdrop of Ophelia's later act of courage, her suicide, in particular, Kahn's reading seems apt. Ophelia's lines should be interpreted as an objection to male attempts at painting an image of her that does not do her justice – to being exclusively constructed through and by the male gaze.

In critical reception, Ophelia's suicide is always tied to a discussion of her descent into madness. Since she forms a contrast to Hamlet's pretence, she is regularly referred to as Hamlet's "mad double."[9] A commonly debated issue is the question of what is responsible for her madness. The King believes that "it springs / All from her father's death" (4.5.75–76), and earlier critics in particular have followed this interpretation by attributing her madness to the death of Polonius.[10] Notwithstanding the sequence of blows Ophelia has to take, the most plausible interpretation is another: Ophelia goes mad because she is consistently silenced, reduced to a token, and denied any form of autonomous presence. As Showalter's seminal work on the subject has shown, madness is in itself a gendered concept. In *The Female Malady*, she explores the cultural history of psychiatry and madness, starting with the premise of "a cultural tradition that represents 'woman' *as* madness, and that uses images of the female body [...] to stand for irrationality in general."[11] Ophelia has always had a major influence on this cultural history of madness as a female malady, as manifested in an absurd blurring of the boundaries between art and life that reached its peak in the Victorian age. When taking pictures of female asylum inmates, photographers commonly staged them in the (stereo)typical Ophelia pose.[12] This is only one of the many examples of how in the reception of *Hamlet*, the concepts of 'femininity' and 'madness' are used interchangeably. Thus, by extension, by following the critical tendency of reducing Ophelia to her madness, one simultaneously defines her by her gender role.

The early modern period in particular was fascinated with madness, a concept that at the time gradually shifted away from the medieval paradigm of madness as a juncture of the divine, human, and diabolic. Instead, Renaissance Humanism began to secularise madness and address it in medical, legal, political, psychological, and social terms.[13] This burgeoning re-conceptualisation coincided with a flourishing of treatises on what today would be categorised as symptoms of clinical depression. Not only Burton's famous *Anatomy of Melancholy*, which subsumes all forms of mental disorder, but also Edward Jorden's treatise on hysteria, *The Suffocation of the Mother*, and Timothy Bright's *Treatise of Melancholy* were read widely. However, already the all-male frontispiece on Burton's book betrays a gendered concept of madness. Whereas melancholy is primarily associated with male scholars, female melancholy aligns with sexual frustration, marital status, and class.[14]

As Maurice and Hanna Charney explain, female madness on the early modern stage generally indicated an increase in dramatic agency because even though in itself a conventional figure, the madwoman bears the potential for unconventional subversion.[15] Yet, Ophelia's language of madness is fragmented, full of repetitions, as well as what Neely dubs "'quotation'." Ophelia speaks in borrowed voices, and so the question arises as to whether her madness marks an improvement with regard to her self-expression. Besides, Neely also stresses that, whereas Hamlet's madness is presented as "fashionably introspective and melancholy," Ophelia's is "alienated, [...] somatized and its content eroticized."[16] She is perceived as more alien, and simultaneously more powerful, precisely because her madness is eroticised. Clearly, such would be an ideologically questionable definition of agency. On the other hand, Ophelia's madness opens up the possibility of subversion, of defying boundaries and interpretation. Like the Andronicus family, who are unable to read Lavinia's bleeding body and, thus, turn to grotesque ventriloquism, all the characters present in the mad scene struggle with the image of the mad Ophelia. Laertes's "Thought and afflictions, passion, hell itself / She turns to favour and to prettiness" (4.5.185–186) is particularly misplaced. Instead of attempting to calm her down, he reduces the threat of the 'Other' by re-defining her as beautiful.

Whereas this eroticisation is imposed on Ophelia from the outside, her mad songs and speeches have a similar effect. They permit innuendo and social critique, forms of insight and expression that remain suppressed during her sanity. "Tomorrow is Saint Valentine's Day" (4.5.48–55) mingles images of grief with overtly sexual connotations, aligning her madness with the early modern context of hysteria, and, hence, the King and Queen repeatedly try to interrupt her shocking outbursts or censor her words by excusing them as "the poison of deep grief" (4.5.57).[17] A likewise sexualised ritual occurs in 4.5.173–183 when Ophelia distributes the flowers symbolising remembrance, thoughts, flattery, infidelity, repentance, and unrequited love.[18] This is a figurative deflowering, and so Margreta de Grazia draws a connection to what she believes to be the actual reason for her madness: "Has Ophelia lost her mind or that part for which *mind* functioned as both euphemism and synonym? Has she had a breakdown or has she been deflowered?"[19] A further ambiguity lies in the iconography of Flora, the flower goddess, which this scene obviously relates to. Depending on the two competing versions of the myth, the figure of Flora could either be the goddess of spring or a Roman prostitute. This ambiguity of interpretation is fitting for Ophelia, whose representation oscillates between these two extremes.[20] No matter how one decides to decode Ophelia's image during the mad scene, this is her final appearance on-stage while she is still alive. The argument of her suicide as an act of agency begs the question as to why, then, this final appearance shows her to be mad. At first glance, this seems counterintuitive – the very opposite of agency. But in addition to an image of distraction and victimhood, what the mad scene also does is suggest an alternative ending for Ophelia in the play. Without suicide, this would be the scenario reserved for her: mad, ostracised from society, and with no control over her fate whatsoever. The mad scene, therefore, paints a picture of reality that not only makes her suicide plausible, but also establishes it as a choice for freedom.

Generally, a popular way of committing suicide throughout the early modern period, drowning was known as a specifically feminine way of killing oneself, and, thus, provides a fitting end for a character whose death results from being imprisoned in restrictive gender norms.[21] Symbolically, too, with its associations of menstrual blood, mother's milk, and tears, water is an inherently female element. When discussing Ophelia's death, some critics relate to the death of a young girl, conveniently named Katherine Hamlett, who accidentally drowned in the river Avon on 17 December 1579.[22] In accordance with such an interest in possible real-life precedents, the account of Ophelia's death is often analysed apropos of its apparent lack of realism. J. M. Nosworthy, for instance, writes that "it has to be admitted that the Queen's story, as such, is one that will not endure the test of common sense,"[23] which makes him believe Shakespeare must have inserted these lines at a later point. Apart from not acknowledging dialogue as part of a dramatic and, therefore, not necessarily plausible construct, such readings miss the point that Gertrude's speech is undeniably implausible and unrealistic, yet deliberately so.

With regard to the crucial question of why Ophelia dies offstage, B. G. Tandon provides three explanations. He muses that either Shakespeare hid Ophelia's death offstage in order to shorten the overall running time (as if in a play as long as *Hamlet* another five minutes would have been unbearable), or because an onstage death would put undue emphasis on Hamlet and Ophelia's relationship rather than the revenge plot. Tandon's third attempt at analysing the scene is not only the least plausible but, furthermore, has nothing to do with Ophelia herself. For him, the speech functions as a means of redeeming Gertrude, and he argues that "[b]y putting the most splendid lines of poetry into her mouth, Shakespeare made her more queenly, by making her describe the death tearfully he made her more tender and therefore more womanly."[24] Tandon's arguable reading of the play's gender politics aside, this is precisely not what happens. Gertrude does not describe Ophelia's death "tearfully," which, at least on the surface, complicates sympathising with her.

Tandon forgets to mention the most pragmatic reason for an offstage suicide: it would be difficult to stage a death by drowning convincingly. But even if practical limitations of the playhouse necessitate a reported death, it would not have to be reported in this manner:

> QUEEN: There is a willow grows askant the brook
> That shows his hoary leaves in the glassy stream.
> Therewith fantastic garlands did she make
> Of crow-flowers, nettles, daisies, and long purples,
> That liberal shepherds give a grosser name,
> But our cold maids do dead men's fingers call them.
> There on the pendent boughs her crownet weeds
> Clamb'ring to hang, an envious sliver broke,
> When down her weedy trophies and herself
> Fell in the weeping brook. Her clothes spread wide,
> And mermaid-like awhile they bore her up,
> Which time she chanted snatches of old lauds,
> As one incapable of her own distress,
> Or like a creature native and endued
> Unto that element. But long it could not be
> Till that her garments, heavy with their drink,
> Pull'd the poor wretch from her melodious lay
> To muddy death.
>
> (4.7.166–183)

The speech is confusing for two reasons. First, if Gertrude was present at Ophelia's drowning, why did she not intervene? This incongruity has led critics to believe that Gertrude cannot have been a witness herself and that she only repeats what someone else has informed her of; anything else would simply be negligent.[25] Second, and more importantly,

Gertrude's speech appears both strangely romanticised and detached. In line with the Elizabethan ideal of *ut pictura poesis*, she aestheticises the dying Ophelia in the same way as Marcus's words transform Lavinia's body into a work of art. What could otherwise be imagined as agony looks like a peaceful, aesthetically beautiful surrender or indeed embracing of death.

Since the painting is based on Gertrude's speech, her words could just as well be a description of one of the most iconic paintings in the history of British art. John Everett Millais's Pre-Raphaelite painting *Ophelia* is closely modelled on the corresponding passage from the play and its suggestive nature imagery, even though Millais added some of the flowers.[26] But primarily, the painting captures the tone of Gertrude's speech. Ophelia's eyes are staring into a void, and she seems to be caught in a trance or state of apathy, as if she were sleepwalking. Ronk discusses the scene's striking visual presence and names it one of the two prime factors for why Ophelia has become such an iconic figure of identification. The other reason, Ronk proposes, is the mysterious lacuna surrounding her death as created by the text.[27] Millais fills this gap and lets the audience assume Gertrude's position of staring at Ophelia's body. Hence, in a similar way as with the bleeding Lavinia, Shakespeare's text – and as the intermediate instance Millais's painting – makes them voyeurs in Susan Sontag's sense.[28] Discussing Millais's painting, Stuart Sillars makes an observation that is revealing in the context of Sontag's approach. For him, Ophelia's posture resembles a crucifixion.[29] This may not resonate immediately, but possibly solely because flowers and Ophelia's pretty face substitute the pain and blood of Christ. The process of a crucifixion necessarily implies a voyeuristic crowd; only in Ophelia's case, the brutality of this image is disguised as idyllic, peaceful, and aesthetically pleasing. If anything, this aestheticisation is even more unsettling.

Kahn identifies Millais's painting as the starting point of a history of both visual and critical representation that victimises Ophelia.[30] Showalter, too, has commented on the fact that Ophelia may be the painting's subject but not its centre; it appears "cruelly indifferent to the woman's death."[31] Yet, in the same way as Millais, Gertrude's account overwhelms Ophelia as a subject and pushes her into the background, as if she only served as a plot element to trigger this speech. Her death is narrated, that is, constructed by and mediated through someone else. It is conveyed through Gertrude's picture-like account of what she has possibly not even witnessed herself – how much more framed, filtered, and silenced can Ophelia's voice be? Millais's *Ophelia* adds a further dimension, which renders the painting a (presumably undeliberate) meta-image of the play's constant mediation of various images of Ophelia. It is vital that Ophelia's death is merely reported in such a way, but it is equally important that of all possible figures, Gertrude is the one who gives this account. Like Ophelia, she is disparaged and stigmatised by her sexuality. She is the incestuous, adulterous whore to Ophelia's innocent virgin. The fact that a woman reports another's – in fact the only other woman's – death aligns the two. But simultaneously, Gertrude seems unable to 'feel' this female alliance and convey the news in a less detached way, which highlights the play's oppressively patriarchal power structures. Rather than speaking up for Ophelia, the speech makes Gertrude complicit in silencing Ophelia's voice. Gertrude's own gender is important on another level, as Ronk observes: "one of the reasons this moment is so unsettling is that vis-à-vis Ophelia, Gertrude stands in what is so frequently in these plays a male position, or at least one that renders her a distant and voyeuristic observer."[32] But not only Gertrude's voyeuristic position draws attention to gender as a category. De Grazia points towards the central image of the willow tree, whose barren branches function as "the fruitless emblem of sterility, the bleak inverse of the genealogical oak" but simultaneously communicate "whore-like adulteration."[33] Reassessing Gertrude's speech through the lens of de Grazia's comment, the passage no longer appears poetic but, especially since the audience adopt the position of bystanders, deeply disturbing.

The problem of whether Ophelia's death is to be considered suicide or accident has been treated with debatable results, sometimes half murder mystery and half psychoanalysis. Peterson compares Gertrude's words to the figure of an unreliable narrator. Her position in the play is neither that of a choric figure nor does it imply any other form of distance or omniscience. She may not even have witnessed the scene herself.[34] Many critics overlook this cautionary note and instead try to find a definitive answer to a question the text deliberately obscures. To name but a few, Lagretta Lenker speculates that Gertrude's evasiveness may be either an attempt to spare Ophelia's family the damning stigma of a suicide or a means of deflecting from Hamlet's moral responsibility in a potential suicide.[35] Dane believes Ophelia's drowning to be "the clearly non-intentional act of an eroticized child,"[36] while Barbara Smith reads it as "neither accidental nor intentional."[37] All these readings dismiss what is more likely the point, namely that the conflicting reports and information concerning Ophelia's death are inconclusive for a reason. All interpretations that try to fill this epistemological gap result in what everyone else in the play does: mould Ophelia into an image and take control over her death narrative.

Any reading that treats Ophelia's death as a suicide – a self-determined action instead of an accident – naturally raises the question of agency. Scott Trudell deems this moment "the nadir of Ophelia's conscious agency,"[38] which renders her an entirely passive creature. Ranjini Philip offers a different opinion, naming her suicide "an intelligible response in her patriarchal world. It is an existential act of partial self-awareness."[39] Even though his phrasing might be criticised for being not only defeatist, but also problematic regarding its implications towards gendered power structures, Philip touches on a key issue, that is, the nature of Ophelia's agency. If self-destruction is the only active choice the play leaves her with, the use of the term 'agency' itself may seem absurd. But when reading Ophelia's death as suicide, the notion of agency is relevant in another way. As a madwoman, she is denied any form of self-determination by definition. Her suicide, within this line of argument, may be construed as an act of despair committed in a moment of mad frenzy, but not a conscious decision. As Michel Foucault makes clear in *Madness and Civilization*, from the early seventeenth century onwards, madness increasingly turned into a social construct rather than an actual illness, as a means to demarcate the normal from the abnormal. That way, "confinement had become the abusive amalgam of heterogeneous elements,"[40] a way for society to exercise their power to ostracise and suppress voices that could potentially disturb the hegemony. Ophelia's madness, then, is both cause and effect of her outlawing. Rather than an inherent defect that renders her incapable of performing action, it has to be understood as a social construct *sensu* Foucault. The stigma 'madwoman' justifies Ophelia's exclusion from the play and grants the power to those who apply it. Against this backdrop, committing suicide is Ophelia's only active decision or action. Within the realm of the play and its patriarchal, if not misogynist, ideology, this is, of course, defeatist to the extreme. Ophelia is objectified and silenced, and if killing herself is the only way out of this situation, such a definition of agency is questionable. From the point of view of an audience, however, this may be perceived differently. Rather, like Lavinia's mutilation, Ophelia's exclusion, objectification, and silencing are too disturbing and hyperbolic. They create a Brechtian form of alienation.

No matter whether suicide or accident, next to her mad scene, the floating Ophelia is the character's most powerful presence throughout the play, and so it should not be surprising that this image has dominated her iconography. The play awkwardly tiptoes around Ophelia, unable to address the brutality of how she is treated. "Instead of this imbroglio and the disturbing questions it raises," Kahn concludes, the play provides "a neat, sentimental finality – the girl is drowned, how sad, end of story – instead conveys an affecting cluster of images, easily reiterated."[41] Although Kahn's cynicism captures the critical history surrounding Ophelia's character, the tendency of wrapping her up in one single image, painted by either Gertrude or Millais, also works in another direction. Reductive and restrictive as this may be, it eternally defines her by her one moment of active agency: her suicide. As Carol Rutter establishes in *Enter the Body*, the majority of critics overlook that Gertrude's narrated version of the drowning is not actually Ophelia's final scene in the play and that she is also featured in the burial scene. In particular, Rutter takes issue with Olivier's, Zefirelli's, Branagh's, as well as Kozintsev's

(1964) adaptations. Whereas the text places particular emphasis on the presence of Ophelia's body, these films struggle with showing her body. "In the theatre," Rutter observes, "once Ophelia's corpse arrives onstage it is a material fact that the scene must reckon with: the body won't go away. But what these films do is avert the camera's eye from the body and, by taking the spectator with them, they erase the corpse."[42] Even though Zefirelli briefly captures the dead Ophelia's face, in all these interpretations of the burial scene, the focus lies on Hamlet's return to Elsinore. By sweeping over the scene's rivalry between Hamlet and Laertes, both of who feel the need to assert their masculinity during Ophelia's burial, while at the same time 'erasing' the dead Ophelia, these films miss the vital point: the way Shakespeare wrote it, the burial scene functions as a means of deconstructing the tragic hero. And even though Branagh's 'gothicised' burial scene shows Ophelia's body – Laertes even jumps into the grave to embrace her – the scene is dripping with vampire tropes that not only introduce an undue and clichéd sense of the macabre, but also fail to contemplate the image of Ophelia's dead body.[43]

That Ophelia's dead body matters shows when the puzzling account of her death as offered by Gertrude is contrasted with another, equally ambiguous passage. However, the matter-of-fact conversation between the gravediggers could not be more different from Gertrude's lines:

GRAVEDIGGER: Is she to be buried in Christian burial, when she wilfully seeks her own salvation?

OTHER: I tell thee she is, therefore make her grave straight. The crowner hath sat on her and finds it Christian burial.

GRAVEDIGGER: How can that be, unless she drowned herself in her own defence?

OTHER: Why, 'tis found so.

GRAVEDIGGER: It must be *se offendendo*, it cannot be else. For here lies the point: if I drown myself wittingly, it argues an act, and an act hath three branches – it is to act, to do, to perform; argal, she drowned herself wittingly.

(5.1.1–13)

This passage is Shakespeare's most elaborate and accurate discussion of early modern legal and ecclesiastical suicide regulations, for which it has received considerable critical attention.[44] Admittedly, at first, it seems a forthright debate – the coroners have cleared Ophelia's body for a Christian burial, and still, the gravediggers question the verdict. But this account clashes with Gertrude's version of events and instead gives voice to the suspicion of suicide that has already been raised in the minds of the audience. Besides, the discussion ridicules the absurdities of early modern suicide legislation; a comic relief moment, the topic is as inappropriate as it gets. The gravedigger's "*se offendendo*," commonly read as a malapropism for "*se defendendo*,"[45] asserts that in order not to be a suicide, Ophelia would have had to drown herself in self-defence. Ludicrous as the deduction of his argument sounds, this clown figure, as so often in Shakespeare, makes a valid point. Following the reading of Ophelia's suicide as an act of revolt against patriarchal suppression, it can indeed be deemed an act of self-defence. Nonetheless, the concluding lines of this dialogue establish that the actual mitigating factor is another: "Will you ha' the truth an't? If this had not been a gentlewoman, she should have been buried out o' Christian burial" (5.1.23–25).

The following information that Ophelia is to be buried in the graveyard without full burial rites complicates the scenario even further:

> PRIEST: Her obsequies have been as far enlarg'd
> As we have warranty. Her death was doubtful;
> And but that great command o'ersways the order,
> She should in ground unsanctified been lodg'd
> Till the last trumpet: for charitable prayers
> Shards, flints, and pebbles should be thrown on her.
> Yet here she is allow'd her virgin crants,
> Her maiden strewments, and the bringing home
> Of bell and burial.
>
> (5.1.224–232)

Like the previous passage, this one echoes early modern debates surrounding suicide, even though the Church provided only poor advice on the exact burial procedure.[46] Yet, the key to this, as well as to the previous dialogue, is not so much its pseudo-accuracy with regard to historical context that scholars have been so careful to outline as its argumentative inconsistencies. Audiences are deliberately left confused about what has happened. The term 'doubtful', thus, calls attention to the general need to make conscious decisions, as the play leaves so much up for interpretation. Along these lines, the controversy surrounding Ophelia's death acquires a choric function. As part of the play's meta-dramatic discourse, both speeches engage in ethical, cognitive, and epistemological questions with regard to the process of dying as well as agency of the individual.

It is not enough that the gravediggers and the priest consider Ophelia's death "doubtful." Gertrude, who could testify that it was an accident, remains silent. Moreover, the possible mitigating factor of Ophelia's madness is not even touched on. As Wymer argues, audiences would have expected the mad Ophelia to receive a Christian burial, which leads him to the conclusion that the withholding of full rites marks a deliberate counterpoint.[47] According to Michael MacDonald, however, *non compos mentis* verdicts were extremely rare, if not even unheard of. Furthermore, the horrifying stigma attached to suicides predominated by far, overshadowing any possibility of mitigation. As Ophelia's madness is implied but not explicitly used to condone her suicide, the play refrains from taking a moral stance. For this reason, MacDonald concludes that *Hamlet* investigates and challenges the early modern concept of suicide without finally resolving its underlying tensions and contradictions.[48] Within the debate of whether Ophelia's death is a suicide or an accident, the text also suggests another, more pertinent reason for suppressing any information about Ophelia's madness: to read it as an accident out of mad frenzy would compromise her agency. Instead, it is meant to be understood as a wilful action.

If looked at more carefully, the debate between Laertes and the priest at Ophelia's interment conflates questions regarding Ophelia's mental health and her virginity. The priest emphasises Ophelia's "virgin crants" and "maiden strewments," and with his appeal that "from her fair and unpolluted flesh / May violets spring" (5.1.237–238) Laertes refers to her being a virgin rather than to the stigma of suicide. As Valerie Traub comments, "[f]etishized to the extent that it is utterly divorced from the rest of her being, Ophelia's chastity embodies, as it were, a masculine fantasy of a female essence wonderfully devoid of that which makes women so problematic: change, movement, inconstancy, unpredictability – in short, life."[49] Such a masculine fantasy not only underpins anxieties concerning female sexuality in *Hamlet*, but also, as I will elaborate, equally surrounds the deaths of Desdemona, Goneril, and Lady Macbeth. The ideal woman, these plays suggest at least on the surface, is a dead one.

When Hamlet asks what man lies in the grave, the gravedigger responds that it would be neither man nor woman, but "One that was a woman, sir; but rest her soul she's dead" (5.1.134–135). Although this attempt at banter sounds like another comic relief moment, Leggatt remarks that "[a]s Lavinia's identity is blurred by her rape, Ophelia's is blurred by death."[50] What he does not carve out strongly enough is that identity here means gender identity. After the rape, Lavinia fits none of the stereotypical female roles anymore, neither that of wife, daughter, nor whore. But even though she is increasingly objectified, the play reiterates her status as woman. Ophelia, by contrast, has turned into "One that was a woman" in the past tense and, hence, seems to have managed what Lady Macbeth can only wish for: she has un-sexed herself. Something similar happens in *Julius's Caesar* when Antony eulogises Brutus with the words "'This was a man!'"(*Julius Caesar* 5.5.75). But, whereas Antony's words may suggest a touch of reservation, the implication that the days of glory are now over, in the case of Ophelia, her 'un-gendering', is implied as something positive and liberating. This is probably the only moment in the play in which she is not defined by her gender role. Through her suicide, Ophelia eventually escapes the object of male staring and control, even after her death. Ophelia has had one of the richest afterlives, be it in literature, art history, or popular culture. In many ways, this has been much more diverse than Hamlet's. Her name has graced a wide range of consumer products, and apart from numerous visual representations in painting, she has also been translated into much more liberating contexts, emancipated from the patriarchal oppression she suffers in the play.[51] It seems as if this possibility of re-writing Ophelia and her tragic ending exists precisely because Shakespeare writes her an exit out of the play. Hamlet, by comparison, stays forever imprisoned in his own tragedy.

"The Dread of Something after Death": Hamlet's Delay of Suicide

As mentioned at the beginning of this chapter, arguing that Hamlet engages in a discussion of suicide would sound tired. According to common interpretation, "To be, or not to be" weighs the pros and cons for suicide, leading to the assumption that *Hamlet* is the play in which, as Barbara Smith argues, "the morality and consequences of suicide are discussed thematically [...] as they are in no other Shakespearean play."[52] This is what it is most famous for, and so the point needs no further elaboration, it seems. However, it is well worth re-addressing the connection between Hamlet's suicidal nature, his lack of action, and the attached implications in terms of gender, especially as compared to the deaths of both Ophelia and Horatio.

Summing up critical assumptions of how to approach Hamlet's iconic soliloquy, it is either an argument against suicide, a discussion of whether to take action against Claudius, or a mixture of the two.[53] With its strikingly different editions, the textual history of *Hamlet* is contested like that of no other play (only *King Lear* being a possible exception), and it equally offers room for controversy with regard to Hamlet's most famous soliloquy.[54] The rediscovery of Q1 in 1823 has been key in this respect. There, the speech is preceded by Claudius's "See where he comes, poring upon a book" (7.110),[55] which allows for a reading that sees Hamlet's following soliloquy as a comment on what he has just read. These reservations notwithstanding, it seems most convincing to side with those who have found that Hamlet is, in fact, talking about suicide; but the question remains as to how abstract a debate he enters. Vincent Petronalla argues that even though the speech centres on suicide, "it need not necessarily be spoken by one who is intensely suicidal" because "the contrasting and the reflecting are done in such a way as to offer us a fusion of the general and the particular."[56] However, the speech does not offer such a fusion of the general and the particular. Rather, the entire soliloquy contains neither a single 'I' nor any reference to the concrete problems Hamlet is confronted with. As a result, it appears strangely generalised and applicable to a number of contexts or situations, which Harold Jenkins believes to be the prime reason for its fame.[57] These contradictions suggest that instead of being a reflection on the dramatic situation, Hamlet's words have to be read on a meta-level. They do not further the plot but instead they have a choric function, singling out suicide as one of the play's predominant themes.

Suicide is a pre-eminent motif in the revenge tragedy genre in which the tragic hero finds himself confronted with the dilemma of either accepting or rejecting the task pre-determined by his dramatic role. This is particularly true for *Hamlet*, since in Kyd's *The Spanish Tragedy*, one of *Hamlet's* more overt hypotexts, Hieronimo is confronted with the options of both suicide and revenge after having found his son murdered in an orchard.[58] Both *Hamlet* and *The Spanish Tragedy* are early revenge tragedies, yet, unlike Hamlet, Hieronimo already seems to be aware of this generic legacy. He eventually opts for revenge because "in revenge [his] heart would find relief" (*The Spanish Tragedy* 2.4.103).[59] In a revenge tragedy, the act of revenge is the hero's *raison d'être*, but Hamlet is a reluctant avenger who rejects suicide in the same way he defers taking action. But since he cannot win the battle against the genre, he can circumvent neither his inevitable death nor revenge.

Many critics have traced Hamlet's argumentative steps through close readings in order to unlock the "To be, or not to be" soliloquy, but his overall train of thought is quite simple.[60] Whether or not he talks about suicide, Hamlet juxtaposes the possibilities of either continuing to suffer whatever fate he has to suffer or to take some form of action against it. The paradoxical image of taking "arms against a sea of troubles" (3.1.59) connotes forceful, if not violent, action, which fits the portrayal of suicide as action rather than defeat, in *Hamlet* and elsewhere in the canon. At the same time, the image carries a tone of resignation because opposing natural forces is a futile endeavour. He describes both death and what comes after death as a dream, a variation on the 'life-as-a-dream' metaphor. During the Renaissance, such metaphors were equally used with reference to the afterlife, which was either conceptualised as an on-going dream or, conversely, the sudden awakening into reality.[61] While Hamlet's description of death or the afterlife as a peaceful dream sounds so much more desirable than "heart-ache and the thousand natural shocks" (3.1.62), he gives an explanation as to why death still is not the more preferable option: "the dread of something after death [...] makes us rather bear those ills we have / Than fly to others that we know not of" (3.1.78–82). Who would not take the easy way out by committing suicide, Hamlet asks. Still, he opts for life, however unbearable this might seem, out of fear that death or a horrible afterlife might be even worse: "Thus conscience does make cowards of us all, / And thus the native hue of resolution / Is sicklied o'er with the pale cast of thought" (3.1.83–85). It is ironic that he envisions "a bare bodkin" (3.1.76) as his weapon of choice. Given that he defers any form of decision, a dagger connoting masculinity, violence, and drastic action would seem an unlikely choice for Hamlet, one that merely fits his rhetoric on suicide.

The majority of commentators have analysed the soliloquy with reference to its religious implications. While it is justifiable to say that the concept of an afterlife points towards a religious framework, the religious references provided by Hamlet are implicit at best. Here, too, the different textual editions complicate this debate even further. Depending on which result they seek to obtain, critics often refer to Q1, which is more specifically Christian in its implications. Q1 explicitly refers to the Last Judgement, which Julian Rice considers the result of a direct attempt to Christianise the rather agnostic Folio version.[62] Even though the speech is most striking for betraying Hamlet's troubling misogyny, religion is more pertinently emphasised in Hamlet's first soliloquy, which in turn influences the interpretation of "To be, or not to be." Hamlet hopes that his "too too solid flesh would melt," which would conveniently release him from the burden of killing himself. As this is obviously not possible, he wishes that "the Everlasting had not fix'd / His canon 'gainst self-slaughter" (1.2.129–132).[63] Compared to the vague "dread of something after death," Hamlet references medieval and Renaissance suicide ethics. As a result, Burton Ralph Pollin maintains that only Hamlet's "deep sense of religion" prevents him from killing himself and finds Hamlet's words to be "saturated with a religious stream of references."[64] Recently, however, David Scott Kastan has revisited the play's portrayal of death, challenging the critical myth of *Hamlet* as "some dramatic *ars moriendi*."[65] The influence of religious debates on death and dying has been overestimated, Kastan indicates, which is certainly true with regard to the nexus of suicide and religion.

All opposing claims of religious impediments as the reason for Hamlet's hesitation presuppose that he considers suicide an option he might actually want to pursue. The text, by contrast, subverts this notion. Instead, early on, it is visible that Hamlet's character convolutes religion with debates on gender. Claudius condemns Hamlet's behaviour as "unmanly grief" (1.2.94), and this danger of appearing effeminate is also acknowledged by Hamlet himself, who later in the play admits that he is filled with "such a kind of gaingiving as would perhaps trouble a woman" (5.2.215). In his essay "The Woman in Hamlet," David Leverenz revisits Goethe's claim that Hamlet can be deemed feminine, which Goethe felt to be a major source of weakness. Unlike Goethe, Leverenz does not equate femininity and weakness in this manner but identifies in Hamlet a susceptibility to feelings, which sounds less different from Goethe's claim than Leverenz indicates. He reduces Ophelia to a casualty of tragic inevitability, arguing that her death "signifies the necessity of drowning both words and feelings if Hamlet is to act the role prescribed for him."[66] To paraphrase Leverenz's words, feelings and femininity correlate with passivity, whereas masculinity collocates with action.

Due to the ostensibly androgynous nature of its tragic hero, together with its debates on feminine and masculine gender roles, Hamlet has had a long-standing history of cross-gender casting. As early as the nineteenth century, Hamlet was sometimes played by female actors.[67] Most radically, this debate has been taken up by the several Hamlets since the late twentieth century, from Frances de la Tour (1979, dir. Robert Walker), to Angela Winkler (1999, dir. Peter Zadek), and Maxine Peake (2014, dir. Sarah Frankcom). Whereas on the one hand the move towards cross-gender casting provides the welcome and timely possibility to broaden the Shakespearean repertoire for female actors, its primary virtue is the potential to investigate a play's construction of gendered power structures. As Tony Howard remarks in his performance history *Women as Hamlet*, with a female actor in the title role, audiences automatically stumble across issues they would normally accept as a given: "the theatrical conventions we might otherwise not question, the political banalities masking Elsinore's lies, and the structures of power and gender that normally trap women in Hamlet in the roles of Mother, Virgin, and Whore. The female Hamlet is a walking, speaking alienation effect."[68] By exposing categories such as 'masculine' and 'feminine' as purely performative, female Hamlets challenge assumptions like the one made by Leverenz and, furthermore, highlight where the play, too, undermines them.

Against the background of gender constructions, Hamlet's actual death is revealing. He dies with a considerable amount of gusto, and the sword-fight, killing four people in quick succession, clashes with his previous lethargy. While dying, he even kills Claudio twice, as it were; first with the sword, then with the poisoned cup. All of a sudden, anxieties with regard to his manliness are substituted by assertions of masculinity. And yet, Hamlet's death is not exactly that of a heroic warrior killed in battle. He dies not from Laertes's sword but from the King's poison, a conventionally gentle weapon that had already emasculated Romeo a few years earlier. Hamlet seems relieved that he no longer needs to kill himself and languishes in the process of dying: "Had I but time (as this fell sergeant Death / Is strict in his arrest) – O, I could tell you" (5.2.343–344). The vehemence with which he reiterates "I am dead" and "I die" even brings to mind Bottom's Pyramus, who keeps talking even after he has officially died. The famous final line "The rest is silence" (5.2.364) may suggest that the rest will remain untold since he will now remain silent. Alternatively, reviewing "To be, or not to be," it may indicate that there is no afterlife.[69] Either way, these words reintroduce the notion of high tragedy but only weakly cover up the scene's incongruous undertones.

Hamlet's death is juxtaposed with Horatio's suicide attempt a few lines later. Several scholars consider Horatio an underdeveloped character and, hence, mostly address him in relation to his function within the play. Drew Daniel, for instance, describes him as "as a flexibly useful foil to Hamlet's persistent need for admirers, advisors, caretakers, gulls, and assistants."[70] Pale a figure as he may be, in the last scene, Horatio gains significance as a counterexample to Hamlet's non-suicide. When he reaches for the poisoned cup with the words "I am more an antique Roman than a Dane. / Here's yet some liquor left" (5.2.348–349), this is primarily a meta-reference to the classical concept of suicide, testimony to his scholarly education. But since poison is considered 'un-Roman' and trivial, this is a dissonant performance of Roman *virtus*. Furthermore, Horatio's comment appears histrionic and out of touch with the dramatic situation. Daniel captures this dissonance, arguing that by "doing what the Romans do precisely when he is *not* in Rome, Horatio showily demonstrates a kind of excessive affinity for an aesthetic mannerism that is deliberately out of place and out of date."[71] De Grazia critiques that Horatio's line has been unjustly neglected by editors of the play who identify the reference to the classical concept of suicide but fail to note that Horatio's preference for suicide surfaces at the very moment he has to submit to a foreign regime.[72] The fear of being humiliated through submission is a common feature of the Roman plays, most evidently of *Antony and Cleopatra*. However, such a reading runs counter to events as presented in the play. In all textual versions of *Hamlet*, the news of Norway's victory arrives after Horatio has delivered this line, and so this temporal discrepancy suggests a private rather than a political motivation.

Throughout, Horatio is defined by his status as Hamlet's best friend, a concept that Renaissance discourse commonly envisioned as 'a second self' or 'one soul in two bodies'.[73] Within this context, notions such as platonic and erotic are fluent. The circumstance that early modern thought frequently prioritised same-sex bonds (both erotic and non-erotic) over heterosexual bonds constitutes what Laurie Shannon names "the gaping distance between early modern 'homonormative' affects and contemporary heterosexual, erotic normativity."[74] Against this backdrop, Francis G. Schoff interprets Horatio's gesture as logically motivated by his love for Hamlet; he simply does not want to live without his friend.[75] Love here means loyalty, but this distinction also suggests a different reading, chiefly in the light of Horatio's last words to Hamlet: "Good night, sweet prince, / And flights of angels sing thee to thy rest" (5.2.365–366). For Jeffrey Masten, these words sound misplaced, even though in the early modern context, the connotation of sweetness as effeminising did not exist in the same way is it does today. Nevertheless, they clash with the tone of the final scene as well as the play at large. The tenderness of Horatio's words comes after what Masten aptly describes as "all the butch heroics of the preceding scenes."[76] Supporting this view, Lars Engle draws a connection to Eros, who kills himself because he does not want to face a life without Antony, his revered master. Simultaneously, Engle concludes that "[Horatio's] interest is less a political one in the Danish regime than an erotic one in Hamlet."[77] While this reference to *Antony and Cleopatra*, in which the boundaries between erotic love and loyalty become remarkably blurred, is justified, Horatio also has a predecessor in an earlier play: Juliet, who seeks to die from the same poison that has killed her beloved Romeo. Hamlet's response to Horatio's suicide attempt is telling: "As th'art a man / Give me the cup. Let go, by Heaven I'll ha't!" (5.2.349–350). According to this argument, not suicide but survival is the heroic, manly gesture, but only because Horatio needs to survive and set the record straight. Daniel, therefore, deduces that "[w]hat is at stake is the maintenance of a masculinity whose primary characteristic is not in this case violent aggression, but rather steadfast obedience."[78] On the whole, then, Horatio's gesture, together with the context in which it occurs, addresses the question of what makes a 'manly' death. Most importantly, though, his attempt to grasp the poisoned cup further stresses Hamlet's inaction and lack of consistency when it comes to killing himself.

It is true that suicide is a major concern for Hamlet, to the extent that his death can be read as a quasi-suicide. Yet, not only Ophelia's offstage suicide, but also, to some extent, Horatio's near-suicide make the tragic hero's inaction all the more apparent. Analysing the correlation between suicide and gender in *Hamlet*, Lenker concludes that "[f]inally, the male protagonist can assert himself against the forces that bind him. The emblematic female, whose life is interpreted by others, cannot free herself from her constraints and isolation. These circumstances enable one character to turn from suicide to action, whereas the other degenerates into madness and self-destruction."[79] Her choice of words indicates an understanding of suicide as degenerate, passive, and bad. The text suggests a different reading, though. Whereas Hamlet does not take arms against his too solid flesh, it is possible to interpret Ophelia's suicide as forceful action rather than a mad accident. Whereas Hamlet wavers, Ophelia actively chooses not to be. Suicide enables her to break free from patriarchal control and a heteronomous existence, albeit at the cost of sacrificing her life in the same breath. Thus, even more emphatically than presenting Ophelia's suicide as an act of agency, the play scrutinises the nature of that agency. Through Hamlet and Ophelia, it juxtaposes a male character who talks about suicide at great length without ever acting in this direction with a female character who generally remains rather silent but, unexpectedly, commits the most drastic of all actions; tragic power structures are reversed here. Ophelia's female agency remains limited, of course, because all she can do is leave the world of the play in order to avoid life as a madwoman. But what her suicide communicates is a subversion of conventional concepts of masculinity and femininity as synonyms for action and passivity. Further, and similarly to the suicides of Portia, Goneril, and Lady Macbeth, it challenges the common understanding of the offstage space as unimportant and marginalising. That Ophelia's dead body pushes back onto the stage, as if to object to her confinement, only signals more clearly that in this play, he who talks most does not automatically deserve all the attention.

Notes

1 Stephen Greenblatt, *Hamlet in Purgatory*, rev. ed. (2001; reprint; Princeton, NJ: Princeton University Press, 2013), 240.
2 Most strongly, this shows in earlier critical responses. In *Characters of Shakespeare's Plays* (1817; reprint; London: J. M. Dent, 1906), William Hazlitt named her "a character almost too exquisitely touching to be dwelt upon" (85). In *Shakespearean Tragedy* (1904; reprint; London: Penguin, 1991), Bradley insisted that her role was deliberately underwritten and diminished so as not to interfere with the main revenge plot. He felt that "in the love and the fate of Ophelia herself there was introduced an element, not of deep tragedy but of pathetic beauty, which makes the analysis of her character seem almost a desecration" (154).
3 Dympna Callaghan, *Shakespeare without Women: Representing Gender and Race on the Renaissance Stage* (London and New York: Routledge, 2000), 90.
4 Kaara Peterson, "Framing Ophelia: Representation and the Pictorial Tradition," *Mosaic* 31.3 (1998): 8.
5 Elaine Showalter, "Representing Ophelia: Women, Madness, and the Responsibilities of Feminist Criticism," in *Shakespeare and the Question of Theory*, ed. Geoffrey H. Hartman and Patricia Parker (London and New York: Routledge, 1985), 91.
6 Martha Ronk, "Representations of Ophelia," *Criticism* 36.1 (1994): 24.
7 Gabrielle Dane, "Reading Ophelia's Madness," *Exemplaria: A Journal of Theory in Medieval and Renaissance Studies* 10.2 (1998): 407.
8 Coppélia Kahn, "Afterword: Ophelia Then, Now, Hereafter," in *The Afterlife of Ophelia*, ed. Kaara L. Peterson and Deanne Williams (New York: Palgrave, 2012), 233.
9 Jacquelyn A. Fox-Good, "Ophelia's Mad Songs: Music, Gender, Power," in *Subjects on the World's Stage: Essays on British Literature of the Middle Ages and the Renaissance*, ed. David C. Allen and Robert A. White (Newark: University of Delaware Press, 1995), 223; Ranjini Philip, "The Shattered Glass: The Story of (O)phelia," *Hamlet Studies* 13.1/2 (1991): 78.
10 As Thompson and Taylor's note to 13.6–8 of the 1603 text indicates, in Q1, the Queen explicitly attributes Ophelia's madness to her father's death. The corresponding passage from Q1 reads as follows: "But this mischance of old Corambis' death / Hath pierced so the young Ofelia's Heart / That she, poor maid, is quite bereft of her wits." *Hamlet: The Texts of 1603 and 1623*, ed. Ann Thompson and Neil Taylor, The Arden Shakespeare Third Series (London: Arden Shakespeare, 2006). In support of this reading see Levin L. Schücking, *The Meaning of Hamlet* (Oxford: Oxford University Press, 1937), 153; John Draper, *The Hamlet of Shakespeare's Audience* (1939; reprint; London: Frank Cass, 1966), 61.
11 Elaine Showalter, *The Female Malady: Women, Madness, and English Culture, 1830–1980* (London: Virago, 2008), 4.
12 Ibid., 86–98; also, see Showalter, "Representing Ophelia," 85–87.

13 See Carol Thomas Neely, *Distracted Subjects: Madness and Gender in Shakespeare and Early Modern Culture* (New York: Cornell University Press, 2004), 1–25; Michael MacDonald, *Mystical Bedlam: Madness, Anxiety, and Healing in Seventeenth-Century England* (Cambridge: Cambridge University Press, 1981).

14 Carol Thomas Neely, "Documents in Madness: Reading Madness and Gender in Shakespeare's Tragedies and Early Modern Culture," *Shakespeare Quarterly* 42.3 (1991): 320.

15 Maurice Charney and Hanna Charney, "The Language of Madwomen in Shakespeare and His Fellow Dramatists," *Signs* 3.2 (1977): 459.

16 Neely, "Documents in Madness," 323; 326.

17 On the materiality of Ophelia's songs and their subversive potential, see Leslie C. Dunn, "Ophelia's Song in *Hamlet*: Music, Madness, and the Feminine," in *Embodied Voices: Representing Female Vocality in Western Culture*, ed. Leslie C. Dunn and Nancy A. Jones (Cambridge: Cambridge University Press, 1994), 59; Fox-Good, "Ophelia's Mad Songs," 222; Caralyn Bialo, "Popular Performance, the Broadside Ballad, and Ophelia's Madness," *SEL* 53.2 (2013): 294.

18 William Shakespeare, *Hamlet*, ed. Ann Thompson and Neil Taylor, The Arden Shakespeare Third Series (London: Arden Shakespeare, 2006), note to 4.5.169–178.

19 Margreta de Grazia, *Hamlet without Hamlet* (Cambridge: Cambridge University Press, 2007), 118.

20 Bridget Gellert Lyons elaborates on this iconographic tradition in "The Iconography of Ophelia," *ELH* 44.1 (1977): 63–70. She, furthermore, discusses the corresponding scene in *The Winter's Tale* in which Perdita turns into Flora – the flower goddess – and explains why, unlike with Ophelia, this scene does not lend itself to such a distinctly ambivalent interpretation.

21 Michael MacDonald, "Ophelia's Maimèd Rites," *Shakespeare Quarterly* 37.3 (1986): 311. Macdonald reports that drowning was the second most frequent cause for suicides in general and the most common for female suicides.

22 J. M. Nosworthy, "The Death of Ophelia," *Shakespeare Quarterly* 15.4 (1964): 345. See also B. G. Tandon, "Why Does Ophelia Die Offstage?" *The Aligarh Journal of English Studies* 15 (1993): 2.

23 Nosworthy, "The Death of Ophelia," 346.

24 Tandon, "Why Does Ophelia Die Offstage," 3.

25 Peterson, "Framing Ophelia," 4; Nosworthy, "The Death of Ophelia," 346.

26 See Michael Benton and Sally Butcher, "Painting Shakespeare," *Journal of Aesthetic Education* 32.3 (1998): 57. Benton and Butcher also discuss the painting's Pre-Raphaelite aesthetics as well as its wider context in the history of paintings modelled on Shakespeare's texts.

27 Ronk, "Representations of Ophelia," 27.

28 Susan Sontag, *Regarding the Pain of Others* (London and New York: Penguin, 2003), 85.

29 Stuart Sillars, *Painting Shakespeare: The Artist as Critic, 1720–1820* (Cambridge: Cambridge University Press, 2006), 206.

30 Coppélia Kahn, "Afterword: Ophelia Then, Now, Hereafter," in *The Afterlife of Ophelia*, ed. Kaara L. Peterson and Deanne Williams (New York: Palgrave, 2012), 232.

31 Showalter, *The Female Malady*, 85.

32 Ronk, "Representations of Ophelia," 30.

33 De Grazia, *Hamlet without Hamlet*, 119.

34 Peterson, "Framing Ophelia," 6.

35 Lagretta T. Lenker, "Suicide and the Dialectic of Gender in *Hamlet*," in *Youth Suicide: A Comprehensive Manual for Prevention and Intervention*,

ed. Barbara Barrett Hicks (Bloomington: National Educational Service, 1989), 109.

36 Dane, "Reading Ophelia's Madness," 420.

37 Barbara Smith, "Neither Accident nor Intent: Contextualizing the Suicide of Ophelia," *South Atlantic Review* 73.2 (2008): 97.

38 Scott A. Trudell, "The Mediation of Poesie: Ophelia's Orphic Song," *Shakespeare Quarterly* 63.1 (2012): 46–76, 75.

39 Philip, "The Shattered Glass," 75.

40 Michel Foucault, *Madness and Civilization: A History of Insanity in the Age of Reason*, (1964; reprint; New York: Vintage, 1988), 45.

41 Kahn, "Ophelia Then, Now, Hereafter," 236.

42 Carol Chillington Rutter, *Enter the Body: Women and Representation on Shakespeare's Stage* (London and New York: Routledge, 2001), 44.

43 Ibid., 45–52.

44 See, for instance, Macdonald, "Ophelia's Maimèd Rites," 309–317; Roland Mushat Frye, *The Renaissance Hamlet: Issues and Responses in 1600* (Princeton, NJ: Princeton University Press, 1984), 297–309.

45 Thompson and Taylor's note to 5.1.9 in the Arden Third Series.

46 MacDonald, "Ophelia's Maimèd Rites," 310.

47 Rowland Wymer, *Suicide and Despair in the Jacobean Drama* (Brighton: Harvester, 1986), 35.

48 MacDonald, "Ophelia's Maimèd Rites," 313; 316.

49 Valerie Traub, *Desire and Anxiety: Circulations of Sexuality in Shakespearean Drama* (London and New York: Routledge, 1992), 32.

50 Alexander Leggatt, *Shakespeare's Tragedies: Violation and Identity* (Cambridge: Cambridge University Press, 2005), 75.

51 Kaara Peterson and Deanne Williams, "Introduction: The Afterlives of Ophelia," in *The Afterlife of Ophelia*, ed. Kaara L. Peterson and Deanne Williams (New York: Palgrave, 2012), 1. The entire edited collection discusses the character in film, performance, popular culture, and the new media. On the various Ophelia paintings, see Peterson, "Framing Ophelia," 1–24.

52 Barbara Smith, "Neither Accident nor Intent," 96.

53 Vincent F. Petronella gives a detailed overview of the speech's critical reception in "Hamlet's 'To be or not to be' Soliloquy: Once More unto the Breach," *Studies in Philology* 71.1 (1974): 72–77.

54 On the status of and relationship between the different quarto and Folio editions, see Ann Thompson and Neil Taylor, Introduction to *Hamlet*, by William Shakespeare, ed. Ann Thompson and Neil Taylor, The Arden Shakespeare Third Series (London: Arden Shakespeare, 2006), 74–94.

55 *Hamlet: The Texts of 1603 and 1623*, ed. Thompson and Taylor.

56 Petronella, "Hamlet's 'To be or not to be' Soliloquy," 78.

57 Harold Jenkins, "'To be, or not to be': Hamlet's Dilemma," *Hamlet Studies* 13.1/2 (1991): 11.

58 On *Hamlet*'s possible literary sources see Harold Jenkins, Introduction to *Hamlet*, by William Shakespeare, ed. Harold Jenkins, The Arden Shakespeare Second Series (London: Arden Shakespeare, 1982), 82–122.

59 Thomas Kyd, *The Spanish Tragedy*, in *Four Revenge Tragedies*, ed. Katharine Eisaman Maus (Oxford: Oxford University Press, 1995). The lines in which Hieronimo mentions suicide are in Latin, but Maus's translation of line 142 reads as follows: "I shall perish with you: thus, thus it would delight me to go into the shadows. But nevertheless I shall resist surrendering to a swift death, since in that case no revenge might follow your death."

60 See, for example, Jenkins, "Hamlet's Dilemma," 9–14 as well as Petronella, "Hamlet's 'To be or not to be' Soliloquy," 79–88.

61 Julian C. Rice, "Hamlet and the Dream of Something after Death," *Hartford Studies in Literature* 6 (1974): 109.

62 Rice, "Hamlet and the Dream of Something after Death," 115. The corresponding Q1 passage reads as follows: "To be, or not to be – ay, there's the point. / To die, to sleep – is that all? Ay, all. / No, to sleep, to dream – ay, marry, there it goes, / For in that dream of death, when we're awaked / And borne before an everlasting judge / From whence no passenger ever returned – / The undiscovered country, at whose sight / The happy smile and the accursed damned. But for this, the joyful hope of this, / Who'd bear the scorns and flattery of the world" (*Hamlet: The Texts of 1603 and 1623*, 7.115–124).

63 As I consider the Folio variant of 'solid' rather than 'sallied' (Q1,Q2), or even 'sullied' with its suggestion of contamination (cf. Jenkins's corresponding note in the Arden Second Series) more logical as a contrast to the concept of 'melting', this quotation is taken from *Hamlet*, ed. Philip Edwards, The New Cambridge Shakespeare (Cambridge: Cambridge University Press, 2003).

64 Burton R. Pollin, "Hamlet, A Successful Suicide," *Shakespeare Studies* 1 (1965): 249.

65 David Scott Kastan, *A Will to Believe: Shakespeare and Religion* (Oxford: Oxford University Press, 2014), 143.

66 David Leverenz, "The Woman in Hamlet: An Interpersonal View," *Signs* 4.2 (1978): 303.

67 On female Hamlets in the nineteenth century, specifically on Sarah Bernhardt, see Tony Howard, *Women as Hamlet: Performance and Interpretation in Theatre, Film and Fiction* (Cambridge: Cambridge University Press, 2007), 98–134.

68 Ibid., 5.

69 Thompson and Taylor's note to 5.2.342 in the Arden Third Series states the annotations of "Rest = residue, remainder, repose, but this might be heard as a pun, 'th'arrest'."

70 Drew Daniel, "'I am more an antique Roman than a Dane': Suicide, Masculinity and National Identity in Hamlet," in *Identity, Otherness and Empire in Shakespeare's Rome*, ed. Maria del Sapio Garbero (Farnham and Burlington: Ashgate, 2009), 82. See also Francis G. Schoff, "Horatio: A Shakespearean Confidant," *Shakespeare Quarterly* 7.1 (1956): 53.

71 Daniel, "'I am more an antique Roman than a Dane'," 83.

72 de Grazia, *Hamlet without Hamlet*, 70.

73 On early modern constructions of friendship, see Laurie Shannon, *Sovereign Amity: Figures of Friendship in Shakespearean Contexts* (Chicago: University of Chicago Press, 2002), notably 1–11.

74 Ibid., 1.

75 Schoff, "Horatio: A Shakespearean Confidant," 56.

76 Jeffrey Masten, "Toward a Queer Address: The Taste of Letters and Early Modern Male Friendship," *GLQ* 10.3 (2004): 368–369. On the use of the term 'sweet' in *Hamlet* as well as in other Shakespearean plays see 370–377.

77 Lars Engle, "How is Horatio Just?: How Just Is Horatio?" *Shakespeare Quarterly* 62.2 (2011): 262.

78 Daniel, "'I am more an antique Roman than a Dane'," 86.

79 Lenker, "Suicide and the Dialectic of Gender in *Hamlet*," 113.

5 Before We Go
Othello

On Friday 17 June 1994, Shakespeare became a voice-over for a moment of American cultural history. Reporting that a suicidal O. J. Simpson lay in the back of his Ford Bronco holding a gun to his head, CBS television anchor Dan Rather glossed the flickering image of the vehicle, parked before Simpson's Brentwood home, by saying that he was reminded of *Othello*, in which a black man, suspecting his white wife of adultery, kills her and then himself. As though shopping for a good story, Rather had mined the literary archive to imagine an ending that, by courting the obsessive fictions that attach to Othello's colour, could mask the culture's racism in Shakespearean suicide and its attendant admission of guilt.[1]

With this anecdote, Barbara Hodgdon begins her essay on how screen adaptations of *Othello* have dealt with the question of race. In the events following this TV announcement, Hodgdon continues, *Time Magazine*'s 27 June cover showed an artificially darkened version of Simpson's police mug shot that brought to mind the famous 'dirty still' from Laurence Olivier's *Othello* (1965), which shows a black stain of Olivier's make-up on Maggie Smith's white cheek. The magazine headlined "An American Tragedy."[2] Apart from its implications regarding racism in mid-90's US media, with regard to Shakespeare's tragedy, this cover made a strong claim: there is a direct correlation between Desdemona's death, Othello's suicide, and the colour of his skin.

The question of whether *Othello* is a racist play or rather a play about racism has been widely discussed.[3] But no matter how divided on this issue, the majority of critics – with the exception of those who consider the notion of race hugely anachronistic in the context of early modern England – agree that it is impossible to separate the play from its racial discourse.[4] This shows most clearly when looking at performance history. There have been a number of attempts at colour-blind staging in order to circumvent or subvert the question of race.[5] Similarly, directors have reacted to the black-facing debate by experimenting with make-up and casting. Such attempts ranged from Michael Kahn's 'photo negative' production at the Shakespeare Theatre in Washington, D.C. (1997), starring Patrick Stewart in the title role as the only white cast member, to Jette Steckel's staging at Deutsches Theater Berlin (2011), in which the title role was played by a female actor in a gorilla suit.[6] Nonetheless, it seems that none of these attempts have provided any radically new insight other than the realisation that race matters; if anything, they have brought to the fore how much exactly.

In all the other tragedies discussed in this book, 'Otherness' usually means 'Other' to the male norm; to be a woman in patriarchal Rome, labelled madwoman, or simply a female character in a tragedy. In *Othello*, the state of being 'Other' is twofold. Both the tragic hero and the heroine are 'Other' to hegemonic discourse; Othello because he is a black military leader in white Venice and Desdemona because she is a woman, furthermore, one that has crossed the taboo of miscegenation. The chapter at hand, therefore, explores the ways in which in the death of Desdemona and Othello's suicide questions of gender and race are intertwined, beginning with the peculiar case of Desdemona's resurrection after death. I will discuss the manifold implications of staging the two deaths side by side and, furthermore, as implied by the chapter's title, pay special attention to both their final words. While both deaths are conditioned by the domineering structures surrounding Desdemona and Othello, I suggest that as individual responses to these forces, the two suicides send converse messages.

"Who Hath Done this Deed": Desdemona Has the Last Word

Desdemona does not commit suicide, but nevertheless, her death is worth looking at from the same angle. Her death scene is one of the most painful in all of Shakespeare and difficult to watch in performance. Next to Lavinia, hers is the only onstage murder of a female character. She is wholly innocent of the charges brought against her, which is why *Othello* has a rich history of audience members trying to intervene and stop Othello from killing her.[7] For its shock value, it should not be surprising that from the Restoration until the late nineteenth century, in performance, the murder tended to be hidden behind curtains. This strategy, however, mainly pursued one effect: to mask its uncomfortable eroticisation and make sure that Desdemona does not rival Othello for dramatic interest.[8]

Beginning with the setting, so appropriate for a domestic tragedy, Othello's preparation of the bedchamber already evokes Renaissance symbolism of approaching death. The question of whether Desdemona has prayed, the locking of the door, as well as his kiss while she is still asleep all indicate an almost ritualistic event. Othello's description of her is equally telling: "I'll not shed her blood / Nor scar that whiter skin of hers than snow / And smooth as monumental alabaster" (5.2.3–5). Alabaster usually suggests a quality of stillness and lucidity often associated with royal effigies of husband and wife, later completed by Othello's dead body lying next to Desdemona's.[9] Othello's words, therefore, resemble the description of an effigy rather than his still-breathing wife. Pascale Aebischer addresses another uncomfortable, gendered quality of Othello's words, pointing out that his "reluctance to break through that surface and shed her blood is a sudden unwillingness to assume the full implications of his voyeuristic gaze, trying to fetishize Desdemona's body at the very moment at which he is punishing it."[10] This is an apt description since the audience are prying into the bedchamber. Moreover, Aebischer's words recall the notion of voyeurism equally attached to the mutilated Lavinia and floating Ophelia. In the case of Desdemona, Othello and the audience are not staring at mutilated female bodies, but the mere anticipation of death and potential violence seems to be no less thrilling. As the growing tension suggests, the murder of Desdemona, not Othello's suicide, is the climactic moment of the play.

Of course, Desdemona's smothering in the bedroom is symbolic, the strangling resembling a sexual act. Her death scene, therefore, functions as a wedding night in which actual death substitutes the metaphorical, sexual dying. Desdemona is killed on the marriage bed she is suspected of having violated, which reduces her to the double female role of wife and whore. Since she dies on the bed, her body would be elevated from the stage for everyone to see. With such a focus first on her sleeping body and subsequently her corpse, she forms what Dympna Callaghan dubs the "dead centre" of the tragedy. The stage tableau of this scene alone implies that the murder of Desdemona is a major dramatic moment, possibly as important as the tragic hero's death. "It is in this way that it is possible to see the female corpse as central to tragic denouement," Callaghan writes, "even though that centrality is constructed via the male gaze."[11] Apart from Desdemona, the only other major female figures who die onstage are Juliet and Cleopatra, both of who equally challenge their respective tragic heroes for dramatic interest.

Like Othello's suicide, Desdemona's death is embedded in larger discourses of race and gender, so much so that she functions as what Emily Bartels calls "a site of ideological production" with regard to both these issues.[12] During the entire play, Desdemona is misrepresented by others. She is referred to by way of clichés, and the tendency to read her as one-dimensional can still be found in criticism. While David Mann holds that she "never emerges even briefly as a recognizable human being, but remains a cipher,"[13] Arthur Kirsch considers her "too good to be true, too innocent to be a wife or too wifely to be innocent."[14] Even though in performance Desdemona has been increasingly played as a strong woman since the mid-twentieth century, Ayanna Thompson notes a shifting representation in the new millennium. Whereas previous productions tended to emphasise her emancipation, now the focus lies on her naivety and inexperience again, which, amongst other things, speaks of a prioritisation of the central conflict between Othello and Iago.[15]

When Brabantio voices his disbelief that his daughter has not only married without his consent but, to make it worse, has chosen a black man as her husband, he describes her as "A maiden never bold, / Of spirit so still and quiet that her motion / Blushed at herself" (1.3.95–97). But the first time Desdemona enters the stage shows a contradictory image to that given by her father, and she makes it clear that she is not the shy and passive creature she has been introduced as. In her speech about the "divided duty" between father and husband (1.3.181–189), she respectfully but assertively outlines her transition from one role to another, namely from daughter to wife. As Bartels notices, Renaissance women are always envisioned within the stereotype of being silent and submissive. It is rarely conceded that such positions may be deliberate acts, which enabled them "to speak out through, rather than against, established postures and make room for self-expression within self-supporting roles."[16] Desdemona is exemplary of this strategy, and so Bartels argues that "[i]t is clear from the start that Desdemona is an actor, as adept as Iago [...] at manipulating the system from within."[17] The problem is that the system only lets itself be manipulated to a limited extent, a reality that Desdemona overlooks and that ultimately proves fatal.

That Desdemona does not perform wifely submissiveness shows even before her appearance onstage. According to Othello's account of their first meeting, she was at least "half the wooer" (1.3.176). He recalls that "she wished / That heaven had made her such a man" (1.3.163–164), which may be interpreted as either 'made her a husband like Othello' or 'made her a man herself'.[18] In marrying Othello, Desdemona seems to achieve both. He provides her with the opportunity to escape the corseted life of her father's household and experience a freedom that she herself as a woman cannot achieve. Of course, she still remains under patriarchal control, but she is able to bask in the glow of his heroic reputation. However, Othello's account of their courtship also suggests an attraction on her part that is primarily sexual. Rather than to a kindred spirit, Desdemona seems to be attracted to Othello's exotic masculinity, which ultimately makes her complicit in the play's larger narrative of racial 'Otherness'.

Conversations between her and Othello portray her as dominant, revealing quick wit and rhetorical power. To her adamant insistence on Cassio's good character, Othello can only resign "Prithee, no more. Let him come when he will, / I will deny thee nothing" (3.3.75–76). She denies him the manly prerogative of speech, which makes her the opposite of the demure and silent Renaissance wife. More specifically, Desdemona performs a hybrid of two contrastive male fantasies of early modern femininity: shrew on the one hand, demure subordinate on the other.[19] Again, this speaks of a fascination with the 'Other', this time of Othello's attraction to Desdemona's unconventional dominance. Of course, this fantasy can only be sustained as long as power relations remain officially in place. However, Othello's "I will deny thee nothing" suggests that for her sake, he is willing to do everything, even if that includes reconsidering professional decisions and thereby subverting his authority as a general.

The most revealing scene, in terms of both Desdemona's character and her critical reception, shows her in not entirely playful banter so as to counter Iago's sexist view of women: "You rise to play, and go to bed to work" (2.1.115). Although he is actually talking to his wife, Desdemona takes Emilia's side and puts herself in the firing line: "What wouldst that write of me, if thou shouldst praise me?" (2.1.117). M. R. Ridley, editor of the 1958 Arden edition, deems this "one of the most unsatisfactory passages in Shakespeare" and finds that "it is distasteful to watch [Desdemona] engaged in a long piece of cheap backchat with Iago, and so adept at it that one wonders how much time of the voyage was spent in the same way."[20] In line with its critical reception, 2.1 has rarely been fully performed onstage. Lois Potter, therefore, names Desdemona the Shakespearean woman who "suffered most at the hands of theatre practitioners" and adds that especially on the British and US stages for a long time, directors, though wanting to challenge the dominant reading of the angelic and innocent Desdemona, were reluctant to re-think the role because such experiments bear the potential of discovering a side to her that may be too radical and, hence, equally unwanted.[21] It is true that a feisty or potentially even flirtatious Desdemona might not seem as easily reconcilable with purity and sexual innocence, notions critical discussions have concentrated on almost obsessively.[22] Yet, whereas such reservations are unsurprising within earlier performance history, in the context of twenty-first century productions or criticism, they have to be considered surprising at best.[23]

Desdemona's death is anticipated by another scene that tends to be cut in performance, probably because it is set apart from the rest of the play. The 'willow scene' in 4.3 is a visual and static rather than dramatic moment, and so directorial explanations for cutting this scene might address its considerable length as well as the fact that it does not further the action. As Denise Walen assumes, there is a simple reason for its existence. In the early modern playhouse, the unpinning of Desdemona's elaborate dress would have taken quite some time, and hence, this musical interlude is necessary in order to bridge this gap.[24] But in addition to her literal undressing, the scene also visualises Desdemona's figurative unpinning. Since visual allegory already featured heavily in Renaissance iconography, audiences would have been prepared for her impending death. Moreover, it is made clear that Desdemona herself knows she will die.

Drawing on symbols of grief, unrequited love, and innocence, the willow song remembers the maid Barbary whose lover abandoned her and who died singing the willow song. As Barbary's fate parallels that of Desdemona, she uses the story as an allegory of her own fate. The foremost themes, of both the song and the conversation between Emilia and Desdemona, are infidelity and men's view of women. Against this background, it should not go unnoticed that apart from Othello's and Lodovico's few lines at the beginning, 4.3 is a scene between two female characters; male voices are shut out. As Carol Rutter, who extensively discusses the role of Emilia, phrases it, the scene "privileges women's talk, women's bodies, women's thoughtful work upon the cultural imperatives that organize their lives, reflections that, while they do not release women from patriarchal confines, at least claim some space for manoeuvre, some terms of survival and settlement within them."[25] Furthermore, it offers a different kind of access to Desdemona. She never soliloquises, but here, the focus shifts towards the interior.

By aligning herself with Barbary, one could assume, Desdemona fashions herself as the loyal, innocent, and wrongly accused woman. Especially her "Let nobody blame him, his scorn I approve" (4.3.51) could be read as a performance of the submissive and helpless woman yielding up to her fate without further resistance.[26] However, to argue thus would be to overlook the peculiar nature of Desdemona's song. Much like a play-within-the-play, the song disrupts the action and invites critical reflection. As Martha Ronk illustrates, at this point, "Desdemona remakes her character [...] by a turn to the visual, asking the audience to examine her and the images which represent her."[27] So, rather than affirming the ostensible parallels to Barbary's fate, the willow song foregrounds the differences. In the song, it is the male lover who is unfaithful and causes the woman's pain. Desdemona, thereby, reverses the roles of perpetrator and victim as presented in Othello's narrative. She ventriloquises a male voice, thus indicating that Othello, not she, is the one who is unfaithful. For this reason, and not least in the face of her portrayal at large, it is much more justifiable to understand her song as a revolt against the male privilege of interpretation.

The question as to in which form this scene occurs – if it occurs at all – is of crucial importance, as a brief glance at textual history indicates. Whereas the Folio depicts Desdemona and Emilia as complex characters engaged in profound conversation, the radically shortened Quarto version alters the representation of the two women and casts them as mere stereotypes: "Desdemona as the patient Griselda and Emilia as the shallow, saucy maid."[28] As can be taken from this textual comparison alone, the play's, and by extension, any production's, stance towards gender stands and falls with this scene.

What is most peculiar about Desdemona's actual death scene, however, is what happens after Othello has smothered her. She revives and utters a few final lines, and so it seems as if she dies twice. While it is not uncommon for Shakespeare's heroes to continue to speak after they have been killed, Desdemona's apparent resurrection, often passed over in scholarly discussions, is unique:

DESDEMONA:	O falsely, falsely murdered!
EMILIA:	O lord, what cry is that?
OTHELLO:	That! what?
EMILIA:	Out and alas, that was my lady's voice:
	[*She draws the bed-curtains.*]
	Help, help, ho, help! O lady, speak again,
	Sweet Desdemona, O sweet mistress, speak!
DESDEMONA:	A guiltless death I die.
EMILIA:	O, who hath done
	This deed?
DESDEMONA:	Nobody. I myself. Farewell.
	Commend me to my kind lord – O, farewell!
	[*She dies.*]

(5.2.116 –125)

If taken literally, her claim "I myself" is simply a lie. Desdemona re-defines the murder as suicide, allocating all blame to herself. Simultaneously, however, she asserts her claim to agency. By pretending to have killed herself, she rejects the role of the victim. This brings up the related question of why Desdemona would risk the stigma of a suicide. Why craft such odd last words, especially since on their dying beds, dramatic figures conventionally speak the truth?

According to Thomas Rymer's notorious 1693 attack on *Othello*, these lines are proof of the cliché "that a Woman never loses her Tongue, even tho' after she is stifl'd."[29] Even though from a critical perspective such an assumption may sound amusing, Rymer overlooks and trivialises the effect Desdemona's last words have – to speak nothing of the misogynist implications of his statement. A number of later critics have expressed the opposite view of a Desdemona shutting up too quickly and discussed her in terms of the lamb willingly led to the slaughter, an understanding that is still (too) often expressed on both page and stage. Given the alleged lack of defence on Desdemona's part, some even question her credibility as a character. Amongst others, this notion is inherent in Harold Bloom's view that "operatically, Shakespeare gives Desdemona a dying breath that attempts to exonerate Othello, which would indeed strain credulity if she were not, as Alvin Kernan wonderfully put it, 'Shakespeare's word for love'."[30] A comparable understanding resonates in Eric Langley's analysis, which suggests that Desdemona should be approached as a romantic heroine. In his view, the two deaths

attempt to write the couple back into the systems of kindness and reciprocation that Iago's machinations have untuned. Just as we saw in

> *Romeo and Juliet* and *Antony and Cleopatra*, there is an attempt made
> by the dying lovers to conceptualize themselves as literal manifestations
> of the romantic model. [...] [A]s she reclaims her murder as an act of
> self-slaughter Desdemona repositions herself back into the role of star-
> crossed heroine, back into a romance tragedy tradition. Commending
> herself to her 'kind' lord [...] she presents the opportunity for a kindly
> conclusion, playing the first part in a sequence of mutual suicide.[31]

Langley's interpretation is tempting, if too easy, because it complements
Othello's self-stylisation as the tragic lover. Taken together, the two
deaths could form a nice pattern. One could also argue in favour of
Langley's view by reading Desdemona's lie as an attempt to spare Othello. If she has killed herself, he does not have to fear legal prosecution.
Her last words "Commend me to my kind lord – O, farewell" are directed towards him. It seems her utmost concern to prove to him that she
has always been faithful. She performatively creates herself as the loyal
wife. Still, such a line of argument paints a much more one-dimensional
picture of Desdemona than that offered by the text.

Seen from the opposite perspective, her fight against death and tem-
porary resurrection can be considered a display of assertiveness and
strength, character traits she shows throughout the play. In addition, she
is even given the chance to provide her own death narrative and, thereby,
influence the way she will be remembered. As Joan Holmer emphasises,
Desdemona does not "passively submit after appearing dead; instead,
she revives to use, presumably in some pain, the only weapon barely left
her – her voice – so that her woman's words 'out-tongue' (1.2.19) man's
deeds."[32] In defying any form of labelling, as either victim or whore,
she undermines his narrative of guilt and sacrifice. Othello's version of
events is false, she says, and so he cannot re-define the murder as honourable obligation but needs to see it for what it is. By claiming to have
killed herself, Desdemona furthermore pre-empts any simple conclusion
the Venetian officials might want to draw. It is an attempt to resist interpretation, something Desdemona tries throughout the play and shares
with the other tragic heroines discussed in this book. Thus, even though
at first glance it may seem otherwise, Desdemona's death – unlike Othello's suicide – does not at all signify surrender and submission. By opposing the dominant, male-constructed narrative, she opposes the Venetian
patriarchy. For a character often considered flat by both others in the
play and literary critics, this is an astonishing way to die.

Even though, or maybe precisely because, it is such a puzzling moment, Desdemona's revival is often cut in productions. Most notably,
three of the latest screen adaptations – Oliver Parker's version starring
Laurence Fishburne and Kenneth Branagh (1995), Tim Blake Nelson's
re-imagined 'O' (2001), and Geoffrey Sax's production for ITV (2001) –
all deny her the last word. The decision to omit her final lines in the

play is a serious directorial intervention, changing the way that audiences read Desdemona. In the same way that the cutting off Lavinia's tongue and Portia's suicide are both symbolic and literal extinctions of the female voice, it is hardly coincidental that Desdemona is smothered or strangled; after the men's constant ignoring and quieting of her voice, she is now also physically silenced. Emilia, too, is killed before she can speak out fully against either Iago or Othello. Her wish "O lay me by my mistress' side" (5.2.237) secures both her personal bond with Desdemona and acknowledges their union as females. Of all these silenced women, Desdemona is the only one who literally speaks out against the attempt of silencing; she is the only one to raise her voice after someone has killed or tried to kill her, if only for a brief moment.

In addition to reading Desdemona's active interpretation of her death as an act of female empowerment, the scene can, and should, be approached through the lens of race. Unsurprisingly, this leads to a much less progressive conclusion. Gratiano describes the bed on which the bodies lie with the lines "[t]he object poisons sight, / Let it be hid" (5.2.364–365). Does this simply mean that the tragic image is too painful to endure? As Michael Neill points out with reference to examples of critical reception and performance history, the shock value of Desdemona's death lies not so much in the fact that she has been unjustly and brutally murdered; rather, it is the image of a white woman lying next to a black man, conjuring up the horror of miscegenation felt by white (early modern) audiences.[33] Neill's argument is bolstered by Othello's opening words of this scene, emphasising the whiteness of Desdemona's alabaster skin. What early modern as well as other racially prejudiced audiences would have considered outrageous is that – metaphorically speaking, and very much like in the 'dirty still' of Olivier's 1965 film adaptation – the moment Desdemona lies down with Othello, he stains her previously white and innocent skin. To explain away this ostensible threat, in a manoeuvre comparable to the assumption that the marriage has never been consummated, scholars have argued that the exact degree of Othello's 'blackness' is difficult to pin down.[34] The smudging of Desdemona, either intentional or accidental, frequently happened during blackface practice. This seemingly rather amusing anecdote is as much a testament to *Othello*'s underlying comic structures, as Paul Menzer indicates, as it is, from an ideological viewpoint, deeply disquieting.[35]

An ending that so drastically demarcates black from white raises the question of whether the play allows for a reading that construes Desdemona's death as a direct consequence of filial disobedience or indeed crossing the taboo of miscegenation. At least Rymer understood it that way, naming *Othello* "a caution to all Maidens of Quality how, without their Parents consent, they run away with Blackamoors."[36] The final scene may not end on as explicitly moralistic a note as Brabantio's words in the 'trial scene' 1.3, but the sense of a moral is nevertheless implied.

Within this context, Desdemona's "I myself" may be said to acquire an altogether different meaning, namely an admission that she herself is partly to blame. She was warned not to marry a black man but decided to ignore all the danger signs. In that case, it is all the more significant that Desdemona dies onstage in plain view. That way, the murder and subsequent display of her body work as powerful deterrents. Thus, while Desdemona's quasi-resurrection should be considered an act of empowerment with regard to gender, it is difficult to sustain such a progressive reading as far as racial implications are concerned. What is more, it seems that progressive readings with regard to both gender and race cannot coexist, which is Desdemona's dilemma. By defining her suicide as an act of self-empowerment and rejecting victimhood, she enables racist (mis)representations of her death as brought on by her own fault.

"Perplexed in the Extreme": Othello as Murderer and Victim

Othello's suicide is one of the more prominent examples; in fact, he is the only of the four great tragic heroes to commit suicide. What equally sets him apart from Hamlet, King Lear, and Macbeth is that he is given a lengthy farewell speech just before he kills himself. Since Cassio's final words on Othello fall short of a grand and eloquent tragic valediction, Othello's own monologue preceding his suicide is sometimes attributed a quasi-eulogy status.[37] Like a eulogy, it provides an indication of how to interpret Othello's death and, retrospectively, his character as such:

> Soft you, a word or two before you go.
> I have done the state some service, and they know't:
> No more of that. I pray you, in your letters,
> When you shall these unlucky deeds relate,
> Speak of me as I am. Nothing extenuate,
> Nor set down aught in malice. Then must you speak
> Of one that loved not wisely, but too well;
> Of one not easily jealous, but, being wrought,
> Perplexed in the extreme; of one whose hand,
> Like the base Indian, threw a pearl away
> Richer than all his tribe; of one whose subdued eyes,
> Albeit unused to the melting mood,
> Drops tears as fast as the Arabian trees
> Their medicinable gum.
>
> (5.2.338–351)

To begin with, the speech reads like a final press conference Othello is holding in order to take control over his death narrative, thereby exploiting the potential of suicide to define a lasting image. He tries to influence how both the others onstage and the audience will remember him; he asks them to reconsider their final verdict. Thomas McAlindon does not sense any dissonance. For him, Othello's "valedictory speech-act is intensely felt but controlled and sonorous. It asks for and aims at truth, neither more nor less."[38] Of course, any perceived self-stylisation and theatricality is also a question of dramatic convention. Othello is not a psychological character, and so it is no wonder that a search for coherence or realism may remain unsuccessful. After all, the perceived theatricality is typical of 'the noble death', a convention of Renaissance tragedy.[39]

On the other hand, what can be taken from the speech is that Othello wants to die thinking well of himself. A more cynical view, famously that by T. S. Eliot, therefore, sees Othello as weak and overly sentimental: "What Othello seems to be doing in making this speech is cheering himself up. [...] Othello succeeds in turning himself into a pathetic figure, by adopting an aesthetic rather than a moral attitude, dramatizing himself against his environment. He takes in the spectator, but the human motive is primarily to take in himself."[40] In contrast to his appearance in the second half of the play, at times declined into incoherence and epileptic fits, in this instance, Othello's language is eloquent and assured. He even still considers himself in the position to give commands. In a performance of heroic masculinity, he pleads for mitigating circumstances by enumerating his military merits. Afterwards, he switches to the role of the husband, but his self-image seems distorted, if not self-delusional, here. Anyone speaking of Othello 'as he is' would probably not characterise him the way he does himself. For McAlindon, the notion of self-betrayal is of "doubtful dramatic relevance; to argue thus is to introduce a kind of mundane calculus which seems out of place in a tragedy of titanic emotion."[41] However, with such a carefully choreographed gesture that constructs the final image by which to remember Othello, it is difficult to gainsay that readings such as Eliot's are justifiable. The dissonances of Othello's words cannot be overlooked, no matter how grand and, therefore, possibly stylised a tragic moment his suicide is.

By trying to downplay his guilt, Othello causes even more frowns. He euphemistically describes the events of the play as "unlucky" and reiterates his belief that what he has done happened "all in honour" (5.2.294). His lack of *anagnorisis* complicates sympathising with him. Other than this, throughout the entire speech, he appears detached from himself and his guilt, using "one" instead of "I." The line referring to Desdemona by the exoticising term "pearl" not only reaffirms her status as an object – a valuable accessory – but also exaggerates Othello's situation. The Folio gives the variant "Judean" instead of "Indian" and, thus, draws a parallel to Judas Iscariot, who committed suicide out of despair for having betrayed Christ.[42] Such a reading indeed renders Othello's speech hyperbolic and artificial, and so his alleged self-revelation loses its sincerity. Even understood within the context of convention, it appears overly theatrical.[43]

If this were the end of Othello's final speech, it would be justifiable to follow the rather unsympathetic reading suggested by Eliot. But Othello continues to speak for another six lines, giving the monologue an altogether different twist:

> Set you down this,
> And say besides that in Aleppo once,
> Where a malignant and a turbanned Turk
> Beat a Venetian and traduced the state,
> I took by th' throat the circumcised dog
> And smote him – thus! [*He stabs himself.*]

(5.2.351–356)

Concerning the content of his speech, what Othello says is that he once killed a Turk for beating a Venetian man as well as disgracing or slandering the state. Now he kills himself in exactly the same way. Most unsettling about these vividly lyric lines is Othello's internalised racism. As Derek Cohen has argued in great detail, Othello's suicide is fuelled by immense self-hatred. Rather than solely by the attempt of restoring himself to former glory, as is usually the case, he is driven to suicide because the domineering discourse has destroyed him.[44] Othello has no ego, no voice of his own to refer to himself. So throughout, he uses the racialising language of the white ruling class. His description of the turbaned, "circumcised dog" evokes orientalist stereotypes of Muslims as 'Other'. Thus, he transforms into the play's own stereotype of the brutal, uncivilised black man, not guided by law and Western culture. Both the earlier killing he refers to and his suicide are presented as additions to his lists of military achievements. Like the Turk he killed in Aleppo, Othello himself has turned into an enemy of the Venetian state, he implies. As Cohen, therefore, remarks, the most unsettling part of Othello's farewell speech is that he perceives himself as a traitor to both cultures, black and white; he realises that he belongs in neither of these two worlds.[45]

For his subsequent suicide, Othello chooses a Roman, soldierly death. On the one hand, this choice re-emphasises his masculinity. It is suggestive that Rowland Wymer, referencing Rymer, describes Othello's suicide as the only convincing performance of conventional masculinity throughout the play.[46] On the other hand, the Roman death Othello chooses is deeply engrained into Western tradition. For this reason, Cohen concludes that "[w]ith his suicide Othello proclaims the triumph of the white civilization he has traduced. And, indeed, it is the *mimetic* nature of his suicide hat supplies the crucial evidence of the defeat and the failure of the Moorish and Turkish cultures in the play. Othello kills himself, as white cultural tradition dictates he ought to do. But in his self-abasement – recovering his own blackness – he offers that white civilization, as on a platter, a powerful vindication of itself."[47] Surely, this tragic ending balances any earlier impression of self-delusion and otherwise unsympathetic demeanour. In the concluding part of his speech, Othello crystallises his fatal dilemma into one disturbing allegory. He has committed an appalling crime, but he is also a victim himself, betrayed by the machinations of white hegemony.

The double role Othello performs in his suicide – tragic lover on the one hand and victim of racist discourse on the other – is established from the beginning of the play. Proud of his military prestige, he performs masculine gender identity associated with the role of the soldier through his words and actions, so his authority enables him to calm a tavern brawl within an instant (2.3.161–170). Even though such a claim runs counter to how Othello is perceived onstage, he repeatedly stylises himself according to the stage convention of the soldier as plain and honest: "Rude am I in my speech / And little blest with the soft phrase of peace" (1.3.82–83). At the same time, Othello is plainly marked as 'Other', and not only regarding his skin colour. His rank, his commanding presence as a military leader, and his young, white wife all set him apart from the rest of the *dramatis personae*. Although these characteristics could be called saving graces in the white-dominated world of Venice, they in fact highlight Othello's status as outsider even further. His elevated military status puts a magnifying glass on the fact that he, as a black man, is curiously misplaced. The most blatantly racist slurs include Iago's warning to Brabantio that "an old black ram / Is tupping your white ewe" (1.1.87–88) as well as Roderigo's description of the "gross clasps of a lascivious Moor" (1.1.124), but these are not the only characters who address Othello's 'Otherness'. He even does so himself, albeit in a less derogatory way, when relating the story of his adventurous past. As Stephen Greenblatt comments, "his identity depends upon a constant performance, [...] of his 'story,' as a loss of his own origins, an embrace and perpetual reiteration of the norms of another culture. It is this dependence that gives Othello, the warrior and alien, a relation to Christian values that is the existential equivalent of a religious vocation."[48] Thus, not only in his suicide Othello subjects himself to Venice's racist ideology, performing the exotic 'Otherness' projected onto him and, hence, feeding into that very ideology.

Othello's private identity is equally defined by race. Even before Desdemona enters the stage, he implicates her into his strategy of exoticising his life story and introduces her as part of his ego: "She'd come again, and with a greedy ear / Devour up my discourse [...]. She loved me for the dangers I had passed / And I loved her that she did pity them" (1.3.150–169). He patronisingly presents her as the woman mesmerised by the man's adventurous stories; his description of the situation sounds more like a father talking to an eager child. He treats Desdemona as an audience, dramatising his life-story only for her and in order to impress her. He seems flattered by her favourable response and loves her back for admiring him. As Alexander Leggatt points out, Othello considers their match "a complementary partnership of opposites" both of them profit from and that ultimately completes them, personally and socially.[49] In view of the rigidly patriarchal and prejudiced structures of Venice, this speaks of idealism and naivety on both Othello's and Desdemona's parts. In Othello's view, his white Venetian wife helps him adapt to Venice's cultural and racial politics. But if Desdemona is a part of his ego, then her alleged failure and loss of honour is inextricably linked with himself.

The somewhat narcissistic image of their relationship painted by Othello ultimately proves fatal. Within his self-concept, the murder of Desdemona and his own suicide are blurred into one tragic act. In his work on the correlation between suicide and narcissism, Langley suggests that both the narcissistic and the suicidal exhibit a tendency towards self-absorption and self-assertion because both groups aim at an individuation from society. In doing so, they strive to form an identity that is detached from others, entirely dependent on the self, and, thereby, seek to gain autonomy. Nevertheless, the construction of identity or in-dividuality is dependent on the communication with, and the reflection through, others. Langley thus writes that "the ultimately unattainable or self-defeating objective for narcissist and defiant self-slaughterer alike is to find a way in which one can be a self on one's own, in which one could depend only upon oneself and therefore assume ownership of one's own action and ends."[50] Othello's dilemma in this respect is twofold: he cannot individuate himself from the dominant culture around him, and he can only be a self in relation to Desdemona. Thus, by killing her, he also kills a part of himself. For this reason, Othello's murder of Desdemona can be considered a suicidal act itself, destroying not only her but also part of his own existence.[51]

At the end of his painful surrender to the white ruling class, Othello stabs himself. Concluding on such a powerfully symbolic gesture, this would be a suitable moment for Shakespeare to let his tragic hero die. Yet Othello lives on to speak a few further lines, and these introduce anew the earlier, more divisive undertones. He revisits the role of the husband, thus turning his final and lasting image into that of the deluded and tragic lover: "I kissed thee ere I killed thee: no way but this, / Killing myself, to die upon a kiss" (5.2.356–357). According to the Folio, this line is again a reference to Judas and Christ.[52] Given that he has just brutally murdered his wife, Othello's gesture appears almost offensive. He seems unwilling or unable to realise the consequences of his actions. Langley speaks of savage irony, adding that Othello appropriates "the old fond paradoxes and by-the-book kisses of Petrarchan desire in order to establish some system, some meaningful order."[53] At this point, the potential stage tableau has to be taken into account as well. Neither the Folio nor the Quarto stage directions provide any indications as to whether Othello dies next to his wife's dead body or whether he actually kisses her. For this reason, such directorial choices are most likely to be culturally and ideologically charged. Whereas for a long time Othellos died next to the bed and, hence, separated from their wives, since the second half of the twentieth century, the majority of productions show them lying next to one another on the bed.[54]

If both Othello and Desdemona die on their marriage bed, the staging echoes a love-suicide in the manner of Romeo and Juliet, a parallel that adds to the impression of Othello's self-delusion. Clearly, in having murdered his innocent wife, he is not the actual victim. Simultaneously, in staging himself as a second Romeo, Othello repeats his strategy of identifying through Desdemona. Like Romeo, Othello needs his female counterpart to uphold the image of who he is. Thus, it seems that Othello's lost identity can only be regained through dying a 'masculine death' as well as through a "symbolic reunion with the dead female figure," as per Callaghan.[55] Throughout the play, he has struggled with his role as the husband but now irrevocably returns to that identity in death.

As a tragic convention, eulogies spoken by others help audiences arrive at a final verdict of the tragic hero. Cassio's eulogy of Othello is puzzling: "This did I fear, but thought he had no weapon, / For he was great of heart" (5.2.360–361). These two short lines appear anticlimactic in that they transport neither the love Horatio feels for Hamlet nor the dignified respect Octavius conveys for Brutus. Even Macbeth is given a more emotional, if distinctly negative, farewell. Unlike in the other tragedies, Cassio's eulogy immediately succeeds Othello's death, and, hence, it is necessarily too rushed to be as dramatic, moving, or solemn a moment.[56] At the same time, these two lines are spoken by someone who has always held Othello in high esteem and who knows him well. This is even signalled by Cassio himself, who indicates that he expected him to commit suicide. In order to explain this incongruence and lack of emotional reaction, Balz Engler suggests a different reading for Cassio's phrase "great of heart." Whereas the predominant interpretation translates this as either 'magnanimous' or 'proud',[57] Engler establishes that 'beside himself' or 'desperate' would be more appropriate.[58] Apart from semantic accuracy, what speaks in favour of this reading is that it completes the picture of Othello's troubled, fractured identity.

After Othello's death, the status quo is re-established suspiciously quickly. Othello's possessions are transferred to Gratiano and, conveniently, all evil is located in Iago. Ludovico announces that he will convey the true version of this "heavy act" (5.2.371) to the Venetian state, which raises the question of what this official version of events might look like. In all probability, it will depict the catastrophe as inevitably brought about by a dangerous mixture of "black naiveté, female sexual appetite, and the forces of good and evil."[59] If the catastrophe has been predetermined this way, the authorities should not be surprised by its outcome. In this respect, Cohen is right in naming Othello's suicide "the most conformist gesture of the play. It indicates powerfully the limits of individual action, and in doing so it reintegrates Othello into the social nexus."[60] Whereas Desdemona's revival after death marks a moment of female empowerment, Othello's suicide has to be considered as surrender. He does not revolt against the ruling class but subjects himself to it, even in pre-emptive obedience. By killing himself the way he does and speaking the lines he speaks, Othello submits to the narrative of his barbaric nature that the Venetians seek to construct. He thus tragically reinforces their racist ideology.

Probably more than any other deaths in the tragedies, both Desdemona's death and Othello's suicide are, therefore, open to conflicting interpretations. On the one hand, it is possible to take the play at face value and argue that it endorses patriarchal ideology, especially as far as its original context of production is concerned. After all, Deborah Kehler concedes that "Desdemona's death is [...] tragically natural and arguably inevitable in the patriarchal, racially prejudiced world of *Othello*."[61] If her death is presented as inevitable – as a tragic necessity – it is no more than resignation. However, Desdemona's resurrection as well as her final words before she eventually dies suggest otherwise. By re-defining her murder as suicide, she speaks up against male attempts at silencing female voices. She explicitly rejects victimhood and claims agency instead.

There are certainly enough indications to justifiably call *Othello* a racist text. Both Desdemona's and Othello's deaths overflow with racialised imagery and fear of the 'Other'; and in his suicide speech, Othello himself subscribes to a reading that blames his skin colour, which brings his tragic dilemma to the fore. At the same time, it is difficult to ignore the several textual fissures, those vital moments in which the play resists a straightforward interpretation of either/or. From a twenty-first-century perspective in particular, it is almost impossible not to notice such contradictions within power structures that crushes everybody who is 'Other' to the system. Along these lines, it may be possible, even if bold and optimistic, to argue that eventually both deaths criticise the patriarchal and racist forces in the play: Othello's suicide since it shows him to be a victim himself and Desdemona's precisely in opposing the role of the victim. That as a woman Desdemona can only do so at the cost of making herself complicit with the racist ideology of the forces she rebels against is a sad realisation, but one that make the cracks in the play's ideological stance all the more obvious.

Notes

1 Barbara Hodgdon, "Race-ing *Othello*: Re-Engendering White-Out," in *Shakespeare, the Movie: Popularizing the Plays on Film, TV and Video*, ed. Lynda E. Boose and Richard Burt (London: Routledge, 1997), 23.

2 Ibid., 23–24.

3 On racism in *Othello* see Ayanna Thompson, Introduction to *Othello*, by William Shakespeare, ed. E. A. J. Honigmann, revised ed., The Arden Shakespeare Third Series (London and New York: Arden Shakespeare, 2016), 54–66; Dorothea Kehler, "*Othello* and Racism," in *Understanding Racial Issues in Shakespeare's Othello: Selected Critical Essays*, ed. Solomon Iyasere and Marla Iyasere (New York: Whitston, 2008), 155–69; Martin Orkin, "Othello and the 'plain face' of Racism," *Shakespeare Quarterly* 38.2 (1987): 166–188. On the often controversial treatment of race in both the play's critical reception and performance history, see Michael Neill, "*Othello* and Race," in *Approaches to Teaching Shakespeare's Othello*, ed. Peter Erickson and Maurice Hunt (New York: MLA, 2005), 37–52; Lois Potter, *Othello in Performance* (Manchester: Manchester University Press, 2002). On race in *Othello* on screen, see Hodgdon, "Race-ing *Othello*," 193–219 as well as Pascale Aebischer, *Shakespeare's Violated Bodies: Stage and Screen Performance* (Cambridge: Cambridge University Press, 2004), 123–121.

4 Some argue that in early modern England, the notion of race did not yet exist and, hence, should not be overestimated. In *The Complexion of Race: Categories of Difference in Eighteenth-Century British Culture* (Philadelphia: University of Pennsylvania Press, 2000), Roxann Wheeler acknowledges the existence of generalised discourses of racial 'Otherness' but argues that "[t]he assurance that skin color was the primary signifier of human difference was not a dominant conception until the last quarter of the eighteenth century" (7). Others insist that even though the term did not carry the same meaning as it does today, race and racial tensions mattered a great deal. Seminal works in early modern studies include Ania Loomba's *Gender, Race, Renaissance Drama* (Manchester and New York: Manchester University Press, 1989) and *Shakespeare, Race, and Colonialism* (Oxford and New York: Oxford University Press, 2002) as well as Kim F. Hall's *Things of Darkness: Economies of Race and Gender in Early Modern England* (Ithaca and London: Cornell University Press, 1995). This on-going controversy peaked in the 2013 meeting of the Shakespeare Association of America, which encouraged the *Shakespeare Quarterly* to dedicate an entire issue to the re-thinking of race in early modern studies. See editors' Peter Erickson and Kim F. Hall's introductory essay "'A New Scholarly Song': Rereading Early Modern Race," *Shakespeare Quarterly* 67.1 (2016): 1–13.

5 On the production history of colour-blind casting of *Othello* see Angela C. Pao, "Ocular Revisions: Re-Casting *Othello* in Text and Performance," in *Colorblind Shakespeare: New Perspectives on Race and Performance*, ed. Ayanna Thompson (New York and Abingdon: Routledge, 2006), 27–45.

6 See Potter, *Othello in Performance*, 79–184; Thompson, Introduction to *Othello*, 97–102. On attempts to arrive at an adequate representation of race, specifically within the German context, see Doris Kolesch, "Wie *Othello* Spielen?" *Shakespeare Jahrbuch* 152 (2016): 87–103.

7 Thompson, Introduction to *Othello*, 42–43.

8 Aebischer, *Shakespeare's Violated Bodies*, 137. For an overview of how stage and film productions (1949–1995) have handled Desdemona's death, see 134–150.

9 Michael Neill, *Issues of Death: Mortality and Identity in English Renaissance Tragedy* (Oxford: Clarendon, 1997), 297.

10 Aebischer, *Shakespeare's Violated Bodies*, 131.

11 Dympna Callaghan, *Woman and Gender in Renaissance Tragedy: A Study of King Lear, Othello, The Duchess of Malfi and The White Devil* (New York: Harvester Wheatsheaf, 1989), 91.

12 Emily C. Bartels, "Strategies of Submission: Desdemona, the Duchess, and the Assertion of Desire," *SEL* 36.2 (1996): 424.

13 David Mann, *Shakespeare's Women: Performance and Conception* (Cambridge: Cambridge University Press, 2008), 152.

14 Arthur Kirsch, *The Passions of Shakespeare's Tragic Heroes* (Charlottesville: The University of Virginia Press, 1990), 46.

15 Thompson, Introduction to *Othello*, 96.

16 Bartels, "Strategies of Submission," 419.

17 Ibid., 424.

18 Honigmann notes that "Romance heroines sometimes wish they were men [...], but this could also mean 'made such a man *for her*'. William Shakespeare, *Othello*, ed. E. A. J. Honigmann, The Arden Shakespeare Third Series (London: Arden Shakespeare, 1997), note to 1.3.164.

19 Bartels, "Strategies of Submission," 426.

20 William Shakespeare, *Othello*, ed. M. R. Ridley, The Arden Shakespeare (London: Arden Shakespeare, 1958), note to 2.1.109–166.

21 Potter, *Othello in Performance*, 66. On the stage history of playing Desdemona until the end of the nineteenth century, see 48–67; on the more recent performance history, see 106–217.

22 See Albert Frederick Sproule, "A Time Scheme for *Othello*," *Shakespeare Quarterly* 7.2 (1956): 217–226; T. G. A. Nelson and Charles Haines, "Othello's Unconsummated Marriage," *Essays in Criticism* 33.1 (1983): 1–18; for an overview of this debate, see Michael Neill, "Unproper Beds: Race, Adultery, and the Hideous in *Othello*," in *Understanding Racial Issues in Shakespeare's Othello: Selected Critical Essays*, ed. Solomon Iyasere and Marla Iyasere (New York: Whitston, 2008), 15–53.

23 Of course it remains speculation as to why exactly directors have cut the scene, but one recent production where significant cuts to the scene coincided with the portrayal of a very young and naïve Desdemona is Nicholas Hytner's at the National Theatre (2013).

24 Denise A. Walen, "Unpinning Desdemona," *Shakespeare Quarterly* 58.4 (2007): 490. Walen also comments on the process of cutting and/or editing this scene in textual editions.

25 Carol Chillington Rutter, *Enter the Body: Women and Representation on Shakespeare's Stage* (London and New York: Routledge, 2001), 145.

26 See Kenneth Gross, *Shakespeare's Noise* (Chicago and London: The University of Chicago Press, 2001), who argues that in becoming Barbary, Desdemona "takes on herself the slanderous label that Iago had turned on Othello and makes it her own name, the sign of a gentler madness than Othello's" (123–124).

27 Martha Ronk, "Desdemona's Self-Presentation," *English Literary Renaissance* 35.1 (2005): 62.

28 Walen, "Unpinning Desdemona," 487. Again, Walen's explanation is not ideological but practical. She puts forward that "an examination of theatrical practice suggests that F prints a version of the play as performed at the Globe and that Q represents a separate, generally later, version that shows signs of the cuts made in F to accommodate performance at Blackfriars" (489).

On the difference between the Q and F text, see also E. A. J. Honigmann, *The Texts of Othello and Shakespearean Revision* (London and New York: Routledge, 1996), 92–102.

29 Thomas Rymer, "From *a Short View of Tragedy* (1693)," in *Shakespeare: Othello: A Casebook*, ed. John Wain (Basingstoke and London: Macmillan, 1994), 45.

30 Harold Bloom, *Shakespeare: The Invention of the Human* (London: Fourth Estate, 1999), 473. Aebischer, who advocates that one should "follow Desdemona's prompt and resist Othello's and his academic backers' attempt to define the murder as a sacrifice and excuse it as an act done 'all in honour'," discusses theatrical interpretations of the question 'sacrifice or murder' on pp. 131–134 of *Shakespeare's Violated Bodies*.

31 Eric Langley, *Narcissism and Suicide in Shakespeare and His Contemporaries* (Oxford: Oxford University Press, 2009), 259.

32 Joan Ozark Holmer, "Desdemona, Woman Warrior: 'O, These Men, These Men!' (4.3.59)," *Medieval and Renaissance Drama in England* 17 (2005): 139.

33 Neill, "Unproper Beds," 16.

34 See Ibid., 23–25.

35 Paul Menzer, *Anecdotal Shakespeare: A New Performance History* (London and New York: Arden Shakespeare, 2015), 67–98.

36 Thomas Rymer, *A Short View of Tragedy* (1693), quoted in E. A. J. Honigmann, introduction to *Othello*, by William Shakespeare, ed. E. A. J. Honigmann, The Arden Shakespeare Third Series (London: Arden Shakespeare, 1997), 29.

37 Balz Engler, "Othello's Great Heart," *English Studies* 68 (1987): 130.

38 Thomas McAlindon, *Shakespeare's Tragic Cosmos* (Cambridge: Cambridge University Press, 1991), 145.

39 Ibid.

40 T. S. Eliot, *Selected Essays 1917–1932* (New York: Harcourt, 1932), 110. F. R. Leavis supported this view, feeling that "in that magnificent last speech of his Othello does tend to sentimentalize [...]. Contemplating the spectacle of himself, Othello is overcome with the pathos of it. But this is not the part to die in: drawing himself proudly up, he speaks his last words as the stern fighting man who has done the state some service." "Diabolic Intellect and the Noble Hero: A Note on Othello," *Scrutiny* 6 (1937): 274–275.

41 Thomas McAlindon, "What is a Shakespearean Tragedy?" in *The Cambridge Companion to Shakespearean Tragedy*, ed. Claire McEachern (Cambridge: Cambridge University Press, 2002), 14.

42 Honigmann's critical apparatus and textual note to 5.2.345 in the Arden Third Series. As Rowland Wymer stresses, 'Judean' is the reading most favoured by recent scholarship. *Suicide and Despair in the Jacobean Drama* (Brighton: Harvester, 1986), 92.

43 As McAlindon cautions, this perceived theatricality "is part of the Stoic style and can be matched in Seneca [...]. Claims that we should take the theatricality of Shakespeare's suicides as self-deceiving egotism ignore not only the Stoic tradition in pagan literature but, more importantly, the Christianized Stoicism exemplified in the political executions, martyrdoms, and martyrologies of the sixteenth century." "What is a Shakespearean Tragedy," 15–16.

44 Derek Cohen, "Othello's Suicide," *University of Toronto Quarterly* 62.3 (1993): 323.

45 Ibid., 325.

46 Wymer, *Suicide and Despair in the Jacobean Drama*, 93.

47 Cohen, "Othello's Suicide," 326.

48 Stephen Greenblatt, *Shakespearean Negotiations: The Circulation of Social Energy in Renaissance England* (Oxford: Clarendon, 1988), 245.

49 Leggatt, *Shakespeare's Tragedies*, 117.

50 Langley, *Narcissism and Suicide*, 3.

51 See also Kirsch, *The Passions of Shakespeare's Tragic Heroes*, 65.

52 Honigmann's note to 5.2.356 in the Arden Third Series.

53 Langley, *Narcissism and Suicide*, 259.

54 Philip C. McGuire, "Whose Work Is This: Loading the Bed in *Othello*," in *Shakespearean Illuminations: Essays in Honor of Marvin Rosenberg*, ed. Jay L. Halio and Hugh Richmond (Newark: University of Delaware Press, 1998), 70–73. McGuire also discusses directorial choices with regard to Emilia's role in this scene because several productions have included her in the bed's "tragic loading" (78–80).

55 Callaghan, *Woman and Gender in Renaissance Tragedy*, 91.

56 Engler, "Othello's Great Heart," 131.

57 Honigmann's note to 5.2.360 in the Arden Third Series suggests either 'high-spirited' or 'proud'. Michael Neill additionally lists 'magnanimous'. See William Shakespeare, *Othello*, ed. Michael Neill, The Oxford Shakespeare (Oxford: Clarendon, 2006). Norman Sanders does not gloss this line at all. See *Othello*, ed. Norman Sanders, The New Cambridge Shakespeare (Cambridge: Cambridge University Press, 2003).

58 See Engler, "Othello's Great Heart," 133–136.

59 Cohen, "Othello's Suicide," 331–332.

60 Ibid., 332.

61 Kehler, "*Othello* and Racism," 166.

6 Promised Ends
King Lear

With Gloucester's suicide attempt at the cliffs of Dover, *King Lear* contains one of the most peculiar scenes written by Shakespeare, and not only as far as suicide is concerned. Next to Lavinia, Gloucester is the second character who is denied suicide, a denial that amounts to a form of torture. Under Lear's rule, increasing violence equals the gradual descent into total chaos. Perhaps unsurprisingly within such a context, death is a pivotal theme; as Michael Neill remarks, the "entire action is triangulated around three great negatives: 'nothing', 'no cause', and 'never'."[1] Apart from Gloucester and Goneril, whose respective deaths will be discussed on the following pages, three additional figures can be associated with the context of self-killing.

To begin with, Lear himself commits a form of emotional as well as political suicide, even if he only realises that in hindsight. Lori Anne Ferrell critiques that scholars have treated Lear's fatal division of his kingdom as a catastrophic political decision that is either prompted by or attests to his growing mental decline, "but none see it simply for what it is: an immediate and conclusive act of governmental self-murder."[2] The story of the king dividing his kingdom and his three daughters is rooted in folklore. By the play's time of composition, this tale existed in various versions, many of which may have influenced Shakespeare. Whereas in Geoffrey of Monmouth's *Historia Regum Britanniae*, Holinshed's *Chronicles*, John Higgins's input to *The Mirror for Magistrates*, and Spenser's *Faerie Queene* Cordelia commits suicide, either by stabbing or hanging herself, in Shakespeare's play, she is hanged in prison.[3] Instead, Shakespeare introduces Goneril and Edmund's plan to disguise Cordelia's death as suicide in order to "lay blame upon her own despair, / That she fordid herself" (5.3.252–253). Within the amalgamation of Christian and pre-Christian beliefs, this addition by Shakespeare is relevant insofar as it would increase Lear's suffering even further. If Cordelia were believed to have killed herself, he would have to bear the loss of his favourite child, the shameful stigma attached to suicide, and her eternal damnation. It would irrevocably taint Cordelia's reputation. The third character worth considering in the context of suicide is Kent. The epitome of the loyal servant, he exits the play on a vague note:

"I have a journey, sir, shortly to go; / My master calls me, I must not say no" (5.3.320–321). R.A. Foakes glosses this line "following Lear beyond the grave,"[4] and though not entirely clear, it is possible to read Kent's lines as indication that he is going to kill himself.

In the following, however, the focus lies on the two characters that definitely commit suicide, or at least believe they are doing so. Beginning with the less frequently discussed case of Goneril, this chapter sets out to challenge the scholarly misconception that her offstage death constitutes her final surrender, a justified exclusion from the play as punishment for her evil. Instead, it considers the way she exits the play as a dignified refusal to bow down to patriarchal oppression. Gloucester and Goneril represent diametrically opposed world orders: an exclusively patriarchal, even misogynist one versus a more inclusive, female one. By contrasting Goneril's distinctly unspectacular suicide with Gloucester's spectacular but humiliating would-be-suicide, I suggest that it is Gloucester's, not Goneril's, suicide that can be read as a form of punishment. As I will show, the manner in which both suicides are staged (or not staged) criticises rather than affirms the very ideology both Lear and Gloucester stand for. In its juxtaposition of male and female suicides, *King Lear* eventually challenges male supremacy.

"The Laws Are Mine": Goneril's Last Revolt

Scholarly discussions mostly brush over Goneril's offstage suicide or ignore it entirely. Ferrell, for instance, claims that it is worth critical attention only insofar as it interrupts the rescue of Lear and Cordelia and thereby, ironically, hinders Edward from 'sparing' Cordelia, whose murder he originally planned to disguise as a suicide.[5] Put differently, she reads Goneril's death as a strategic means of allowing for the final tragic image of Lear carrying Cordelia's dead body onto the stage. Goneril is, thus, reduced to a prop within the grand finale, no more than a casualty of tragic convention. Alternatively, there is the assumption that her 'depraved' ending, a stigmatised death by suicide, mirrors her 'evil' nature. For Melvyn Donald Faber, her suicide forms "a most damnable conclusion to a most damnable career, and the hot, smoking dagger with which the Gentleman re-enters Act V to announce her end speaks for [...] the hell-fires awaiting her."[6] Not even Shakespeare's most bloodthirsty villains are described as drastically. In a less stigmatising way, Claudette Hoover locates the prototypes of Goneril and Regan in the heroines of classical drama. Female figures such as Hecuba, Clytemnestra, and Antigone repeatedly assume traditionally masculine qualities to achieve their goals, a strategy that – within the realm of these plays – is condemned as unnatural but simultaneously turns them into heroines. According to Hoover, in Goneril's suicide, Shakespeare follows these classical precedents, yet unlike, for example, Antigone's death, Goneril's suicide does not assert values but simply puts an end to a series of terrible crimes. "If, then, *King Lear* glances, however obliquely, at the classics," she concludes, "the effect is neither to elevate nor explain his own masculine women. On the contrary, the fact that Goneril and Regan parade as heroines but lack both grandeur and cause simply magnifies their inhumanity and compounds our confusion."[7] The implication is striking. Shakespeare's masculine, that is, strong tragic women need to be elevated because their ostensible un-femininity degrades them. The strength of character that they exhibit needs to be explained or justified in order for them to count as credible dramatic figures.

The second point Hoover makes, that of Goneril and Regan as purely evil and lacking a cause, is a widespread critical view. But if this assumption pre-determines any reading of Goneril's suicide, it deserves scrutiny. The tendency to diabolise the two sisters originates in the play's gender ideology at large, which subtly presents itself as natural. Other than by Goneril and Regan themselves – characters that are presented as unlikeable – gender hierarchies are never questioned. Similar to the reception of Lady Macbeth, their demonisation has turned into a critical commonplace found in both early and later responses. A. C. Bradley already dedicated an entire page to his disgust for Goneril, describing her as "the most hideous human being (if she is one) that Shakespeare ever drew."[8] And while David Mann still considers both Goneril and Regan "unchanging, unnatural monsters,"[9] Linda Bamber raises the question of how one could "account for these terrible portraits, charged as they are with sexual antagonism."[10] Bamber's comment is particularly suggestive since she explicitly ties Goneril and Regan's 'evil' to their transgressive gender performances.

In the title of an essay, Ann Thompson provocatively asks "Are there any women in *King Lear*?" For Thompson, the critical neglect of the two sisters results from a phallocentric bias of new historicist and cultural materialist readings.[11] Since the 1980s, they have been re-evaluated, often through the lens of psychoanalysis. In *Re-Visioning Lear's Daughters*, published in 2010, Lesley Kordecki and Karla Koskinen aim to emancipate scholarly discussions from their "innate gender bias" and illustrate that the play very well "*can* accommodate feminists, who no longer need to sit uncomfortably through staged productions that often shut down the full humanity of Lear's daughters."[12] So, on the stage, too, the focus has shifted. Simultaneously, though, there is a tendency towards sexualisation. "This foregrounding of the sisters as sexual predators," Kevin Quarmby puts forward, "seems counter to their serious re-examination in a feminist context. Nevertheless, their sexuality also highlights the dramatic currency of the characters as fetishized commodities for twenty-first century stage consumption."[13] Thus, while the critical reception of the two sisters has shifted towards a more sympathetic view, directors seem compelled to find expressions for their 'evil' that do not stigmatise them too much but nevertheless show them as the opposite of Cordelia. Additionally, what strikes Pascale Aebischer "as rather perverse" is that most stage productions taking a sympathetic view towards Regan and Goneril feel the need to reconstruct a family history that hints towards a troubled past.[14] Most vigorously, this reconstruction or reclaiming of a family history was realised in Jane Smiley's novel *A Thousand Acres* (1991), a retelling from Goneril's perspective in which the play's indications of a problematic upbringing are manifested in domestic violence and sexual abuse.[15] Such extra-textual additions or interpretations suggest that in order to view Goneril and Regan as tolerably sympathetic characters, one needs to work against or branch out of Shakespeare's text. As will be elaborated, however, the manner in which Shakespeare builds up and dramatises Goneril's suicide equally interrogates their 'evil' and contextualises their transgressions as reactions against a masculinist system.

The groundwork for considering Goneril and Regan innately evil characters is laid in the opening scene. Compared to the modest Cordelia, they appear to be greedy flatterers and hypocrites. But their insincere speeches are encouraged by Lear's absurd and narcissistic question: "Which of you shall say we say doth love us most" (1.1.51). It is telling that in his speech laying out his "darker purpose" (1.1.35), Lear addresses Cornwall and Albany rather than his daughters. From the outset, women's voices are ostracised. Furthermore, in boasting their love for their father, Goneril and Regan merely follow the politics of the court. It does not take too much effort to understand that a separation into two equal halves cannot be in Goneril's interest. As the eldest daughter, she might have expected to be the sole heiress of Lear's kingdom, and so her dissatisfaction with the outcome is understandable. Yet, what has the highest potential of creating sympathy for them is that, although they can hardly be named ideal daughters, Lear treats them appallingly. Most blatantly, this manifests when he curses Goneril's female body: "Into her womb convey sterility, / Dry up in her the organs of increase" (1.4.270–271). Anticipating Lady Macbeth's "Unsex me here" speech, Lear conjures higher spirits to unsex Goneril's body by taking away what undeniably marks her as female: her reproductive organs. This is a verbal sterilisation. Similar to what happens to Lavinia's body after her rape and mutilation, Lear abjects Goneril in Julia Kristeva's sense.[16] In order to reduce her threat, he transforms the female body into a waste product, a distorted body that mirrors her depravity. Since Lear never soliloquises in the strict sense of the term, he remains the most inaccessible of all tragic heroes. For E. A. J. Honigmann, Lear's hateful outbursts can, therefore, be named "soliloquy at one remove."[17] They have a quasi-soliloquy function, thus indicating that Lear's misogyny is internalised rather than an immediate reaction to perceived misbehaviour on Goneril's part.

Primarily, Goneril threatens Lear because he feels emasculated, which can be taken from his reproach "I am ashamed / That thou hast power to shake my manhood thus" (1.4.288–289). Her assertiveness, sense of entitlement, as well as her idea of power are conventionally masculine qualities; they exceed the boundaries of conventional femininity. As Alexander Leggatt notes, this anxiety extends to all three of his daughters "because he fears and loathes their flesh-and-blood involvement with him, fears and loathes the woman in himself."[18] But not only Lear feels threatened in his manhood. In a way that, again, anticipates Lady Macbeth in the taunting of her husband, Goneril names Albany a "Milk-livered man, / That bear'st a cheek for blows, a head for wrongs." (4.2.51–52). In return, she earns Albany's "See thyself, devil: / Proper deformity shows not in the fiend / So horrid as in woman" (4.2.60–62), a line that echoes Lear's misogynist rants and, thus, seems to serve as a motto of the play's gender ideology at large.

It is worth noting that Lear's above curse on Goneril's body is a reaction to her discontent with the misbehaviour of Lear's entourage. If they are truly "so disordered, so debauched and bold" (1.4.233) as she says, this would be a reasonable complaint. The stage directions are unclear about any potential misbehaviour and the exact number of knights. When Lear enters at 2.2.195, the Folio stage direction only lists a single knight. The Quarto mentions no knights at all.[19] For this reason, the question of whether Goneril exaggerates is a significant choice to make for a director. Adrian Noble's 1993 production with the RSC, which was particularly indifferent towards the female characters and reduced them to mere types, sided with Lear by showing the knights as "well-behaved cheerful gentlemen," thereby discarding Goneril's accusations as unsubstantiated.[20] Peter Brook's 1962 production with the RSC was among the earliest that took the women's part by supporting Goneril's claim, and more recent productions tend to follow suit. In Sam Mendes's 2014 staging at the National Theatre, Simon Russell Beale's "shaven-headed, thuggish, Stalinesque dictator" was constantly surrounded by a large and imposing circle of riotous knights dressed in black uniforms, thus contributing to its conceptualisation of Lear as the leader of a totalitarian regime.[21] Gregory Doran's 2016 production with the RSC sympathised with Goneril even more overtly. Doran equally depicted Lear's entourage as roaring drunkards who knocked over tables, but he furthermore had Goneril giving away food to the poor, thus showing a caring and softer side to her that the text withholds.

The convoluted ways in which the play, primarily its reception, define concepts such as 'evil' and female agency forms the backdrop against which to consider Goneril's death. Her suicide in 5.3 is reported by the Gentleman, and the bloody dagger he brings onstage serves as a visual reminder that something violent has happened:

GENTLEMAN: Help, help, O, help!
EDGAR: What kind of help?
ALBANY: Speak, man.
EDGAR: What means this bloody knife?
GENTLEMAN: 'Tis hot, it smokes,
              It came even from the heart of – O, she's dead!
ALBANY: Who dead? Speak, man.
GENTLEMAN: Your lady, sir, your lady; and her sister
              By her is poisoned; she confesses it.

(5.3.221–226)

At first glance, this dialogue merely conveys the information that both sisters are dead and that Goneril has poisoned Regan. Whether Regan has stabbed Goneril first or whether Goneril has used the knife against herself is left open. The suspicion of suicide only hardens when considered against Albany's earlier fear "Go after her; she's desperate, govern her" (5.3.159). Kordecki and Koskinen put forward another, even more convincing reason as to why Goneril's suicide should not surprise. Since suicide is, amongst other things, traditionally associated with military leaders, it is a fitting end for Goneril as a ruling monarch unwilling to acknowledge defeat.[22] Critics routinely overlook her status of a monarch. Taking this into account, her self-determined ending seems fitting. In addition, the above passage contains other relevant information, namely that Goneril has poisoned her sister but killed herself with a knife. In doing so, she is the reverse image of Romeo, who uses a masculine weapon (sword) to kill but one of feminine connotation (poison) on himself. The fact that she chooses a weapon of masculine connotation can be understood as an expression of her dissatisfaction with her role as a female as well as her constant attempts to break free from these constraints.

In a play that has no space for women and femininity at all, it should not surprise that Goneril's suicide takes place offstage. She is marginalised from the centre of attention, a mere body that needs to be removed quickly before the final scene. In the realm of the play, everything female is eradicated. More precisely, the female eradicates itself. Goneril and Regan kill each other. With regard to female agency, this appears to be the bleakest ending of all the tragedies. Ophelia, Portia, and Lady Macbeth also die offstage, and their bodies remain hidden. The bodies of Goneril and Regan, by contrast, are brought onstage. Albany even gives the command "Produce the bodies, be they alive or dead" (5.3.229), as if they were trophy bodies in a triumphal procession. So, whereas Ophelia emerges from the offstage space concealed in a coffin, here the two female bodies re-enter in plain view. Foakes argues that if Goneril's and Regan's deaths appear "somewhat melodramatic," this can be explained by the necessity to close with a scene that shows Lear surrounded by the three bodies of his daughters, all of them tragedies of his own making.[23]

If the display of the three bodies enhanced Lear's pain, this would be a melodramatic move indeed. If taken for what it is – three dead female bodies displayed on a stage – this image is a poignant one. These dead bodies matter. All three of them are "dead centres" of tragic denouement in Dympna Callaghan's sense, undermining woman's "progress from transgressor to saint" and demolishing "neat schematisations of tragic form which have been posited by the hallowed traditional tragic paradigm."[24] Even though the play allocates the roles of transgressor and saint to Goneril/Regan and Cordelia respectively, eventually these categories converge. The three women lie next to each other, almost exchangeable in the face of what they represent. At the same time, in its sheer display, this stage tableau of female victimisation challenges tragic convention, as Callaghan suggests. By directing the audiences' gaze towards the three female bodies, the play subtly turns it away from the tragic hero.

Sean Lawrence draws attention to the fact that Goneril's suicide is prompted by a refusal to be ruled by others. In the first place, her last words in the play, "the laws are mine, not thine. / Who can arraign me for't" (5.3.156–157), are directed at Albany. As the Queen, she is above the law, Goneril says.[25] Yet, simultaneously, she renounces any male power more generally, exemplified in her rejection of male-constructed laws. Whereas in the Folio Goneril exits after speaking this line, in the Quarto she replies to Albany's subsequent question of whether she is informed about the letter. She then leaves the stage with "Ask me not what I know" (5.3.158), which in the Folio is assigned to Edmund. This allocation seems illogical because the immediately preceding lines already indicate that she knows about it.[26] But more importantly, the Folio allocates her a much more graceful exit. She leaves the play with her head held high, opposing male control one last time. With reference to Edwin Shneidman's interpretation of the Freudian position towards suicide,[27] Faber terms Goneril's suicide a "murder in the one-hundred and eightieth degree," an act of aggression not only directed at the self but also society and its extensions – in this case, the father.[28] He is right in stressing this double edge. By killing herself, Goneril not only attacks her own body, but also the society she feels imprisoned in. John McLaughlin elaborates that "[m]uch of the behaviour of Goneril and Regan can be explained by what Adler called the 'masculine protest', a refusal by women to accept the weakness of the feminine role. [...] [Goneril] denies her husband's authority and reserves for herself alone the absolute power of monarchy. Like Lear, she considers herself above the law. The sister who has dethroned her as a child she has already dispatched with a woman's weapon, poison, but it is significant that she takes her own life with a masculine weapon, a knife. Suicide is her ultimate rejection of an inferior feminine role."[29] Unlike Lady Macbeth, whose suicide will be discussed along similar lines, Goneril does not turn mad; her 'evil' alone justifies her exclusion from the play. Furthermore, unlike all the other women who die offstage, she exits with a final line that hints at how her suicide should be understood. If this seems a feeble revolt against the patriarchy for the simple fact that she does not die onstage, thus not sharing the tragic hero's limelight, such an interpretation may be countered with regard to the play's depiction of Gloucester's non-suicide. By not showing something that happens while simultaneously dragging out onstage something that does not actually happen, *King Lear* subverts the notion of an offstage death as reserved for the weak.

"That Benefit to End Itself by Death": Gloucester's Punishment

Another suicide that does not happen is that of *King Lear*, although, given Lear's state at the end of the play, suicide might well have been an imaginable alternative. This alternative scenario appears most clearly if Lear's demise is compared to the other tragedy Shakespeare wrote in the years of 1605/1606.[30] *Timon of Athens* resembles *King Lear* in its depiction of the hero's descent into poverty and madness, its investigation of human ingratitude, as well as its almost exclusively male world. But, whereas Lear's rage is primarily directed at the women surrounding him, Timon's hatred develops into more general misanthropy. When the Athenian senators visit him in his self-imposed exile in the woods, he shows them one of the trees and tells them: "whoso please / To stop affliction, let him take his haste, [...] And hang himself" (*Tim.* 5.1.209–212). Although primarily a means to express his contempt, this monologue is indicative of Timon's mind-set at the close of the play. As Richard Fly remarks, "the universe seems increasingly to be a place in which only self-destructive acts are possible. Suicide, either direct or indirect, becomes the rule of all life, including his own."[31] Atypical of Shakespeare's tragic heroes, Timon dies offstage, and the manner of his demise is left peculiarly unresolved. Only a lengthy and somewhat cryptic epitaph read out by Alcibiades confirms his death. However, Timon's final words suggest that he may have killed himself: "Graves only be men's works and death their gain; / Sun, hide thy beams, Timon hath done his reign" (*Tim.* 5.1.222–223). Honigmann, too, considers these lines a hint towards a possible suicide,[32] and Fly holds that the implication of suicide appears more pronounced when considered against the end of the play, at which Timon's existence takes on an increasingly verbal quality. "For Timon, to cease speaking is to cease to be, and in his final address to the world – 'Lips, let four words go by and language end' [*Tim.* 5.1.220] – he unequivocally acquiesces in this form of self-annihilation."[33] To read Timon's death as a possible suicide certainly fits the nihilistic and misanthropic vision of the play. But also, it raises the question as to why Lear, who believes himself in a similar position, does not even consider killing himself.

As Kathleen McLuskie has pointed out in her essay on the potential and limits of a feminist reading of *King Lear*, the play presupposes a patriarchal and indeed misogynist ideology and structure. In
order to be able to empathise with the tragic hero, one needs to suppress all discomfort elicited by the deeply troubling constructions of
gender and acquiesce an "equation between 'human nature' and male
power."[34] Otherwise, the tragedy simply does not work, at least not
for a present-day (feminist) audience. This equation of human nature
and male power McLuskie mentions is personified by two characters,
divided into two separate yet connected plots: Lear and Gloucester.
Typical of Renaissance drama, the subplot is considered a commentary
on or parallel to the main plot. Some of these analogies are more, others
less, obvious.[35] First, both follow a similar trajectory – a descent into
madness and subsequent return to relative sanity. Second, both represent an older generation or world order that is upturned by children they
consider ungrateful. Third, while Lear's view of Cordelia changes in an
instant from "our joy" (1.1.82) to "a stranger to my heart" (1.1.116),
Gloucester insists "I loved him, friend, / No father his son dearer"
(3.4.164–165). Hence, they are furthermore united in a problematic
concept of fatherly love.

Other than this, Lear and Gloucester are linked by their misogyny.
Lear's lines are the most powerfully sexist in Shakespeare, leaving no
room for interpretation as to what he thinks of women: "Down from
the waist they are centaurs, though women all above. But to the gir-
dle do the gods inherit, beneath is all the fiend's: there's hell, there's
darkness, there is the sulphurous pit, burning, scalding, stench, consumption" (4.6.121–125). Here, as elsewhere in the tragedies, female
sexuality equals evil and depravity, something that has to be feared and
silenced. Compared to Lear's rants, Gloucester's seem less shocking, but
his chauvinism is no less pronounced. Since he only has sons, he reverts
to their mother who, like Lear's wife, merely features *in absentia*. The
first information provided on Gloucester is the fact that he has fathered
an illegitimate son, a scandal he, by way of a bawdy joke, readily blames
on Edmund's mother: "Do you smell a fault?" (1.1.15). Foakes suggests
a reading of "smell a sin or wrongdoing, with a punning allusion to the
female genitals" and indicates that Gloucester hereby anticipates Lear's
misogyny later on.[36] To extend the analogy between the two, one could
argue that whereas Lear suffers emotionally, Gloucester is physically
tortured on Lear's behalf. This line of thought is particularly suggestive in view of the symbolism underlying Gloucester's blinding. Peter
Rudnytsky notices that Gloucester's eyeballs are referred to as "precious
stones" (5.3.189), a phrase also used to connote testicles. In the same
way, the phrase "bleeding rings" (5.3.188) develops the metaphor of
eyes and jewels but, furthermore, relates to the female genitals, a connotation that renders the blinding a symbolic castration.[37] If Lear and

Gloucester are considered two sides of the same coin – two souls united in a shared patriarchal world-view – no doubt this ideology is queried by the text.

To stretch the argument of Lear and Gloucester as two sides of the same coin yet another step further, Gloucester's suicide attempt can be regarded a substitute for the suicide Lear never thinks of. Shakespeare presumably takes the overall subplot surrounding Gloucester, including the mock-suicide at the cliffs of Dover, from the second book of Sidney's *Arcadia*. In Sidney's text, the former Prince of Paphlagonia asks his son Leonatus to lead him to the top of the rocks so that he can commit suicide. Leonatus refuses and instead reveals himself to his father.[38] Thus, again, Shakespeare borrows elsewhere but simultaneously introduces a significant innovation with regard to suicide. Without Gloucester's attempted suicide, the Dover cliff scene would be a relatively uneventful episode.

That *King Lear* has been deemed difficult, if not impossible, to stage certainly owes much to this scene. Generically, letting a character die and then revive is a comic device. With Gloucester, Shakespeare translates this convention to a tragic context, but the comic element, in terms of both genre and tone, are still traceable. G. Wilson Knight emphasised the play's use of the grotesque, to which the Dover cliff scene provides the climax. In his opinion, "[t]he core of the play is an absurdity, an indignity, and incongruity."[39] Bradley, on the other hand, believed that, whereas in a play like *Othello* such absurdities would be dissonant, they are appropriately in line with the spirit of *King Lear*. Furthermore, he added, "contrary to expectation, [Gloucester's suicide] is not, if properly acted, in the least absurd on the stage."[40] Implicit in Bradley's comment resonates, of course, the question of how exactly the scene should be performed onstage.

As Foakes suggests in his introduction to the Arden Third Series, the scene only works if the audience know that there are no actual cliffs. Otherwise, its powerful effect would be lost entirely.[41] Jan Kott addresses the play within the context of the Theatre of the Absurd, more specifically that of Beckett's *Endgame*. For him, the Dover cliff scene in particular is written as pantomime. It is "grotesque, and has something of a circus about it. The blind Gloster who has climbed a non-existent height and fallen over on flat boards, is a clown. A philosophical buffoonery has been performed, of the sort found in modern theatre."[42] Throughout stage history, directors have approached this dilemma in various ways. To name but a few examples, John Gielgud and Anthony Quayle's production in 1950 employed a backcloth showing the cliffs in the background, thereby firmly placing the scene at the actual cliffs of Dover.[43] Peter Brook in 1962, on the other hand, resorted to the technique of mime as insisted on by Kott. As Leggatt describes this production, "[i]n the neutral space that was the set we could have been at Dover Cliff; as the mime created it for us, we almost felt that we were. Then Gloucester threw himself forward and rolled across the floor. He was not at Dover, he was on a stage; or on level ground that could have been anywhere. The ambiguity that the scene would have had in the Globe Theatre was reproduced in the idiom of this production in a way that scenic realism would never have allowed."[44] Jonathan Miller's 1982 screen adaptation for the BBC opts for a middle ground. Although Gloucester and Edgar are climbing up the cliffs of Dover, the camera does not show the space or potential abyss they face. When he falls, Gloucester throws himself out of the camera frame, and the question of whether he has killed himself is suspended for a brief moment.[45]

Much has been said about *King Lear* and its portrayal of different religious beliefs, and a fusion of Christian and pre-Christian beliefs can also be traced within the present scene.[46] From the first line onwards, the scene is heavily indebted to the morality play tradition. Beginning with Gloucester's "When shall I come to the top of that same hill" (4.6.1), invoking the Mountain of Purgatory, Gloucester's suicide attempt can be read as an allegory of fall and subsequent recovery. In a metaphorical analogy to his physical blinding, Gloucester needs to suffer in order to be purged from his despair and 'see clearly' again. The association of suicidal despair with the Devil, common within both the medieval and Renaissance contexts, is made explicit in Gloucester's claim: "'The fiend, the fiend'; he led me to that place" (4.6.79). Edgar, disguised as Poor Tom who assumes the role of Comfort and Mercy, even offers a detailed description of this creature: "As I stood here below methought his eyes / Were two full moons. He had a thousand noses, / Horns whelked and waved like the enraged sea" (4.6.69–71). For Rowland Wymer, the text ultimately suggests an exchange of pagan despair for Christian comfort, hope, and salvation. At the same time, the scene is not what Gloucester believes it to be. There is no miracle of resurrection; everything is just a deception orchestrated by Edgar. This, then, leads to a more pessimistic view, an "identification of religious comfort with illusion."[47] Kott makes a similar point, conceding that "Gloster's suicide does not solve or alter anything. It is only a somersault on an empty stage [...] It is waiting for a Godot who does not come."[48] This nihilistic reading seems much more in tune not only with the absurdity of this particular scene, but also the overall spirit of the play.

Before Gloucester falls, Edgar asks himself in an aside "Why do I trifle thus with his despair / Is done to cure it" (4.6.33–34). Clearly, this is equally directed at the audience because Edgar appears ambiguous, if not malevolent, here. His motivation remains opaque, shrouded in a blend of deliberate cruelty and good intentions. Figuratively speaking, by not revealing his identity, Edgar denies his father the capacity to see again. He repeats the blinding, this time on an emotional level. If Edgar's intention was to cure his father from suicidal despair, this seems to have failed. In line with the idea that neither God nor Christian salvation exist, Gloucester remains weary and tired of life. When Oswald threatens to kill him, he begs "Now let thy friendly hand / Put strength enough to't" (4.6.226–227). The sentiment of life-weariness resurfaces in 5.2 when Gloucester's "No further, sir; a man may rot even here" is countered by Edgar: "What, in ill thoughts again? Men must endure / Their going hence even as their coming hither. / Ripeness is all" (5.2.8–11). Arthur Kirsch fittingly calls this last line "Gloucester's epitaph."[49] The fruit needs to ripen until it naturally falls from the tree. And so, instead of ending his life and suffering through suicide, Gloucester is forced to endure. In that sense, Gloucester's fate echoes that of Lavinia. Both characters are mutilated, and in both cases, these mutilations prevent them from ending their lives. No matter how logical this sounds – because clearly a blind Gloucester could still stab himself with a dagger, if he had one – this is what the text insists on. Unlike Lavinia, Gloucester still has a voice to express his wish to die. His voice is deliberately ignored, and so, here, like in *Titus Andronicus*, the withholding of suicide resembles a form of torture.

Faber draws a more optimistic conclusion, believing that "Gloucester's self-sacrificial willingness to succor the unfortunate Lear, his defiance of Cornwall and Regan, his preference of death to inaction, uncover a prepossessing sweetness, an engaging decency, in his nature" that ultimately redeem him.[50] Faber's rather uncritical reading of Gloucester misses the painfully grotesque undertones captured by Kott, and even Gloucester himself seems to contradict this view by asking "Is wretchedness deprived that benefit, / To end itself by death?" (4.6.61–62). Ferrell rightfully names Gloucester's would-be suicide a "farce at its most painful edge: not simply failing to extinguish one's own life, but also failing to recognize that one has not actually succeeded at this self-sufficient task."[51] Since Gloucester is not the only character who does not manage to kill himself, the latter part of Ferrell's comment is particularly important. Brutus's suicide, too, is not exactly the heroic death he envisioned it to be, and neither is Antony's. But, contrary to Gloucester, who remains blissfully oblivious of the absurd scenario he finds himself in, Antony is aware of his failure. This lack of self-realisation invites as much, if not more, uncomfortable laughter as any other suicide devised by Shakespeare. Furthermore, whereas both Brutus's and Antony's suicides result in some sort of heroic rehabilitation, Gloucester only gets a lukewarm reconciliation with his son. The scene in which Edgar discloses his identity and Gloucester subsequently dies is merely reported, presumably so as not to interfere with the reunion of Lear and Cordelia.[52] That way, any emotional closure or final redemption is denied to Gloucester in a similar way as it is denied to Lear. Both characters stand for a misogynist ideology which is deemed destructive and unfruitful, in the personal as well as the political sense. As Lear's mirror image, Gloucester is punished in Lear's stead for upholding such a worldview, his inability to kill himself being the ultimate torment.

Facing the bodies of Cordelia, Goneril, and Regan, Kent asks "Is this the promised end?" (5.3.261). This line has received due critical attention as a comment on the play's brutally pessimistic ending, which almost exhausts tragic convention and infamously inspired Nahum Tate to re-write it.[53] With regard to both Gloucester's and Goneril's individual endings – his failed attempt to kill himself, as opposed to her offstage suicide – the play holds its promise. In place of Lear, Gloucester is punished for his unrelenting patriarchy. This punishment is epitomised in Gloucester's inability to find relief in suicide. His fruitless struggle to throw himself off the cliffs of Dover is as grotesque and absurd as it is painful to watch. His inability to realise that he has not succeeded invites uncomfortable laughter and ridicule. Vis-à-vis this long and so famous scene, Goneril's offstage suicide at first glance falls flat. Unlike the suicide of Juliet and the death of Desdemona, it does not have much dramatic presence. Further, unlike the news of Portia's suicide, the messenger announces Goneril's death with pure contempt. Yet, despite this depiction, her suicide does not have to be understood as submission, especially not as punishment or final proof that good has trumped evil. With striking frequency, both Lear and critics of the play locate Goneril's evil not in her sometimes undoubtedly sinful actions but in her being an 'unruly woman'. Throughout the play, she fights her subordinate female position, a revolt that culminates in her suicide. She refuses to be defeated, neither by France's invading army nor her own father. For this reason, she exits the world in which everything female and not conventionally feminine values such as ambition are suppressed. Represented through Gloucester and Goneril, the play, therefore, dramatises male supremacy as opposed by women. Within the mercilessly male world of the play, it does not come as a shock that ultimately none of the women succeed at revolt, even if Goneril comes closest. Simultaneously, however, the torture-like quality of Gloucester's failed suicide – and not least Lear's own tragic ending – suggests severe critique, if not the impending demise, of a world order that suppresses one gender entirely.

Notes

1 Michael Neill, "Death and King Lear," in *Shakespeare in Our Time: A Shakespeare Association of America Collection*, ed. Dympna Callaghan and Suzanne Gossett (London and New York: Bloomsbury, 2016), 81.
2 Lori Anne Ferrell, "New Directions: Promised End? *King Lear* and the Suicide Trick," in *King Lear: A Critical Guide*, ed. Andrew Hiscock and Lisa Hopkins (London: Continuum, 2011), 114.
3 On the probable sources see R. A. Foakes, Introduction to *King Lear*, by William Shakespeare, ed. R. A. Foakes, The Arden Shakespeare Third Series

(London: Arden Shakespeare, 1997), 92–110; Kenneth Muir, *The Sources of Shakespeare's Plays* (London and New York: Routledge, 1977), 196–207.

4 William Shakespeare, *King Lear*, ed. R. A. Foakes, The Arden Shakespeare Third Series (London: Arden Shakespeare, 1997), note to 5.3.320.

5 Ferrell, "New Directions: Promised End," 101.

6 Melvyn Donald Faber, "Some Remarks on the Suicide of King Lear's Eldest Daughter," *University Review* 33 (1967): 314.

7 Claudette Hoover, "Goneril and Regan: 'So Horrid as in Woman'," *San Jose Studies* 10.3 (1984): 56–57.

8 Bradley, *Shakespearean Tragedy* (1904; reprint; London: Penguin, 1991), 277.

9 David Mann, *Shakespeare's Women: Performance and Conception* (Cambridge: Cambridge University Press, 2008), 157.

10 Linda Bamber, *Comic Women, Tragic Men: A Study of Gender and Genre in Shakespeare* (Stanford: Stanford University Press, 1982), 2.

11 Ann Thompson, "Are There Any Women in *King Lear?*" in *The Matter of Difference: Materialist Feminist Criticism of Shakespeare*, ed. Valerie Wayne (Ithaca, NY: Cornell University Press, 1991), 117–128.

12 Lesley Kordecki and Karla Koskinen, *Re-Visioning Lear's Daughters: Testing Feminist Criticism and Theory* (New York: Palgrave, 2010), 1. See also Cristina León Alfar, *Fantasies of Female Evil: The Dynamics of Gender and Power in Shakespearean Tragedy* (Newark: University of Delaware Press, 2003), 79–110; Coppélia Kahn, "The Absent Mother in *King Lear*," in *Rewriting the Renaissance: The Discourse of Sexual Difference in Early Modern Europe*, ed. Margaret W. Ferguson et al. (Chicago: University of Chicago Press, 1986), 33–49.

13 Kevin A. Quarmby, "Sexing Up Goneril: Feminism and Fetishization in Contemporary *King Lear* Performance," in *Women Making Shakespeare: Text, Reception and Performance*, ed. Gordon McMullan et al. (London and New York: Bloomsbury, 2014), 326.

14 Pascale Aebischer, *Shakespeare's Violated Bodies: Stage and Screen Performance* (Cambridge: Cambridge University Press, 2004), 174. As an example of a production that sympathised with Goneril and Regan mostly by inventing such a backstory, Aebischer extensively discusses Nicholas Hytner's 1990 staging with the RSC (173–178).

15 See Tim Keppel, "Goneril's Version: *A Thousand Acres* and *King Lear*," *South Dakota Review* 33.2 (1995): 105–117.

16 Julia Kristeva, *Powers of Horror: An Essay on Abjection* (New York: Columbia University Press, 1982), 1–4.

17 Honigmann, *Shakespeare: Seven Tragedies: A Dramatist's Manipulation of Response* (London: Macmillan, 1976), 109.

18 Alexander Leggatt, *Shakespeare's Tragedies: Violation and Identity* (Cambridge: Cambridge University Press, 2005), 158.

19 Foakes's note to 2.2.192 in the Arden Third Series. Foakes also comments on this on p. 67 of his introduction to *King Lear*.

20 Aebischer, *Shakespeare's Violated Bodies*, 153.

21 Jonathan Croall, *Performing King Lear: Gielgud to Russell Beale* (London and New York: Bloomsbury, 2015), 232.

22 Kordecki and Koskinen, *Re-Visioning Lear's Daughters*, 209.

23 Foakes, Introduction to *King Lear*, 43.

24 Callaghan, *Woman and Gender in Renaissance Tragedy: A Study of King Lear, Othello, The Duchess of Malfi and The White Devil* (New York: Harvester Wheatsheaf, 1989), 96.

25 Sean Lawrence, "The Difficulty of Dying in *King Lear*," *ESC* 31.4 (2005): 46. See also note to l. 5.3.156–157 in the Arden Third Series.

26 Foakes's note to 5.3.152–158 in the Arden Third Series.

27 Edwin S. Shneidman, *Definition of Suicide* (Northvale: Jason Aronson, 1985), 34. Rather than discussing suicide in great detail, Freud subsumes it under larger questions of death. In *Beyond the Pleasure Principle*, he formulates the principle of the death-drive as one of two primary human instincts. Death-drives stands in opposition to life-drives, which include the striving for survival, sexual drives, and other life-producing or life-preserving drives (45–102). In *Totem and Taboo*, Freud establishes a connection between suicide and murder, arguing that "impulses to suicide in a neurotic turn out regularly to be self-punishments for wishes for someone else's death" (179). This is the initial thought later developed by Shneidman.

28 Faber, "Some Remarks," 316.

29 John J. McLaughlin, "The Dynamics of Power in *King Lear*: An Adlerian Interpretation," *Shakespeare Quarterly* 29.1 (1978): 41–42.

30 According to Stanely Wells and Gary Taylor, *William Shakespeare: A Textual Companion* (Oxford: Clarendon, 1987), 127–128.

31 Richard Fly, *Shakespeare's Mediated World* (Amherst: University of Massachusetts Press, 1976), 139.

32 E. A. J. Honigmann, "*Timon of Athens*," *Shakespeare Quarterly* 12.1 (1961): 17.

33 Fly, *Shakespeare's Mediated World*, 138.

34 Kathleen McLuskie, "The Patriarchal Bard: Feminist Criticism and Shakespeare: *King Lear* and *Measure for Measure*," in *Political Shakespeare*, ed. Jonathan Dollimore and Alan Sinfield (Manchester: Manchester University Press, 1985), 98.

35 See, for instance, John Ellis, "The Gulling of Gloucester: Credibility in the Subplot of *King Lear*," *SEL* 12.2 (1972): 275–278.

36 Foakes's note to 1.1.15 in the Arden Third Series.

37 Peter L. Rudnytsky, "'The Darke and Vicious Place': The Dread of the Vagina in *King Lear*," *Modern Philology* 96.3 (1999): 293.

38 Sir Philip Sidney, *The Countess of Pembroke's Arcadia (The New Arcadia)*, ed. Victor Skretkowicz (Oxford: Clarendon, 1987), 179–186.

39 G. Wilson Knight, *The Wheel of Fire: Interpretations of Shakespearean Tragedy* (1930; reprint; London and New York: Routledge, 2001), 191.

40 Bradley, *Shakespearean Tragedy*, 230.

41 Foakes, Introduction to *King Lear*, 62.

42 Jan Kott, *Shakespeare our Contemporary* (London: Routledge, 1991), 117.

43 Alexander Leggatt, *Shakespeare in Performance: King Lear* (Manchester: Manchester University Press, 1991), 29.

44 Ibid., 37.

45 See also James P. Lusardi and June Schlueter, *Reading Shakespeare in Performance: King Lear* (Madison: Fairleigh Dickinson University Press, 1991), 112–116.

46 See Jonathan Dollimore, *Radical Tragedy: Religion, Ideology and Power in the Drama of Shakespeare and his Contemporaries* (Brighton: Harvester, 1984), 189–204; Stephen Greenblatt, *Shakespearean Negotiations: The Circulation of Social Energy in Renaissance England* (Oxford: Clarendon, 1988), 96–128; Alison Shell, *Shakespeare and Religion* (London and New York: Bloomsbury, 2010), 95–100; 186–222; Frankie Rubinstein, "Speculating on Mysteries: Religion and Politics in *King Lear*," *Renaissance Studies* 16.2 (2002): 234–262.

47 Rowland Wymer, *Suicide and Despair in the Jacobean Drama* (Brighton: Harvester, 1986), 68–69.

48 Kott, *Shakespeare Our Contemporary*, 119.

49 Arthur Kirsch, *The Passions of Shakespeare's Tragic Heroes* (Charlottesville: University of Virginia Press, 1990), 112.

50 Melvyn Donald Faber, "Suicide in Shakespeare" (PhD diss., University of California, 1963), 451.

51 Ferrell, "New Directions: Promised End," 101.

52 Foakes, Introduction to *King Lear*, 64.

53 On the ending, see Joyce Carol Oates, "'Is This the Promised End?': The Tragedy of *King Lear*," *The Journal of Aesthetics and Art Criticism* 33.1 (1974): 19–32; Jay L. Halio, "The Promised Endings of *King Lear*," in *The Work of Dissimilitude: Essays from the Sixth Citadel Conference on Medieval and Renaissance Literature*, ed. David G. Allen and Robert A. White (Newark/London: University of Delaware Press/Associated University Press, 1992), 235–242; Peter Halter, "The Endings of *King Lear*," in *On Strangeness*, ed. Margaret Bridges (Tübingen: Narr, 1990), 85–98. On the several re-writes, see Foakes, Introduction to *King Lear*, 80–89.

7 Trying the Last

Macbeth

After *Titus Andronicus*, *Macbeth* is Shakespeare's second bloodiest creation, but in contrast to *Titus*, comparatively little blood is shed in front of the audience. Instead, the text is pervaded by blood imagery, much more so than any other Shakespearean tragedy. A play that so mercilessly massacres one character after another should not shy away from staging a suicide. But not only does Macbeth not kill himself, he even provides an explanation as to why he will not do it: "Why should I play the Roman fool, and die / On my own sword? whiles I see lives, the gashes / Do better upon them" (5.8.1–3). These seemingly negligible lines are usually overlooked, even though as a reference to suicide they are just as concrete as Hamlet's "To be, or not to be." With Lady Macbeth, the play also features an actual suicide, but like Ophelia, Portia, and Goneril, she dies offstage.

It is a commonplace that *Macbeth* is obsessed with gender constructions. In *Shakespeare's Culture of Violence*, Derek Cohen comments on the boundless violence that "only produces corollaries such as the breakdown of 'normal' forms. Gender distinctions [...] are close to being erased in *Macbeth*. The power of violence is nearly sufficient to perform such erasure."[1] Simultaneous with this obliteration, however, violence performatively reinforces gender distinctions. Both in conversations between the Macbeths and on the battlefield, aggression and violence are synonymous with masculinity, thus defining what separates man from woman. The present chapter examines the nexus between such violent constructions of masculinity and the play's portrayal of suicide, indicating that both the Macbeths' deaths can be read as commenting on and constructed by the play's debate on gender.

In view of my larger argument of suicide as an act of agency, it is first necessary to untangle the precarious ways in which the play, as well as critical reception, define and also morally evaluate female agency. Hence, this chapter first looks at Lady Macbeth's suicide and interrogates the critical tendency of translating her struggle against domineering power structures into an expression of evil. The fact that she dies offstage is usually treated as an acknowledgement of guilt and defeat, of submission to her inferior role. Contrary to such established readings,

I suggest that her suicide can be understood as her final act of rebellion rather than defeat, as a way of liberating herself from the play's oppressive gender discourse. I will discuss the play's refusal to show Lady Macbeth's suicide against Macbeth's refusal to commit it, thus explaining why the death he dies instead is a much more fitting ending for the character but not necessarily one that establishes him as the stronger and more dramatically compelling of the two.

"By Self and Violent Hands": Lady Macbeth's Gender Trouble

Even though the death of Lady Macbeth is one of the most famous Shakespearean suicides, scholars frequently downplay its significance; after all, it happens offstage and, furthermore, at a moment when the play seems to have lost all interest in her. Angela Pitt describes the suicide as "insignificant in itself" because it neither happens onstage nor influences the course of the action.[2] Rowland Wymer makes a different point, arguing that "her anguish and her suicide are not finally redemptive because there is no real sign of repentance in them."[3] Irving Ribner even deduces a dubious moral: "In her death by suicide there is further emphasis upon the theme which dominates the play: that evil inevitably must breed its own destruction."[4] Comparable to critical views on Macbeth's own death, these opinions reveal certain presuppositions: first, suicides have to take place centre stage, ideally committed by the tragic hero. Second, suicides are only important when they have a redemptive function. Third, suicide is a form of punishment. Apart from the fact that at least the latter two assumptions are mutually exclusive, none of them can be applied convincingly to Lady Macbeth.

Ribner's view of her suicide as punishment – by no means a solitary opinion – needs to be contextualised within Lady Macbeth's history of critical reception. Even though in this play bursting with violent masculinity the tragic hero, too, is portrayed as distinctly ambivalent, she is the one who is routinely singled out as the root of all evil. Such views seem to be the ideological cornerstone on which to build an interpretation of her suicide. Kenneth Muir, for instance, claims that "although it is true that Lady Macbeth is not naturally depraved or conscienceless (any more than Satan was) she deliberately chooses evil, her choice being more deliberate than her husband's."[5] For Linda Bamber, "Lady Macbeth's murderous ambition is more horrible than her husband's because a woman [...] should represent nurture and human connectedness."[6] Bamber, therefore, concludes that "to argue for a redistribution of sympathy in *Macbeth*, as some feminists have done, is a pretty desperate measure."[7] In other words, Lady Macbeth's prime offence lies not in manipulating her husband into murdering the King but in transgressing normative gender roles. Within this context, 'evil' is a synonym for 'ambition', and criticism merely perpetuates the biblical archetype here. Lady Macbeth stands in for Eve, the evil temptress to Macbeth's Adam, an image that is explicitly called upon – if ironically misapplied – in Macbeth's "We have scorch'd the snake, not kill'd it" (3.2.13). While for a long time this monstrous, fiendish image dominated the representation onstage, in the twenty-first century, there seems to be a consensus that such one-dimensionality reduces her dramatic appeal, if not undermines the text.[8] Reducing her to Malcolm's damning epithet supports the play's hegemony, re-iterating the play-inherent attempt to justify an ideology of male supremacy.

Lady Macbeth's taunting of her husband is full of sexual innuendo, and their marriage is presented as passionate. As Joanne Roberts notes, modern stage productions, therefore, tend to sexualise the character, which raises a question that, again, touches on the more problematic undertones of critical reception. Roberts writes "making her sexy on the stage adds an intriguing dimension to her portrait – is her sexuality seductively 'feminine' or frighteningly 'masculine'? Or perhaps both? If her sexuality is not emphasized, she may become even more interesting."[9] But if, as suggested here, the text does not describe her as overtly sexual, rather than making her more complex as a figure, this tendency of sexualising her reinforces the notion of Lady Macbeth as an evil temptress. Within this stereotype, sexuality signifies moral corruption, not only on the early modern stage, but also, with uncomfortable frequency, today. What such interpretations shed light on is not so much the character's representation in the play as the ideologies or politics behind critical reception. She shares this status with Ophelia, with the difference that Ophelia is marginalised through victimisation, not demonisation.

Most powerfully, Lady Macbeth's conflicted femininity is communicated in her second extended soliloquy, the famous "Unsex me here" (1.5.37–53). As several critics have noted, she links herself rhetorically with the witches. Within the play, witchcraft represents a male fantasy of feminine power.[10] But more importantly in the context of suicide and its intricate connection with gender, the speech draws attention to the female body within early modern conceptualisations of corporeality. Specifically, her speech is located within the discourse of Humorism. She wishes her woman's milk to be absorbed by the body and transformed into gall and blood, conventionally masculine fluids.[11] Despite its supernatural associations, her soliloquy is less a ritual of witchcraft than a dramatic speech. As Dale Townshend remarks, "[e]ffected by a linguistic command, unsexing is swift, deliberate and even effortless in nature, [...] inaugurated by a performative speech-act in which the external signs are reabsorbed by the body and summarily directed."[12] If spoken on the Elizabethan stage, these lines, furthermore, add a self-referential level, pointing to the dual presence of the male actor playing a female role. In the original theatrical context in particular, Lady Macbeth's body thus functions as a site of a gradually emerging and, hence, still rudimentary understanding of both sex and gender.[13]

In addition to echoing Renaissance gender discourses, the soliloquy is worth looking at through the lens of Judith Butler, whose theory of gender performativity is so perfectly suitable to explain Lady Macbeth's status in the play that it seems as if Butler must have had her in mind. Butler's understanding of gender as constructed by society's normative discourse, as repeated performances of what is considered masculine and feminine behaviour, can be applied easily: whereas Macbeth's doubts bring him in conflict with the cultural construction of masculinity, Lady Macbeth's ambition and cunning rationality – masculine gender performances – make her an 'unfeminine' woman. Yet, Butler even questions the materiality of sex as a natural category, a notion that particularly helps to shed light on Lady Macbeth's soliloquy. For Butler, sex is not just a given, physical surface onto which gender is projected but rather a normative category and, therefore, a cultural construct itself.[14]

Similar to Butler, Lady Macbeth seems to reject the concept of essentialist femininity defined by physical form, which is why Alexander Leggatt deems the soliloquy a "self-conducted attack on the female body" and rightly draws a parallel to Lear's curse on Goneril.[15] Through relinquishing her menstrual cycle, Lady Macbeth seeks to sterilise herself, not only regarding her ability to give birth, but also her conventionally feminine qualities such as remorse and conscience. At the same time, her wish of being filled "top-full / Of direst cruelty" (1.5.41–42) constructs a paradoxical double image of simultaneous pregnancy, impregnated by the seeds of evil. Equally paradoxical, her "take my milk for gall" (1.5.47) can be read as either 'substitute my milk with gall' or an expression of gall as the appropriate nourishment for evil spirits.[16] In this way, nursing, an archetypically feminine task, becomes either physically impossible or a breeding ground for cruelty. For Janet Adelman, these lines, therefore, echo cultural anxieties of maternal nursery.[17] On the whole, then, Lady Macbeth's gender performance is neither wholly feminine nor masculine. The hybrid state she envisions is ontologically impossible, and it is equally impossible to fathom which gender identity follows which biological marker referred to in her speech. Dympna Callaghan has explored the mechanisms through which the play both comments on and takes part in contemporary gender discourse, which increasingly moves towards a femininity defined by reproductive organs.[18] This participatory dimension of the play noted by Callaghan is a prime factor for Butler, for whom gender performances do not have to be mere repetitions of existing norms but rather change categories and, thereby, modify gender discourse.[19] Within the norms of Lady Macbeth's historical and cultural context, what she performs is unthinkable, in terms of both sex and gender. Her soliloquy expresses this impossibility in a drastic manner because the play's rigid gender categories refuse to be expanded or modified any other way.

Even though Butler does not touch on the context of drama, her concept of gender performativity still involves a notion of theatricality, primarily since her terminology echoes dramatic discourse. As James Loxley explains, theatre as well as performance studies have drawn on and departed from Butler, yet her theory as such is already indebted to the notion of performance in a theatrical sense. Both performance and performativity are so much intertwined that their relation "is [...] best described as asymptotic; an ever-closer proximity without a final, resolving convergence."[20] Lady Macbeth's speech is performative in the way it creates gender, albeit one that explodes the play's limits of intelligibility. But it is also a performance, and her speech appears theatrical. Cristina Léon Alfar compares it to an actor's preparation in the dressing room, the stretching and preparing for the upcoming performance that "seeks the phantasmatic state of mind and body enabling a masquerade."[21] This notion of the masquerade appropriately reflects the speech's function as Lady Macbeth's rejection of a submissive role, of putting on armour before entering the fight for power she so desperately strives for.

In order to illustrate the 'unnatural' cruelty with which she pursues her own ambition, critics almost always revert to "I have given suck" (1.7.54–59), a speech that is as powerful as it is alarming. Lisa Jardine places these lines within the misogynistic tradition of portraying female figures as unwomanly monsters at the very moment they are about to do something evil and, hence, 'unwomanly'. Medea, the murdering mother, is a prime example of what Jardine calls one of the "touchstones of classical not-womanhood."[22] Ever since her classical origin, this figure has proven both fascinating and horrifying. As Katherine Heavey explains in her study on the myth's early modern reception, onstage it originally served to horrify and repel particularly male audience members who saw themselves confronted with the threat of aberrant femininity.[23] In this case, the monologue has sparked the notorious question of "How many children had Lady Macbeth?" because it offers a rare if somewhat cryptic glimpse into the past. Otherwise, the scenario is purely hypothetical. As the play re-iterates so adamantly, the Macbeths are childless. Rather, the drastic image indicates the importance of her commitment to the cause. Macbeth's impressed, though no less disturbing, reaction to her speech shows that the strategy serves its purpose: "Bring forth men-children only! / For thy undaunted mettle should compose / Nothing but males" (1.7.73–75). Again, the play draws on the paradoxical ideal of an all-male world, which is why Adelman argues that it "curiously enacts the fantasy that it seems to deny: punishing Macbeth for his participation in a fantasy of escape from the maternal matrix, it nonetheless allows the audience the partial satisfaction of a dramatic equivalent to it."[24] Clearly, the term 'satisfaction' is ironic. Nothing could be less desirable than the ultraviolent all-male world evoked in *Macbeth*.

Similar to Ophelia's death, Lady Macbeth's suicide is associated with her madness. Her mental decline is often regarded as a mitigating factor, not condoning but at least lessening her 'evil'. The question of why she goes mad – whether of burdened guilt or estrangement from her sole confidant – has been given ample consideration. Sandra Clark and Pamela Mason detect in her madness "the symptoms of psychic distress, the 'torture of the mind', the sleeplessness, the guilt and fear, that had previously been Macbeth's."[25] The Doctor gives a different reason, believing that "More needs she the divine than the physician" (5.1.76). He understands her madness to be religious despair or the Devil's work, an association that reflects early modern abstractions of madness, hysteria, and related forms of mental illness.[26] Others return to her role of a troubled mother figure. Joanna Levin analyses her within the paradigm of the "pathology of the hysterical mother,"[27] and Catherine Couche even detects in her mad speech the symptoms of postnatal psychosis.[28] These latter analyses appear too narrowly fixated on the absence of children, reducing her to the role she seeks to emancipate herself from.

However, one line in particular indicates that, apart from the burdening guilt and resulting nightmares, her gender trouble is indeed key: "The Thane of Fife had a wife: where is she now?" (5.1.43–44). First and foremost, this is an unexpected reference to the murder of Lady Macduff and her children. For this reason, Clark and Mason propose that, contrary to what the text suggests, Lady Macbeth may be aware of these crimes.[29] Yet, within the dynamics of the play, she may just as well refer to herself. Compared to her formerly powerful presence, she is detached from and diminished by her husband. That way, this line also mourns the gradual extinction of all female voices within the play. Derek Cohen remarks that "[o]ne of the many disturbing facts about mad people is that they do not fit into the social, political or economic categories of class, race or gender. Their social loci are thus difficult to determine, and their relation to the social nexus remains unfixed and uncertain."[30] Through her madness, Lady Macbeth develops into an outcast of society, which is mirrored by her gradual exclusion from the play. Yet, even though her powerful presence in the opening scenes suggests the opposite, she is marginalised from the outset. There is no point at which she fits the male-controlled world of *Macbeth*. Within the logic of the play, it is, thus, no wonder that she falls victim to what Elaine Showalter calls a "female malady," a concept that equates the female body with irrationality.[31] Put differently, Lady Macbeth's madness is not the natural result of her guilty conscience. She is not a person but a dramatic character. Rather, Shakespeare makes her mad in order to mark her as 'Other'.

The sleepwalking scene is often read as utter loss of control, as argued by Adelman, who in this moment considers her "entirely absent to herself."[32] Since the sleepwalking scene precedes the news of Lady Macbeth's death, it would be possible to discount her suicide as a direct result of her madness, an action she has committed unconsciously in a moment of delusion. To argue thus would be to deny her any form of autonomy. More adequately, and again in analogy to Ophelia, her madness can be read with Michel Foucault, for whom the label 'mad' serves as a means of controlling and silencing transgressive voices.[33] Foucault's concept of madness as a social construct imposed by the hegemony is especially fitting since the doctor who forms a diagnosis is a representative of those social institutions who define madness. In this respect, it is telling that the male doctor cannot cure her. As Mark Thornton Burnett rightly insists, in her sleepwalking scene, Lady Macbeth continues her earlier opposition against patriarchal norms. "Far from a nadir," he writes, "this is Lady Macbeth's moment of triumph, and she displays strength and resolve as she continues the constraints of sexual difference."[34] Similar to Ophelia, other characters try to read Lady Macbeth, decipher her state of mind, and, hence, define her identity. But even in madness, she fights male control.

That Lady Macbeth's suicide is far from insignificant is supported by the fact that it is Shakespeare's invention, recorded by none of the (presumed) textual sources. While for the play as such, Shakespeare largely follows Holinshed's account of Macbeth in the *Chronicles*, he, furthermore, inserts material from the accounts of two other Scottish Kings: the murder of King Duff (here Macdonwald's murderous wife is a possible influence on Lady Macbeth) as well as King Kenneth II, who murders King Duff's son Malcolm to ensure that his own sons will be kings. Possibly even the account of King Nathoclus, who is murdered by his servant after a witch prophecy, serves as a hypotext.[35] Lady Macbeth features in no more than one brief sentence, and so she is almost exclusively Shakespeare's creation.[36] In Shakespeare's play, the news of her death arrives suddenly, announced by the simple "The Queen, my Lord, is dead" (5.5.16). Also, the news is immediately preceded by the offstage cries of women who do not otherwise appear in the play, which further highlights the strict separation of men and women. Burnett reads these cries as "a female unity, an attempt to find an authentic language" that disrupts the masculine nature of the impeding battle.[37] In addition to this literal rise of the female voice, cries also suggest that Lady Macbeth must have died an unexpected, violent death. But since her suicide happens offstage, the audience do not learn that she has supposedly killed herself until Malcolm's concluding speech: "his fiend-like Queen, / Who, as 'tis thought, by self and violent hands / Took off her life" (5.9.35–37). Until this line, there is no more information as to the nature of her death. Like both the witches and Lady Macduff, she simply disappears from the play. Whereas Macbeth's head is brought onstage as a kind of trophy body, hers is not. Also, there are no indications as to how she killed herself. In the case of both Ophelia and Portia, Shakespeare offers a precise description of how they have died. Given Lady Macbeth's essential role in the play, this remains a peculiar lacuna.

This gap in the text leaves much room for speculation, and often directors or actors feel they have to decide on a specific method that seems appropriate for Lady Macbeth's suicide. Sian Thomas, who played the role in a 2004 production with the RSC (dir. Dominic Cooke), believed it fitting for Lady Macbeth to kill herself in a re-enactment on the murder of Duncan, only this time on herself.[38] In Roman Polanski's 1971 adaptation, Lady Macbeth commits suicide by throwing herself out of a window into the courtyard. In Justin Kurzel's 2015 film version, she does not kill herself at all – at least there are no indications that she might have. Whereas Polanski shows only a brief glimpse of her corpse, Kurzel dwells on her a little longer, draped peacefully and effigy-like on the bed. Rather unusual for a theatrical production, Lucy Bailey's 2010 production at Shakespeare's Globe, too, displayed the dead Lady Macbeth. In an interview, Bailey expressed unease with keeping the body hidden and losing the visual impact of a display, so the bloodied corpse was brought back onto the stage and later carried away through the audience.[39] No matter which solution they provide, all of these examples document a certain discomfort with Lady Macbeth's reported suicide; it is too significant to be passed over as a side note, and the lack of more specific information is too unsatisfying. If by not showing her dead body and withholding the exact circumstances of her death the play builds up a tension that audiences struggle with, this is a key moment in which *Macbeth* interrogates its own structures and implications.

Considering the question of why Lady Macbeth dies offstage, it is worth reviewing the case of Ophelia. Both women die, and in both cases, it is indicated that they have killed themselves. But, whereas scholars frequently construe Ophelia's death as a tragic accident, Lady Macbeth's death is almost always considered intentional. Surely, this is symptomatic of her critical reception. Whereas the innocent Ophelia is denied such drastic agency, in the case of Lady Macbeth, a figure of 'evil', the same action is considered a wilful decision. John Erskine Hankins also extends this logic to comparable female figures, arguing that, whereas Goneril's and Lady Macbeth's suicides mark "the horrible climax to a series of wicked deeds," Ophelia and Portia are "weak rather than morally responsible."[40] Thus, like most critics, Hankins acknowledges Lady Macbeth's agency, in her suicide as in the play at large. Yet, since this agency finds its expression in evil deeds, it must be silenced again.

In addition to Ophelia's triple marginalisation from the play – her being a woman in a tragedy, the label 'mad', and her merely reported death – for Lady Macbeth, the play holds a fourth stigmatising label of exclusion: "fiend-like." This argument of her offstage death as a form of censorship, of punishing the character for her transgressions by denying her the dramatic attention she strives for, equally works if one wanted to make a point of her being victimised this way. In Adelman's view, for instance, Lady Macbeth's suicide signals defeat because "by the end, she is so diminished a character that we scarcely trouble to ask ourselves whether the report of her suicide is accurate or not."[41] Thus, if considered in isolation, Lady Macbeth's offstage suicide could be taken as proof of tragedy's gender bias. If considered in contrast to Macbeth's death and his explicit rejection of suicide, however, such a defeatist conclusion with regard to her level of agency seems premature. Compared to his final appearance, beheaded and paraded around by Malcolm's army, her exit can at least be interpreted as voluntary.

"Why Should I Play the Roman Fool": Macbeth's Rejection of Suicide

The question of why Macbeth does not kill himself has received little critical attention, but those who do engage in the debate refer to a variety of possible reasons. Melvyn Donald Faber takes issue with Ribner, who argues that Shakespeare intentionally denies Macbeth "the heroic gesture of suicide which he grants to Brutus and Othello" because Macbeth's gruesome death much more appropriately mirrors his moral corruption.[42] Faber's response is that Shakespeare "did not deprive Macbeth of a glorious voluntary death. He found it impossible, from the strictly dramatic point of view, to accord him one" because "he hat [sic] gotten himself into a position which made the employment of self-murder as a cathartic vehicle unthinkable."[43] Ribner's and Faber's arguments are problematic for one particular reason. Both presuppose that suicide is always necessarily heroic, reducing all suicides in Shakespeare's plays to a simple formula: the 'good' characters (like Brutus and Othello) get heroic and redemptive suicides, and the 'bad' ones (like King Lear and Macbeth) do not. However, Shakespeare's suicides are neither always glorious nor solely heroic or a cathartic vehicle, as for example the deaths of Hamlet, Cassius, Antony, as well as all female suicides in the canon imply.

Just like Horatio's claim that he is "more an antique Roman than a Dane," Macbeth's refusal to "play the Roman fool" is an explicit reference to the Roman image of suicide. Yet, unlike Horatio, who expresses a longing for these former values, Macbeth distances himself from the Roman context. The question sounds rhetorical; for him, suicide would be foolish, and so he rebuffs the classical associations of honour, nobility, and valour. On the one hand, this rejection speaks of a shift in how to define honour. Kenneth Muir investigates the play's inconclusive uses of the term, which continuously oscillates between a military sense of the term, free honours, and mere mouth-honour.[44] In the late sixteenth and early seventeenth centuries, the term underwent a major change of emphasis until the exact connotation was blurred. Alice Shalvi illustrates that 'honour' effectively became synonymous with 'reputation', a development she identifies as one of Shakespeare's essential points of dramatic interest and criticism.[45] On the other hand, one could argue that Macbeth rejects these positive connotations because he knows that he does not deserve them. He has lost all claims to honour and nobility the moment he murdered Duncan. Alternatively, such values are simply not part of his world picture. For this reason, Macbeth appears a remarkably modern figure, much closer to a twenty-first-century context than to those of ancient Rome, medieval Scotland, or the Renaissance.

According to Jan Kott, for Macbeth suicide is not an option because it is always "either a protest, or an admission of guilt. Macbeth does not feel guilty, and there is nothing for him to protest about."[46] It is true that unlike Shakespeare's other tragic heroes, Macbeth is clear-sighted about his situation. He does not occupy himself with self-delusion, trying to justify his crimes: "I am in blood / Stepp'd in so far, that, should I wade no more, / Returning were as tedious as go o'er" (3.4.135–137). This line echoes a much earlier play, that is, Richard III's "I am in / So far in blood that sin will pluck on sin" (*R3* 4.2.63–64). *Richard III* follows the same trajectory – a tyrant murdering his way to the throne. But while *Macbeth* also depicts the hero's emotional journey, Richard remains largely detached.[47] Even though Richard is a much more static character, he forms an earlier version of Macbeth. His character anticipates Macbeth's conflict and his fragmentation. Richard neither commits suicide nor explicitly talks about it, but at the end of the play, he expresses a nihilism similar to that found in Macbeth:

> What do I fear? Myself? There's none else by;
> Richard loves Richard, that is, I and I.
> Is there a murderer here? No. Yes, I am!
> Then fly. What, from myself? Great reason, why?
> Lest I revenge? What, myself upon myself?
>
> (*R3* 5.3.183–187)

The almost schizophrenic repetition of "I," "myself," and particularly the phrase "myself upon myself" brings to mind Narcissus. As Eric Langley defines the parallel between suicide and narcissism already discussed with regard to Othello, both the narcissist and the suicide exhibit a tendency towards self-absorption and self-assertion because both aim at an individuation from society. In doing so, Langley explains, they strive to form an identity that is dependent on the self, but the construction of identity is naturally dependent on the reflection by others.[48] This is precisely the paradox Richard addresses in his speech. Whereas Macbeth at least initially relies on his wife as a figure of alterity that helps him form an identity, Richard remains isolated from the beginning. Despite several such caricature-like qualities, Richard is given a moment of *anagnorisis*. His famous "A horse! A horse! My kingdom for a horse" (*R3* 5.4.7) acknowledges that he is destined to lose the battle. As Florian

Kläger remarks with regard to Richard's awareness of his own meta-dramatic determinacy, the play emphasises the dialogic nature of the relationship between Richard, the chronicles, the audience, and finally Richard's own historiographical presence.[49] Richard is trapped within his own play. Macbeth, on the other hand, is not. There is no point at which he recognises that he is betrayed by a larger mechanism or ideology. Macbeth's dilemma is self-imposed, and the reason lies at least partly within his corrupted understanding of gender roles.

Jarold Ramsey stresses the subtlety with which the play alternately confirms and undermines "the paradoxes of self-conscious 'manhood',"[50] but the first image of Macbeth conveyed by the text is not exactly subtle. The second scene opens with Duncan's "What bloody man is that?" (1.2.1), a line that is often named programmatic of the entire play and that could just as well refer to Macbeth as to the bleeding captain.[51] *Macbeth* opens and closes with celebrations of military bravery, and even though its eponymous hero is hailed as the ideal warrior, his first description of a man that kills with "brandish'd steel, / Which smok'd with bloody execution" and slashes his opponents "from the nave to th'chops" (1.2.17–22) is not wholly positive. Although Duncan responds to this news with admiration, the image conveyed here is more that of a brutal murdering machine – the butcher that Malcolm speaks of in his concluding speech. Macbeth's first coherent monologue reveals that he already has murder on his mind. The witches' prophecies and their implications are literally hair-raising: "If good, why do I yield to that suggestion / Whose horrid image does unfix my hair, / And make my seated heart knock at my ribs" (1.3.134–136). Far from being rhetorical, this question as much anticipates an audience response as it verbalises Macbeth's state of mind. What the text, therefore, makes clear right at the beginning is that masculinity, as well as its related associations of valour and military honour, is portrayed as an ambivalent concept and one that needs closer scrutiny as the play progresses.

Similarly to Macbeth's initial appearance, Lady Macbeth's first description of her husband as a coward, too, betrays a distorted, perverted understanding of manliness. But, whereas he initially opposes her view and declares "I dare do all that may become a man; / Who dares do more, is none" (1.7.46–47) immediately after his wife's "Unsex me" speech, Macbeth adopts her idea of manhood. This excludes any kind of alleged weakness, that is, moral considerations and conscience. For Macbeth, social convention defines man as ambitious, ultraviolent, and ruthless. As a result, he generates and repeats exaggerated gender performances in order to create the impression of an über-masculine gender core. This may be against his intuition – hence his initial wavering – but he adopts this idea nonetheless. Macbeth's ensuing transformation into a murdering machine does not come as a surprise. The laconic but simultaneously boastful way in which he describes how he will "give to th'edge o'th' sword" (4.1.151) Macduff's children is disturbing. Within the logic of succession, it is no wonder that Macbeth turns his aggression against Macduff's wife and children since his own lack of heirs is the root of his insecurity. His crown is "fruitless", and his sceptre remains "barren" (3.1.60–61), which makes him a weak ruler and questions his manhood. Ergo, Adelman's seminal reading of the play's analogies between political power and sexual potency classifies Macbeth's excessive blood thirst as a "fantasy of escape" from maternal power and, hence, an attempt to erase all mother figures.[52]

In scholarly reception, Macbeth's reaction to the death of his wife is either seen as almost casual, especially in comparison to Macduff's reaction when hearing the news that Macbeth has slaughtered his wife and children,[53] or as utter nihilism and sign of an inner core that is already dead. Also, it is not entirely clear how to understand his "She should have died hereafter: / There would have been a time for such a word" (5.5.17–18). As Clark and Mason suggest, this could either mean that her death was inevitable anyway or that she has died prematurely. "The first interpretation, with 'should' meaning 'certainly would' suits Macbeth's nihilistic mood; the second, with 'should' meaning 'ought', accords with the play's many references to things done out of time."[54] Nihilism and life-weariness are undoubtedly reflected in the "Tomorrow, and tomorrow, and tomorrow" speech (5.5.19–28), which is triggered by the news of Lady Macbeth's death. In the final scenes, Macbeth resembles a monstrous creature and defines himself as such, drawing on the image of bear-baiting: "They have tied me to a stake: I cannot fly, / But, bear-like, I must fight the course" (5.7.1–2). Juliet Dusinberre emphasises that Shakespeare opposes an equation of masculinity with action, which in turn equally contradicts a concept of femininity as weak and unable to fight. "Physical strength," she writes, "is the attribute of a beast unless tempered by judgement."[55] Through cruelty and violence, Macbeth intends to masculinise himself, albeit at the cost – Dusinberre's words imply – of becoming less human.

Several critics consider Macbeth's death to be anticlimactic because it is not given the same dramatic presence as the deaths of Hamlet, Othello, or King Lear. In fact, it has no dramatic presence at all because Macbeth is killed and beheaded offstage. For Bamber, Macbeth's death, like that of Coriolanus, is "lacking in general significance" because they "simply exhaust the possibilities of their mode; they repeat themselves until, like Marlowe's Tamburlaine, they are dramatically played out. Then they die."[56] Arthur Kirsch has a different objection, arguing that although all tragic heroes are necessarily headed towards death, "in no other play is that movement so willfully life-denying, and for this reason *Macbeth* seems the least redemptive of Shakespeare's great tragedies."[57] One of the reasons as to why Macbeth's death might seem less redemptive than others is that he reclaims the audience's sympathy in the play's final moments. His outward brutality is juxtaposed with several soliloquies and other brief windows into his character that reveal a much more sensitive and resigning interior. A prime example is his realisation "I have liv'd long enough: my way of life / Is fall'n into the sere, the yellow leaf" (5.3.22–23). In view of lines such as this, Kirsch contends that "[i]t is common to say that Macbeth's ambition is suicidal. It may be more exact and revealing to recognize that nonbeing is his ambition, [...] that his deepest wish is to annihilate the very self he asserts."[58] But, whereas it is plausible to consider Macbeth's ambition suicidal insofar as it is deemed fatal from the outset, the question remains: if self-annihilation were his deepest wish, then why does Macbeth not kill himself?

Macbeth dies as a soldier in battle, and generally, warrior ethics are a dominant concern in the play.[59] When Macbeth kills young Siward, his father is relieved that he did not die while running away from his attacker. He proudly announces "Had I as many sons as I have hairs, / I would not wish them to a fairer death" (5.9.14–15). This, Siward suggests, is the ideal, heroic warrior death. With regard to Macbeth's own soldierly honour, Thomas McAlindon refers to Macbeth's final words: "I will try the last: before my body / I throw my warlike shield: lay on, Macduff; / And damn'd be him, that first cries, 'Hold, enough!'" (5.8.32–34). For McAlindon, this is "the epitaph that Macbeth gives himself," the words of a man who knows that he has exceeded his own limit.[60] In line with this interpretation, several actors have performed Macbeth's final line as self-damnation, following his general sense of life-weariness and portraying him as suicidal. Derek Jacobi (1993, dir. Adrian Noble), for instance, interpreted Macbeth's "I have liv'd long enough" as a reflection on whether he should kill himself: "I had the dagger in my hand and the idea occurred of simply ending it all – I wonder why I don't just kill myself – until the thought was interrupted by Seyton's entrance and a little of the old blood starts coursing around again."[61] Eventually, Jacobi's Macbeth chose an (ironically rather Roman) onstage suicide, running into Macduff's sword after having uttered his final lines. Simon Russell Beale (2005, dir. John Caird) felt that to play Macbeth as suicidal would essentially contradict the feeling of invincibility he exudes. Nevertheless, the production opted for a form of assisted suicide that Macbeth tricked Macduff into because at this point, survival is no longer preferable to death.[62] Will Keen's Macbeth (2010, dir. Declan Donnellan) died a similar death, surrendering to Macduff and then running into what in this prop-free production was imagined to be Macduff's sword.

Even though at this point of the action Macbeth's endeavour may justifiably be deemed self-destructive, envisioning him as suicidal implies a sense of closure or redemption that the play otherwise withholds. Besides, such a reading contravenes his previous decision against suicide.

Along these lines, Macbeth's "I will not yield, / To kiss the ground before young Malcolm's feet, / And to be baited with the rabble's curse" (5.8.27–29) sounds familiar. Horatio, Cleopatra, and Antony, too, express an unwillingness to be led in captivity, yet they all state this as their main motivation for suicide. Macbeth is neither a Roman nor does he want to play the "Roman fool." Within his worldview, a man does not kill himself. Instead, he will "try the last," namely stand up to Macduff and never surrender.

Not only critics, but directors too, have found Macbeth's death to be anticlimactic and, thus, frequently change the play's ending, so much so that today the final scene is rarely performed according to the original text.[63] Macbeth's death has nothing of the tragic grandeur attached to the deaths of Othello or Lear. Instead, he dies offstage in order for his head to be exhibited in the final scene. Besides, Macbeth is the only great tragic hero without a dying speech. David Garrick in particular regretted this ostensible lack and, hence, interpolated a dying speech that, in true Restoration fashion, separates right from wrong and paves the way for a re-instigation of the political order.[64] Such a revision, however, obscures the ending's effect. In order to achieve his ambition to rule, Macbeth adopts the role of what he considers the most masculine of all men. Within his concept of masculinity, suicide is unthinkable. But his gender performance is so hyperbolic and distorted that it inevitably destroys him. His death is appropriately drastic: he ends the play as a severed head, possibly displayed on a pole. Thus, Macbeth remains not more than a strategically necessary deterrent – a visual premonition of the grisly end awaiting all traitors to the state.

Macbeth's development of power relations is often read as chiastic. The hero's power increases, whereas Lady Macbeth gradually diminishes into total decline and disappears from the play. When taking a look at the way the two deaths are juxtaposed, though, this trajectory is too simplistic. Macbeth succumbs to the play's hegemony by adopting conventional gender norms he exaggerates to the extreme, a strategy that leads to his decapitation and even pushes him off the stage. For Macbeth, the heroic warrior, "trying the last" indicates perseverance. For his wife, it means suicide in order to emancipate herself from the patriarchal stranglehold that has no room for female ambition or power. If her reported death initially suggests a denial of agency and lack of dramatic interest in her, this interpretation is fostered by the complex manner in which critical reception defines her female agency. She is attributed agency, but since this agency enables her to commit evil deeds, it is re-defined and, through associations with diabolical obsession and madness, taken away again. Shakespeare seems to do the same, first exploring the limits of female power and then punishing her for her transgressive actions by writing her off. However, the text does not leave it at that; the textual blank concerning the manner of her suicide breeds curiosity rather than disinterest. To say that her offstage death either punishes her or denies her the limited agency she has left would be to draw a premature conclusion, especially when compared to the death of Macbeth. That he has to be beheaded necessitates an offstage death, but in terms of sheer dramatic presence, he dies as marginalised as his wife. Unlike her husband, whose head is gruesomely exhibited onstage, Lady Macbeth is spared this display. In this way, Shakespeare writes her a dignified, self-determined exit, fitting for the central role she takes in the play.

Notes

1 Derek Cohen, *Shakespeare's Culture of Violence* (Ipswich and New York: St. Martin's, 1993), 127.
2 Angela Pitt, *Shakespeare's Women* (Newton Abbot: David & Charles, 1981), 68; 70.
3 Rowland Wymer, *Suicide and Despair in the Jacobean Drama* (Brighton: Harvester, 1986), 56.
4 Irving Ribner, *Patterns in Shakespearian Tragedy* (1960; reprint; London and New York: Routledge, 2005), 162.
5 Kenneth Muir, Introduction to *Macbeth*, by William Shakespeare, ed. Kenneth Muir, The Arden Shakespeare Second Series, 2nd ed. (London: Arden Shakespeare, 1997), lviii.
6 Linda Bamber, *Comic Women, Tragic Men: A Study of Gender and Genre in Shakespeare* (Stanford: Stanford University Press, 1982), 3
7 Ibid.
8 On the stage history of Lady Macbeth, see Russ McDonald, *Look to the Lady: Sarah Siddons, Ellen Terry, and Judi Dench on the Shakespearean Stage* (Athens and London: The University of Georgia Press, 2005). On different actors' approaches to playing Lady Macbeth, see Alan Hughes "Lady Macbeth: A Fiend Indeed?" *Southern Review* 11 (1978): 107–112; Sinead Cusack, "Lady Macbeth's Barren Sceptre," in *Clamorous Voices: Shakespeare's Women Today*, ed. Carol Rutter (London: The Women's Press, 1988), 53–72; Sian Thomas, "Lady Macbeth," in *Performing Shakespeare's Tragedies Today: The Actor's Perspective*, ed. Michael Dobson (Cambridge: Cambridge University Press, 2006), 95–105.
9 Joanne Addison Roberts, "Sex and the Female Tragic Hero," in *The Female Tragic Hero in English Renaissance Drama*, ed. Naomi Conn Liebler (New York and Basingstoke: Palgrave, 2002), 204.
10 On the witches and Lady Macbeth, see Peter Stallybrass, "*Macbeth* and Witchcraft," in *Focus on Macbeth*, ed. John Russell Brown (Boston: Routledge, 1982), 189–209; Dympna Callaghan, "Wicked Women in *Macbeth*: A Study of Power, Ideology, and the Production of Motherhood," in *Reconsidering the Renaissance: Papers from the Twenty-First Annual Conference*, ed. Mario Di Cesare (Binghamton, NY: Medieval & Renaissance Texts & Studies, 1992), 355–369.
11 Mark Breitenberg, *Anxious Masculinity in Early Modern England* (Cambridge: Cambridge University Press, 1996), 35–68. Although blood was understood in a number of contradictory ways with regard to gender, one of its primary connotations was an affinity with sperm, "a form of rarefied, heated blood (a sort of ultra-blood) that, since Aristotle, represented the masculine principle" (49).

12 Dale Townshend, "Unsexing Macbeth," in *Macbeth: A Critical Reader*, ed. John Drakakis and Dale Townshend (London: Arden Shakespeare, 2013), 183.

13 See also Phyllis Rackin, "Staging the Female Body: Maternal Breastfeeding and Lady Macbeth's 'Unsex Me Here'," in *Corps/Décors: Femmes, Orgie, Parodie*, ed. and intro. Catherine Nesci et al. (Amsterdam: Rodopi, 1999), 17–29; Chelsea Phillips, "'Unsex Me Here': Bodies and Femininity in the Performance History of Lady Macbeth," *Testi e Linguaggi* 7 (2013): 353–361.

14 Judith Butler, *Bodies That Matter: On the Discursive Limits of 'Sex'* (London and New York: Routledge, 1993), 10.

15 Alexander Leggatt, *Shakespeare in Performance: King Lear* (Manchester: Manchester University Press, 1991), 193.

16 On the different interpretations of this line see the note to l. 48 in the Arden Third Series. Cf. also Alice Fox, "Obstetrics and Gynecology in *Macbeth*," *Shakespeare Studies* 12 (1979): 129. Phillips's "'Unsex Me Here'" looks at this particular passage through performance history.

17 Janet Adelman, *Suffocating Mothers: Fantasies of Maternal Origin in Shakespeare's Plays, Hamlet to The Tempest* (New York: Routledge, 1992), 135.

18 Callaghan, "Wicked Women in *Macbeth*," 369.

19 Judith Butler, *Gender Trouble: Feminism and the Subversion of Identity* (London and New York: Routledge, 1990), 202–203.

20 James Loxley, *Performativity*, The New Critical Idiom (London and New York: Routledge, 2007), 140.

21 Christina Alfar León, *Fantasies of Female Evil: The Dynamics of Gender and Power in Shakespearean Tragedy* (Newark: University of Delaware Press, 2003), 125–126.

22 Lisa Jardine, *Still Harping on Daughters: Women and Drama in the Age of Shakespeare* (Brighton: Harvester, 1983), 96.

23 Katherine Heavey, *The Early Modern Medea. Medea in English Literature, 1558–1688* (Basingstoke and New York: Palgrave, 2015), 12. See also Stephanie Chamberlain, "Fantasizing Infanticide: Lady Macbeth and the Murdering Mother in Early Modern England," *College Literature* 32.3 (2005): 72–91.

24 Adelman, *Suffocating Mothers*, 140.

25 Sandra Clark and Pamela Mason, Introduction to *Macbeth*, by William Shakespeare, ed. Sandra Clark and Pamela Mason, The Arden Shakespeare Third Series (London: Arden Shakespeare, 2015), 11.

26 Carol Thomas Neely, "Documents in Madness: Reading Madness and Gender in Shakespeare's Tragedies and Early Modern Culture," in *Shakespearean Tragedy and Gender*, ed. Shirley Nelson Garner and Madelon Sprengnether (Bloomington: Indiana University Press, 1996), 327. See also Paul H. Kocher, "Lady Macbeth and the Doctor," *Shakespeare Quarterly* 5.4 (1954): 341–349.

27 Joanna Levin, "Lady Macbeth and the Daemonologie of Hysteria," *ELH* 69.1 (2002): 38.

28 Christine Couche, "A Mind Diseased: Reading Lady Macbeth's Madness," in *Word and Self Estranged in English Texts, 1550–1660*, ed. Philippa Kelly and L. E. Semler (Farnham: Ashgate, 2010), 135–148.

29 *Macbeth*, ed. Sandra Clark and Pamela Mason, The Arden Shakespeare Third Series (London: Arden Shakespeare, 2015), note to 5.1.45.

30 Derek Cohen, *The Politics of Shakespeare* (New York: St. Martin's, 1993), 124.

31 Elaine Showalter, *The Female Malady: Women, Madness, and English Culture, 1830–1980* (London: Virago, 2008), 4.

32 Adelman, *Suffocating Mothers*, 145.

33 Michel Foucault, *Madness and Civilization: A History of Insanity in the Age of Reason* (1964; reprint; New York: Vintage, 1988), 38–64.

34 Mark Thornton Burnett, "The 'Fiend-Like Queen': Rewriting Lady Macbeth," *Parergon* 11.1 (1993): 16.

35 On the play's possible sources see Clark and Mason, Introduction to *Macbeth*, 82–97; Jonathan Goldberg, "Speculations: *Macbeth* and Source," in *Shakespeare Reproduced: The Text in History and Ideology*, ed. and intro. Jean E. Howard and Marion F. O'Connor (New York: Methuen, 1987), 242–264.

36 Raphael Holinshed, *Holinshed's Chronicles*, vol. ii, 170/2/52, quoted in W. G. Boswell-Stone, *Shakespeare's Holinshed: The Chronicle and the Plays Compared* (New York: Dover, 1968): "The words of the three weird sisters also (of whom before ye haue heard) greatlie incouraged him herevnto, but speciallie his wife lay sore vpon him to attempt the thing, as she that was verie ambitious, burning in vnquenchable desire to beare the name of a queene" (25).

37 Burnett, "Rewriting Lady Macbeth," 17.

38 Thomas, "Lady Macbeth," 105.

39 "Lucy Bailey on the Scottish Play," *Theatre Voice*, podcast audio, May 21, 2010, accessed May 4, 2017, http://www.theatrevoice.com/audio/lucy-bailey-on-the-scottish-play/.

40 John Erskine Hankins, "Suicide in Shakespeare," in *The Character of Hamlet and Other Essays*, ed. John Erskine Hankins (Chapel Hill: University of North Carolina Press, 1941), 234.

41 Adelman, *Suffocating Mothers*, 145.

42 Ribner, *Patterns in Shakespearian Tragedy*, 167.

43 Melvyn Donald Faber, "Suicide in Shakespeare" (PhD diss., University of California, 1963), 493.

44 Muir, Introduction to *Macbeth*, xlv.

45 Alice Shalvi, "'Honor' in *Troilus* and *Cressida*," *SEL* 5.2 (1965): 283. See also Mervyn James, *Society, Politics and Culture: Studies in Early Modern England* (Cambridge: Cambridge University Press, 1986), particularly 308–413. On a dramatic discussion of the concept, see Charles Laurence Barber, *The Idea of Honour in the English Drama 1591–1700* (Stockholm: Almqvist and Wiksell, 1957).

46 Jan Kott, *Shakespeare Our Contemporary* (London: Routledge, 1991), 77–78.

47 On the overall parallels between the two plays, see Margaret Hotine, "*Richard III* and *Macbeth* – Studies in Tudor Tyranny?" *Notes and Queries* 38.4 (1991): 480–486; Marta Gibińska, "Villains on the Throne. Some Remarks on the Dramatic Craft of *Richard III* and *Macbeth*," in *Word and Action in Drama*, ed. Günter Ahrends et al. (Trier: WVT, 1994), 81–91. On the related question of conscience in *Richard III* see Claudia Olk, "Performing Conscience in *Richard III*," *Anglia* 130.1 (2012): 1–18; Daniel E. Hughes, "The 'Worm of Conscience' in *Richard III* and *Macbeth*," *The English Journal* 55.7 (1966): 845–852.

48 Langley, *Narcissism and Suicide in Shakespeare and His Contemporaries* (Oxford: Oxford University Press, 2009), 1.

49 Florian Kläger, *Forgone Nations. Constructions of National Identity in Elizabethan Historiography and Literature: Stanihurst, Spenser, Shakespeare* (Trier: WVT, 2006), 190.

50 Jarold Ramsey, "The Perversion of Manliness in *Macbeth*," *SEL* 13.2 (1973): 286.

51 See Coppélia Kahn, *Man's Estate: Masculine Identity in Shakespeare* (Berkeley: University of California Press, 1981), 150–192; Adrian Streete, "'What Bloody Man Is that?': Questioning Biblical Typology in *Macbeth*," *Shakespeare* 5.1 (2009): 18–35. Street reads this line as echoing Psalm 5.

52 Adelman, *Suffocating Mothers*, 131. On the relationship between performances of masculinity and politics see Amanda Bailey, "Occupy Macbeth: Masculinity and Political Masochism in *Macbeth*," in *Violent Masculinities: Male Aggression in Early Modern Texts and Culture*, ed. Jennifer Feather and Catherine E. Thomas (New York and Basingstoke: Palgrave, 2013), 191–212.

53 See Bamber, *Comic Women, Tragic Men*, 94.

54 Clark and Mason's note to 5.5.16 in the Arden Third Series.

55 Juliet Dusinberre, *Shakespeare and the Nature of Women* (London and Basingstoke: Macmillan, 1975), 285.

56 Bamber, *Comic Women, Tragic Men*, 96.

57 Arthur Kirsch, *The Passions of Shakespeare's Tragic Heroes* (Charlottesville: University of Virginia Press, 1990), 100–101.

58 Ibid., 96.

59 See Donald R. Riccomini, "Warrior Ethic in *Macbeth* and *Henry V*," *The Upstart Crow* 30 (2011): 42–66; Franziska Quabeck, *Just and Unjust Wars in Shakespeare* (Berlin: de Gruyter, 2013), 196–201.

60 Thomas McAlindon, *Shakespeare's Tragic Cosmos* (Cambridge: Cambridge University Press, 1991), 212.

61 Derek Jacobi, "Macbeth," in *Players of Shakespeare 4: Further Essays in Shakespearean Performance by Players with the Royal Shakespeare Company*, ed. Robert Smallwood (Cambridge: Cambridge University Press, 1998), 209.

62 Simon Russel Beale, "Macbeth," in *Performing Shakespeare's Tragedies Today: The Actor's Perspective*, ed. Michael Dobson (Cambridge: Cambridge University Press, 2006), 118.

63 See Clark and Mason, Introduction to *Macbeth*, 116. They cite a number of productions that have either cut Young Siward's death or made considerable cuts to the final scene.

64 Simon Williams, "Taking Macbeth out of Himself: Davenant, Garrick, Schiller and Verdi," in *Shakespeare Survey 57: Macbeth and Its Afterlife*, ed. Peter Holland (Cambridge: Cambridge University Press, 2004), 60. On other changes Garrick made to the play as well on its relation to an earlier adaptation by Davenant, see Williams 59–61. The speech inserted by Garrick reads: "'Tis done! The scene of life will quickly close. "Ambition's vain, delusive dreams are fled, / And now I wake to darkness, guilt and horror. / I cannot bear it! Let me shake it off. – / Twa' not be; my soul is clogged with blood. / I cannot rise! I dare not ask for mercy. / It is too late, hell drags me down. I sink, / I sink – Oh! – my soul is lost forever! / Oh! (*Dies*)" (Williams, "Taking Macbeth out of Himself," 60).

8 Well Done

Antony and Cleopatra

Antony and Cleopatra marks Shakespeare's final and in many ways quintessential dramatisation of suicide. Coincidentally, it also showcases the highest amount of suicides. Apart from the title characters, Eros, Charmian, and Iras all kill themselves next to their respective master and mistress. And although not presented as a suicide, some even consider Enobarbus's death within the same context.[1] The play not only puts emphasis on the preparations for suicide as well as its executions, but also carefully distinguishes between male and female suicides. Whereas female suicide is described as a clean, graceful act that leaves the body almost undamaged, male bodies end up as what Barbara Hodgdon aptly summarises as "broken, ruptured, mangled."[2] The false rumour of Cleopatra's suicide and the two protagonists' actual suicides immediately remind of *Romeo and Juliet*, although re-imagined with a change of key. Accordingly, the play's comic elements, both in the generic and tonal sense, have received extensive commentary.[3] Unlike Romeo and Juliet, Antony and Cleopatra die separately. Whereas Antony already kills himself in 4.15, Cleopatra stays alive until the final scene. The preparations and execution of her suicide are dragged out over the entire fifth act; conventionally, this prominent position is reserved for the tragic hero.

In this reversal of traditional tragic power structures, the masculine world of *Julius Caesar* is challenged by feminine Egypt. Antony finds himself trapped between the two. As Coppélia Kahn remarks, the Rome of *Antony and Cleopatra* is "a Rome drawn to, repelled by, and finally fused with what is Other to it."[4] Taking this fusion of the masculine and feminine as its starting point, this chapter explores how the play repeatedly evokes the ideal of Roman suicide with its associations of honour and male heroism only to undermine it again. Cleopatra's and Antony's suicides are defined in opposition to one another: hers, Shakespeare's most assertive depiction of suicide as a deliberate, carefully choreographed gesture; his, an awkward show of compromised masculinity. While this noteworthy contrast sustains the generic experiment, both in terms of potentially comic tone and an inversion of traditional power structures, I do not suggest that Antony's suicide belittles or degrades him. Rather, the fact that here – like in *Julius Caesar* – it is the female suicide that most deserves the label 'Roman death' challenges the concept of Roman masculinity itself, exposing it as mere rhetoric and cliché. Moreover, since ultimately both suicides achieve the desired effect, I will show that most distinctly of all, this play exploits the quality of what Amy Delynne Craig calls the "power of suicide as a message" and, thereby, establishes suicide as a powerful communicative act.[5]

"After the High Roman Fashion": Cleopatra's Final Victory

Antony and Cleopatra are never alone onstage. Their entire relationship is played out to willing audiences, inside and outside the realm of the play. Within this context of artistry and self-fashioning, Cleopatra's suicide forms her masterpiece. Like Juliet, she gets two suicides – one a stratagem she plays on Antony and the other real. The former, originally Charmian's idea, is presented in the form of a reported death. She gives orders to "Say that the last I spoke was 'Antony', / And word it, prithee, piteously. Hence, Mardian, / And bring me how he takes my death" (4.13.8–10). The strategy of concocting a false death is a conventionally comic trope. In *Much Ado About Nothing* and *All's Well That Ends Well*, Claudius and Bertram, both of who have wronged their respective heroines, are tricked into believing that they have died and eventually realise their earlier mistakes. In the same way, Cleopatra suggests, the news that she has killed herself speaking his name will ease Antony's rage. As exemplified by her first line in the play, "If it be love indeed, tell me how much" (1.1.14), it is her utmost concern to see how Antony reacts, to test whether her emotional hold on him is strong enough. Also, it is a test of how far he will go in the belief that he has lost her. Still, her motivations are not entirely clear – would she in his place have considered suicide an appropriate reaction to the news of her death? If so, why would she take the risk of him killing himself? It seems that she underestimates his feelings because for her, suicide would not have been an option in that situation. Although with different intentions, Cleopatra's stratagem echoes the Friar's plan to spread the rumour of Juliet's death. With this precedent in mind, it is not surprising that, like the Friar's plan, Cleopatra's ploy goes awry. Whereas Romeo falls for the illusion of the seemingly dead Juliet, in Antony's case, the rumour alone is sufficient for him to commit suicide. He does not even question the report. Rather than contemplating the loss of Cleopatra, he feels the pressure to follow suit immediately and requite her presumed artful Roman gesture.

In this play, one suicide always implicates another. Consequently, the news of Antony's suicide affirms Cleopatra's decision to kill herself. From the beginning, she involves her entourage into the careful planning of her last dramatic gesture:

> All's but naught;
> Patience is sottish, and impatience does
> Become a dog that's mad. Then is it sin
> To rush into the secret house of death
> Ere death dare come to us? How do you, women?
> What, what, good cheer! Why, how now, Charmian!
> My noble girls! Ah, women, women! Look,
> Our lamp is spent, it's out. Good sirs, take heart.
> We'll bury him, and then what's brave, what's noble,
> Let's do't after the high Roman fashion
> And make death proud to take us. Come, away.
> This case of that huge spirit now is cold.
> Ah, women, women! Come, we have no friend
> But resolution and the briefest end.

> > (4.15.82–95)

The monologue opens with a reference to the moral value of suicide, a less explicitly religious phrasing of Hamlet's dilemma in the "Too solid flesh" speech. But Cleopatra's question is merely rhetorical; religious impediments are of no concern to the characters. Her domestic metaphor of "the secret house of death" appears paradoxical because unlike Antony's, in true "high Roman fashion" her own suicide is a public act. The final two lines suggest that suicide is the only way out now. However, she does not make it brief. As Robert Wilcher notes, the final act mirrors the classical structure of tragedy and, thereby, forms a contrast to the episodic and cinematic nature of the rest of the scenes.[6] While Antony's death is intermingled with the plotline of Enobarbus, her suicide sits at the centre of dramatic attention. Although the above monologue indicates a firm decision on suicide, Cleopatra's motivation remains opaque. Her "I am his fortune's vassal and I send him / The greatness he has got" (5.2.29–30) is clearly ironic, an attempt to lull Caesar into a false sense of security. She attempts to stab herself on the spot but is disarmed by Proculeius, who warns her "Do not abuse my master's bounty by / Th'undoing of yourself. Let the world see / His nobleness well acted" (5.2.42–44). These lines sound like an indirect appeal to commit suicide. If she had not made up her mind already, Proculeius's words would then convince Cleopatra that she has to die in order to avoid public humiliation.

Judging from her ironically submissive behaviour in this scene, this suicide attempt already seems to be part of the show she stages to trump Caesar. Yet, rather than revealing the details of her plan to the audience, Cleopatra only whispers them to Charmian, which increases dramatic tension. What she is very clear about, however, is her reason for committing suicide. Like Antony, she re-iterates her refusal to be led in triumph, fearing that she will see "Some squeaking Cleopatra boy [her] greatness / I' th' posture of a whore" (5.2.219–220). The most striking issue of this passage is, of course, the reference to cross-dressing as a theatrical convention. Generally, this reality complicates understanding the role of Cleopatra because, to a much greater degree than the other tragedies, the text is aware of the male actor behind the female role. As Juliet Dusinberre writes, the play shows "oscillating constructions of the masculine and the feminine which dominate not only the play, but the conditions of its reception in the consciousness of the audience."[7] In other words, the additional layer of gender confusion caused by the theatrical practices of cross-dressing questions the notion of gender on a meta-level: Shakespeare shows a Cleopatra who performs notions of masculinity while being the ultimate female. Yet, behind the mask of the male actor, Cleopatra's femininity, too, is a performance. This intricate layering eventually suggests that an essentialist and stable concept of 'woman' is, in Dympna Callaghan's words, "a classification of no more substantial existence than the most outlandish fiction."[8] Gender, both feminine and masculine, is exposed as performative according to Butler. But also, the above line highlights another aspect, as Phyllis Rackin indicates:

> Throughout, Cleopatra has been depicted as a showman: showing has been her great defect and also her consummate virtue. In this speech, and in the scene that follows, the question of her worth is directly associated with the question of the worth of shows. Here she seems to set the two at odds: only if we reject the shows we have seen can we accept the unseen greatness of Cleopatra. But in her suicide she will present a new show that validates both, and even in this speech the validation begins. The very fact that Cleopatra can talk about the show and claim that it is a poor parody implies that she has access to a level of reality beyond what has been presented. By implying the inadequacy of the representation, she implies also that she can transcend it.[9]

As Rackin makes clear, it is important not to dismiss Cleopatra's suicide as mere show and, therefore, dishonest spectacle. On the contrary, she is aware of its performance-like nature. She is able to control the performance, thereby making use of its communicative function to the full extent.

It is no exaggeration to say that Cleopatra's suicide forms a stark contrast to Antony's. But apart from its more graceful execution, the main difference to Antony's suicide is its careful planning. Involving her servants Iras and Charmian as dressers, she transforms herself into the stage manager of her own death and orders them "Show me, my women, like a queen. Go fetch / My best attires. I am again for Cydnus / To meet Mark Antony" (5.2.226–228). Marga Munkelt comments on the use of "like a queen" rather than 'as queen' and concludes that Cleopatra transforms herself into a visual monument. It is ironic, Munkelt notes, that in spite of her refusal to be impersonated by actors, Cleopatra, thus, creates a blueprint for all future enactments of the role.[10] This notion of theatricality regularly finds its way into performances of this scene. Whereas both Janet Suzman (1972, dir. Trevor Nunn) and Judi Dench (1987, dir. Peter Hall) transformed into golden statues, Frances de la Tour (1999, dir. Steven Pimlott) carefully applied heavy make-up. "Like *Madam Butterfly*'s brilliant impersonator or an Egyptian Norma Desmond preparing for her close-up, she staked out rights to her own performance, a consummate actor to the last."[11] To begin with, it seems that Cleopatra has turned her mind towards Antony again; no more words about her refusal to be outplayed by Caesar. On the other hand, her request for the "crown and all" (5.2.231) shows that she does not intend her suicide to be a private gesture that speaks of her love for Antony. Dressed in her royal insignia, she seeks to emphasise her political status and, thus, directly insult Caesar. In addition, Wymer remarks, the hint towards an impending reunion with Antony – indicated by lines such as "Husband, I come! (5.2.285) – only reinforces that for Cleopatra, erotic fulfilment and self-display are inseparably linked.[12] That way, her claim of the impending reunion with Antony equally works as a public, Roman gesture. The private and the political are merged into one grand final act.

Unlike Shakespeare, Plutarch remains unclear regarding Cleopatra's choice of weapon. The viper, so deeply rooted in cultural memory as Cleopatra's messenger of death, is only one of the possibilities he mentions.[13] First and foremost, the viper is a weapon that answers to the Roman ideal of bodily integrity. Suicide by poison enables Cleopatra to retain her beauty and grace, as Caesar notices (5.2.344–346). But, of course, Cleopatra is not a Roman empress, and so she appropriately chooses "the pretty worm of Nilus" (5.2.242). Beside its cultural implications, her weapon of choice is gendered. Whenever Shakespeare's characters revert to poison, this comparatively gentle weapon connotes femininity. However, all the others that poison themselves, or at least try to do so, are male. Romeo and Horatio are portrayed as effeminate, and their taking to poison is an indication of compromised masculinity. In Cleopatra's case, too, poison connotes femininity but not in the sense of a troubled gender identity. Throughout the play, she breaks the boundaries of conventional femininity while simultaneously remaining the 'ultimate woman'. With a conventionally feminine weapon as opposed to conventionally masculine resolution and execution, these two sides equally combine in her suicide. Here, too, they do not contradict but supplement each other.

Cleopatra comments on this gendered dimension by reaffirming her decision: "My resolution's placed, and I have nothing / Of woman in me. Now from head to foot / I am marble-constant" (5.2.237–239). On the one hand, her words suggest that she envisions both her suicide and the process of dying as a sensual experience. As Lisa Starks writes, "Cleopatra performs her suicide as an act of passionate love and erotic release – not as a sacrifice, like Antony, but as a transfiguration into an immortal goddess."[14] On the other hand, evocative of Lady Macbeth's "Unsex me here," she construes how death de-feminises her. She does not remodel herself as masculine but "marble-constant," thus eradicating the notion of gender altogether. After Lady Macbeth and Ophelia, Cleopatra is the third female character for whom this is envisioned as something positive, an emancipation from any constraints pertaining to their submissive gender role.

Although anticipating Cleopatra's suicide, it seems that in the final scene, the play is heading towards a comic ending. Similar to the gravediggers in *Hamlet*, the clown not only slows down the action but also forms a grotesque contrast to the severity of Cleopatra's action. More specifically, the scene provides comic relief by overtly delaying Cleopatra's suicide. She repeatedly asks him to leave, and her annoyance shows in her telling him "farewell" four times. She has to push him off the stage, as it were, thereby reclaiming her control over the scene. Secondly, the generic notion of comedy prevails because she perceives her death as a twofold comic resolution: she triumphs over Caesar and is reunited with her beloved Antony:

> Give me my robe. Put on my crown. I have
> Immortal longings in me. Now no more
> The juice of Egypt's grape shall moist this lip.
> [*The women dress her.*]
> Yare, yare, good Iras! Quick! Methinks I hear
> Antony call. I see him rouse himself
> To praise my noble act. I hear him mock
> The luck of Caesar, which the gods give men
> To excuse their after wrath. Husband, I come!
>
> (5.2.278–285)

Again, Cleopatra fashions herself as an actor getting ready for her final and decisive performance. She imagines Antony applauding her "noble act." Similarly, her "Husband, I come" speaks of a love suicide; yet, within the same line, she comes back to Caesar and the effect her suicide has on him. Clearly, the notion of an audience, no matter whether admiring or critical, is crucial to her self-concept. This striving for attention, together with the repeated insistence on her actions as noble and courageous, alienates rather than enthrals E. A. J. Honigmann. He questions the nobility of her suicide because "she tries too hard [...]. She not only gives the performance, she writes the programme-notes."[15] It is certainly justified, if not commendable, to question these ready-made interpretations of her suicide that she provides. Antony, Romeo, Brutus, and most notably Othello are all given final speeches in which they conveniently explain what to make of their suicides. All of them show at least a slight grain of self-delusion, the major difference to Cleopatra being that she sees herself as an actor. Despite his critical view, Honigmann acknowledges the self-consciousness with which she performs and concedes that Cleopatra differs from these tragic heroes "in being a self-conscious performer, as opposed to their unconscious self-dramatisation, which means, very nearly, that she is a conscious deceiver, therefore not a self-deceiver."[16] It is exactly this self-awareness that differentiates her and, as will be shown – in his wry self-commentary – also Antony from the rest of Shakespeare's suicides. As any gifted actor, Cleopatra is conscious of the effect of her performance.

The impression of a comic ending is furthermore bolstered by Cleopatra's initial reaction to Iras's suicide. Although clearly a gesture of absolute loyalty and love for her royal mistress, Cleopatra fears sexual competition: "If she first meet the curled Antony, / He'll make demand of her, and spend that kiss / Which is my heaven to have" (5.2.299–301). These words with which she positions the asp at her breast convey haste and frustration about this suicide *interruptus*. While other plays, most notably *Romeo and Juliet*, already draw a connection between the orgasm as sexual dying and actual death, Cleopatra's suicide goes a step further. Her final words have an ecstatic quality, imagining a symbolic reunion with her lover: "O Antony! [...] What should I stay – [*Dies*]" (5.2.310–311). In the words of Lorraine Helms, Cleopatra's suicide can, thus, be deemed "an achieved rite of passage through eroticism into marriage."[17] Cleopatra's last words evoke an additional image of sexual desire: a mother suckling her baby. Also, with the serpent on her breast she transforms into both Eve and Mary, which echoes the earlier biblical image of her holding the bleeding Antony in her arms. Together with the overall optimistic and eager tone in anticipating death, both these tropes – marriage as well as motherhood – indicate a comic rather than tragic conclusion.[18]

That Cleopatra's suicide is worthy of her status is made explicit by Charmian's eulogy. Echoing Antony's "I have done my work ill" (4.14.106) to the Guard's question "What work is here, Charmian? Is this well done?" Charmian replies "It is well done, and fitting for a princess / Descended of so many royal kings. / Ah, soldier!" (5.2.323–326). Accordingly, Caesar, who has previously named Cleopatra a whore, refers to the dead queen as "Bravest at the last" and "royal" (5.2.333–334). This eulogy also marks Charmian's final words. She dies almost mid-sentence. For Jonathan Bate, her death suggests a complex interiority, forming her into a full-fledged dramatic character rather than a mere cipher.[19] But more importantly, by concerning her last words with Cleopatra, Charmian dedicates her own suicide to her mistress. Iras's earlier death has to be understood along the same lines, even though she kills herself in anticipation of Cleopatra's suicide. Charmian and Iras's degree – their status as servants – demands subservience. Nonetheless, they are not bound to die with her. Whereas Brutus and Antony unsuccessfully try to command their subordinates to kill them by invoking the bond between servant and master, the two women do not need to be reminded of an oath they have sworn. Their loyalty to Cleopatra is absolute, and so they follow her into death without hesitation. Similarly to Titinius's and Eros's suicides out of loyalty towards Cassius and Antony respectively, Iras's and Charmian's deaths, thus, elevate Cleopatra even further and attest to her grandeur. Still, John Wilders is sceptical as to whether Cleopatra's suicide is a lasting triumph, arguing that it can be understood "as she wants us to see it, as a supreme and glorious sacrifice or as an extreme self-indulgence. As in his portrayal of Antony, Shakespeare does not allow us to respond in any simple way. We are at the same time drawn to and distanced from them both."[20] Wilders is right in arguing that her self-indulgent performance needs to be taken with a grain of salt. All of the suicides in the canon are surrounded by doubts. Sometimes – as in Cleopatra's case – a character's self-presentation requires scrutiny, sometimes the reports by others. It is this ambiguity, this need for interpretation, which makes suicide such a powerful tool of dramatic characterisation.

Death brings Cleopatra the desired reunion with Antony. Like their younger counterparts Romeo and Juliet, they are buried next to each other and, hence, united both physically and spiritually. Also, Caesar has to concede that he has been tricked. All has proceeded as Cleopatra intended, it seems. Hodgdon, however, calls attention to the final stage direction, which reads "*exeunt omnes, the soldiers bearing the dead bodies.*"[21] Thus, up to the concluding line spoken by Caesar, the three women's bodies would still be visible onstage and then carried out by Caesar's entourage. In *King Lear*, female bodies are carried back onto the stage, but here, all three suicides happen onstage. Both the dramatic focus and the audience's gazes are shifted towards these female deaths – a stage tableau that no longer casts them as secondary. Whereas in the original early-modern context their joint exodus was a necessary way of clearing the stage before the concluding jig, it simultaneously gives Caesar "the opportunity to put Cleopatra's body to his own political use, to write its history as his own."[22] This implies that in the very last moment of the play, Cleopatra loses the battle against tragedy. Her suicide does not thoroughly provide the comic ending she envisioned. After all, *Antony and Cleopatra* is a tragedy, a genre in which patriarchy is supposed to have the last word. But if looked at more closely, this last word is unusual: "No grave upon the earth shall clip in it / A pair so famous" (5.2.357–358). Fame rather than undying love or anything else seems to be their distinctive criterion, an epitaph that would presumably be much to Cleopatra's liking. So, as Mary Beth Rose rightly points out, it can be argued that through his eulogy of the pair, Caesar "is forced to accept and perpetuate their positive self-conceptions of their own suicides, rather than depriving their legend of triumphant meaning, as Antony does to Brutus with such ruthless success."[23] Caesar has the last word, but like her death, it is scripted by Cleopatra rather than himself. She evades his control even posthumously.

"I Have Done My Work Ill": Antony's Troubled Masculinity

Contrary to Cleopatra's death, Antony's suicide is often described in terms of ridicule. Still, critics are divided about whether it invites audience laughter and, thus, belittles him. Wilders writes that Antony "is most miserably degraded [...] in his failure to perform the decorous suicide which he attempts and which, in retrospect, he likes to think he has accomplished."[24] For Michael Neill, it is a moment of "shocking bathos," which "deliberately courts embarrassed laughter."[25] Reuben Brower, by contrast, holds that Antony's suicide eventually ennobles him, leaving "the audience with the feeling that greatness in victory and greatness in defeat are equally glorious, equally pitiable."[26] Jacqueline Vanhoutte takes a middle position, claiming that Shakespeare neither ridicules nor glorifies Antony's suicide; "instead, he depicts it in agonizing detail."[27] Her emphasis on the dramatic attention Antony's, and much more so Cleopatra's, suicide gets, is apt. No other play dramatises the process of preparing and carrying out a suicide so extensively. Most of these details are already present in North's translation of Plutarch, as is the notion of ridicule,[28] but Shakespeare's dialogue intensifies the grotesque even further. For Kahn, Antony's inadequate suicide is not so much an artistic failure as a tribute to the ideologically charged double status of suicide – its Roman connotations as opposed to those of the Renaissance. "Rather than dismissing Antony's death as a theatrical fiasco," she writes, "we would do better to identify the codes that gave meaning to Roman suicides, in order to determine how, filtered through Renaissance perspective, they might also configure Antony's."[29] What is at stake here, in other words, is not only Antony's own heroic masculinity, but also the ideological forces operating behind it. The concept of Roman suicide as such is put on trial.

The notion of ridicule adheres to Antony from the outset. On the one hand, the Antony encountered in the play is the ultimate warrior hero – the greatest general of all time. Even before his name is mentioned, Philo refers to "his goodly eyes, / That o'er the files and musters of the war / Have glowed like plated Mars" (1.1.2–4), thereby likening him to the god of war. He is the 'Herculean hero,' a Renaissance archetype of masculinity.[30] However, the Antony of *Antony and Cleopatra* deviates from these Roman standards of masculinity considerably. His "dotage" that "O'erflows the measure" (1.1.1–2) is mentioned in the opening line. He is regarded as effeminate – as lacking masculine dominance over her – and so the traditional power relations between the two are turned upside down. When Antony's ships flee the first battle at Actium, Scarus states that he "never saw an action of such shame. / Experience, manhood, honour, ne'er before / Did violate so itself" (3.10.22–24). When they also desert the second battle, his humiliation is so unbearable that he considers suicide for the first time. Yet, in the same manner that Romeo blames his apparent lack of masculinity on Juliet, Antony directs his rage at Cleopatra: "The witch shall die" (4.12.47). In this monologue, he draws on the death of Hercules, whom he claims as his ancestor.[31] First, his premonition "The shirt of Nessus is upon me" (4.12.43) is an indication that he is aware of the fact that death is unavoidable for him now. Second, it refers to his blaming Cleopatra. Analogous to Deianira, who mistakes the poisoned shirt for a love potion and, thereby, accidentally kills Hercules, Cleopatra has destroyed Antony with her emotional hold over him. But the crucial point at which Antony misjudges this convenient image is that like Deianira, Cleopatra has not "sold" him on purpose. In the face of Antony's shameful flight from the battle, suicide provides the opportunity of cutting his losses. By dying a Roman death, his reputation of the heroic Roman general would be at least partly restored. Yet, simultaneously, a suicide would acknowledge that his feelings for Cleopatra have defeated him, which in turn, would not qualify for (re)claiming nobility through suicide. His attempt to redeem his manhood, however, is further complicated by the fact that the execution of Antony's suicide does not meet the standard of a heroic Roman death.

Even though Antony first starts thinking about suicide after the shame of the second battle, it is the false report of Cleopatra's deaths that eventually prompts his action:

> All length is torture; since the torch is out,
> Lie down and stray no farther. Now all labour
> Mars what it does – yea, very force entangles
> Itself with strength. Seal then, and all is done.
> Eros! – I come, my queen – Eros! – Stay for me.
> Where souls do couch on flowers we'll hand in hand
> And with our sprightly port make the ghosts gaze.
> Dido and her Aeneas shall want troops,
> And all the haunt be ours. Come Eros! Eros!
>
> (4.14.47–55)

Within the context of Rome as a shame-oriented culture that uses the imminent threat of public disgrace as a mechanism to control and punish individuals,[32] a suicide to avoid said public disgrace would be acceptable, if not honourable. But Antony's suicidal thoughts are prompted by his despair and wish to be reunited with his lover, and such exclusively private emotions do not qualify for a noble death as per the classical concept of Roman suicide. Whereas Antony had previously felt that "the witch shall die," now his anger seems to be gone, and he idealises them as a couple. But while Virgil's Aeneas leaves Dido in order to become the founding father of Rome, Antony stays with his queen until the end. Antony and Cleopatra not only liken themselves to Virgil's couple, but also aim to transcend them; after all, Aeneas eventually prioritised his political mission over love. As Gordon Braden observes, this "invocation of Dido and Aeneas as a touchstone of undying love is bizarre," especially since Virgil portrays Dido's suicide as a spiteful and bitter rather than a romantic gesture.[33]

Competition remains a key element with Antony. He is driven by the desire to follow her example and even overtake her because he believes that through her alleged suicide, she has outdone him again, disgraced him, and shown him to lack "The courage of a woman" (4.14.61). First, he has ruined his masculine honour on the battlefield, and now, to make it worse, a woman has died in a traditionally masculine way. Echoing the earlier moment of cross-dressing, he rages that "She has robbed me of my sword" (4.14.23) – that is, his masculinity. Antony suggestively evokes the sword as an icon of 'Romanness', of being a soldier, and as phallus. As Craig suggests, he, thus, "exhibits a sense of the value not only of the theatrical presentation, but of the impression that the self-representation that is created will leave behind in history."[34] He needs to be remembered as man of the sword, a symbol now reduced to a mere prop he no longer carries. Even though he is wrong in believing that Cleopatra has 'conquered' herself, Antony confirms that he indeed lacks this courage to kill himself.

Like Brutus, he orders one of his servants to do so. He reminds him "Thou art sworn, Eros" (4.14.63) to release his master from "Th'inevitable prosecution of / Disgrace and horror" (4.14.66–67). The easiest way to avoid disgrace and horror would be a straightforward suicide. With his "Thou strik'st not me; 'tis Caesar thou defeat'st" (4.14.69) Antony tries to ease Eros's burden by referring to the greater political good of such a deed, but his encouragement towards Eros seems at least as much, if not more, directed at himself. It can only be deemed ironic that this servant's name, which Antony so excessively repeats throughout the entire scene, is that of the god of love. Kahn reads Eros as "a displaced allegorical representation of the eros that, fused with honor, would symbolically reconcile 'Egypt' and 'Rome'. Read as *double entendre*, the panting cadences would then suggest that Antony envisions suicide as the very consummation of his passion for Cleopatra."[35] But if this *double entendre* is taken literally, Antony is not killed by his love for her. By extension, the real motivation for suicide must be another, and one that Antony fittingly names in the immediately following lines: "Wouldst thou be windowed in great Rome and see / Thy master thus with pleached arms, bending down / His corrigible neck" (4.14.73–75). The reason he gives here, the refusal to function as a trophy in Caesar's triumphal procession, is one that qualifies for a proper Roman death. Like Cleopatra, Antony fears public humiliation, and it is his prime concern not to grant Caesar this final victory.

Eros, who, forcefully and with further digression, commits suicide in order to avoid having to kill his beloved master, further enhances Antony's lack of command and courage. He, thus, gets in line with other servant figures whose masters appeal to their sense of duty. Whereas Pindarus follows Cassius's request to kill him and Titinius commits suicide in reaction to Cassius's death, Eros pre-emptively performs this gesture of loyalty. In order to make the friction created by the discrepancy between the two suicide performances absolutely clear, Antony himself juxtaposes his own and Eros's behaviour:

> Thrice nobler than myself!
> Thou teachest me, O valiant Eros, what
> I should and thou couldst not! My queen and Eros
> Have by their brave instruction got upon me
> A nobleness in record. But I will be
> A bridegroom in my death and run into't
> As to a lover's bed. Come then! And, Eros,
> Thy master dies thy scholar. To do thus
> [*Falls on his sword.*]
> I learned of thee. How? Not dead? Not dead?
> The guard, ho! O, dispatch me.
>
> (4.14.96–105)

Again, two versions of Antony, the heroic warrior and the lover, compete with each other. He praises Cleopatra and especially Eros for their courage to die nobly, but then he strives to be reunited with his queen and find "a lover's bed" in death. As Brower comments, Antony "speaks with an Ovidian lover's consciousness of playing a historical role, and with a renaissance hero's aim of recovering lost nobility under a new form of action."[36] What Brower touches on specifically is the notion of theatricality. He considers Antony's suicide an act he puts on deliberately, acutely aware of its connotations but to some degree incapable of conforming to them. In this respect, Antony's suicide is not different from those of the other tragic heroes, all of who exhibit an awareness that suicide has the potential to communicate a specific message. In Antony, however, this awareness is most conspicuous, surpassed only by Cleopatra's own elaborately staged death.

The comic or humorous elements of the play generally work against Antony; Honigmann identifies this as a significant departure from Plutarch, where Antony is the initiator of laughter and ridicule rather than its receiving end.[37] The potential for laughter at Antony's expense is palpable, especially in the above passages immediately preceding his suicide. As Lois Potter points out, onstage Roman suicides are always conceivably comic because they necessarily require some sort of assistance.[38] As can be taken from Brutus's suicide, too, it is simply physically impossible to run into one's own sword while holding it. But, whereas Brutus eventually finds reluctant assistance in Strato, Antony tries to commit the deed on his own. Fittingly, he comments on his amateurish execution. His "I have done my work ill, friends. O make an end / Of what I have begun" (4.14.106–107) is probably exactly what the audience would think. As Rozett points out, the self-irony with which Antony acknowledges his failure elevates rather than degrades him in the eyes of an audience.[39] This is especially relevant since these moments of self-awareness are Shakespeare's invention; Plutarch's record of Antony's death does not contain any such comments.

As far as the weapon is concerned, Antony's may be a proper Roman death. Its misfired execution, however, subverts this notion of heroism and nobility. It is humiliating that he needs to beg the other guards to finish the work he has begun, but despite his plea "Let him that loves me strike me dead" (4.14.109), nobody puts him out of his misery. Cynthia Marshall points to the physicality of Antony's body, arguing that through his bleeding and inactive body, Antony is cast in a traditionally feminine position. As a consequence, she writes, "the Antony whose body becomes quite literally an object to be manipulated, troubles an audience's notions of what it means to be a (masculine) hero and even of what it means to be an actor (rather than a body) onstage."[40] Within the realm of the play, Antony's suicide is a performance of compromised masculinity. Furthermore, it reflects its own idiosyncratic condition as a performance within a theatrical performance.

Richard Madeleine cautions that the comedy in Antony's suicide may trigger inadvertent laughter,[41] but the text suggests that reactions such as a mild chuckle or even laughter are not unwarranted at all. In fact, theatrical productions often embrace this capacity for physical comedy, even if to different extents. To name but a few examples, under Michael Benthall's direction (1951), Laurence Olivier "flung his sword from him as he wounded himself only to find, when not dead, that he could no longer reach it and therefore had to call for help."[42] In Jon Scoffield's 1974 TV adaptation of Trevor Nunn's production with the RSC (1972), Antony covers his eyes awaiting Eros's sword. He is caught off guard when he reopens his eyes and learns that Eros has killed himself instead. Dominic Dromgoole's version at Shakespeare's Globe (2006) placed particular emphasis on the farcical elements and played for laughs in

Antony's suicide scene. Summarising critical responses towards the production, Potter notes that "[s]ome reviewers, amazingly, thought that the scene of Antony's suicide was unintentionally funny. Others realized that it positively invited audience laughter but felt that it should not have done so. [...] Antony placed his sword against a pillar and ran at it, finally stumbling onto the weapon at an awkward angle. The tone in which he finally said, 'not dead?' could be translated as 'I might have known I'd make a mess of this'."[43] In Jonathan Munby's production at the same venue (2014), Clive Wood as Anthony gestured towards his rather unimpressive wound and shrugged, unable to suppress laughter at the absurdity of his own situation. As Kahn remarks, such attempts to address the physicality of Antony's body add a level other than ridicule: "If suicide plays out homosocial rivalry to its limits, transforming defeat at a rival's hands into victory, and inscribes collaboration in suicide as autonomy, by rendering Antony physically powerless this scene also exposes the contingencies that attend these cultural fictions."[44] To paraphrase her words, in rendering Antony's suicide a failure, the play calls into question the concept of 'Romanness' or Roman *virtus* with its attached gender ideology.

Physical comedy ensues when news arrives that Cleopatra is still alive, and Antony is carried to her monument. First, the comedy is supported by the presumed stage tableau because the difference in levels mirrors their discrepancy in power at this moment. Cleopatra is in charge because her stratagem is responsible for Antony's miserable situation. Accordingly, she looks down on him from her monument. His claim that "Not Caesar's valour has o'erthrown Antony, / But Antony's hath triumphed on itself" (4.15.15–16) is at odds with the performance he has just delivered. Given the fact that he is still alive only because he has not managed a proper suicide, terms such as "valour" and "triumph" certainly appear euphemistic. The guards' laboriously lifting Antony upwards bridges the difference in heights, and Cleopatra's "Here's sport indeed! How heavy weighs my lord!" (4.15.33) suggests that this involves considerable effort, thus again emphasising Antony's physicality. As Hodgdon reports, one strand of recent performances tended to avoid any aspect of mockery here in order to preserve the notion of Antony as an untainted tragic hero. Such productions generally refrained from any actual lifting of Antony's body and instead reverted to emblematic ways of staging the scene; for example, by lowering Cleopatra down to him.[45] For Katherine Duncan-Jones, however, this scene contains a vital element of black comedy and one that any production should respond to. She, therefore, criticises Munby's production for not playing this out to greatest effect and using the Globe's 'upper' stage to lift Antony up.[46] By comparison, Giles Block's production at Shakespeare's Globe (1999) fully exploited this potential for comedy, suspending Antony in a sling "where he swung, a clumsy, awkward weight which exposed the theatre's machinery as machinery and caused a rupture in the action."[47] Despite the impression of ridicule, the moment Antony is lifted up to the monument he also undergoes an upwards movement in the symbolic sense. His ascension anticipates his eventual restoration as war-like Mars, no matter how 'un-Roman' his suicide.

In the dialogue subsequent to Antony's suicide (attempt), the mode switches from physical to verbal comedy. Not even in his dying moment does Cleopatra grant Antony his masculine prerogative of speech and silences his "I am dying Egypt, dying / Give me some wine and let me speak a little" with "No, let me speak, and let me rail so high / That the false huswife Fortune break her wheel" (4.15.43–46). However painful this may be for the audience to watch, Antony does not seem to suffer greatly. Starks speaks of seemingly masochistic pleasures dramatically refiguring "an erotic economy that destabilizes conventional binaries structuring Western constructions of sexuality, heroism, and masculinity."[48] Thus, again, constructions of 'Romanness' are contested. This comes to the surface again in Antony's last words before he eventually dies:

> The miserable change now at my end,
> Lament nor sorrow at, but please your thoughts
> In feeding them with those my former fortunes
> Wherein I lived the greatest prince o'th' world,
> The noblest; and do now not basely die,
> Not cowardly put off my helmet to
> My countryman; a Roman by a Roman
> Valiantly vanquished.
>
> (4.15.53–60)

As Wilcher points out, Antony fashions two competing versions of himself here, as if aware that they could belong to two entirely different plays.[49] On the one hand, Antony has been cast as the figure overcome by his love for Cleopatra and whose end has been miserable. On the other, he has played the role of "the greatest prince o' th' world."

The final lines of his speech are difficult to decipher. Antony's "a Roman by a Roman / Valiantly vanquished" could simply refer to himself, a Roman, who is defeated by Octavius, another Roman. Alternatively, and since at this moment Antony is primarily concerned with constructing a lasting image of heroic 'Romanness', this may also invoke the Roman concept of suicide and its adherent connotations of nobility. On a purely rhetorical level, he performs Roman virtue. Vanhoutte, by contrast, senses that Antony attempts to emancipate himself from his own cultural background, a context that does not allow for the reconciliation of his two conflicting identities. As she argues, the many Latinate words Antony uses point towards his public persona, but their exact combination "cancels out Roman meaning even as it is invoked: 'valour' destroys 'valour' and 'Roman' annihilates 'Roman'. The suicide may or may not have subdued Antony's 'worthiest self', but it has certainly destroyed his Roman identity."[50] If these Roman values cancel each other out, this, too, unmasks 'Romanness' as nothing more than a cultural fiction. What both readings have in common is that they address Antony's own feeling of having achieved a final victory. Furthermore, he fashions his death as a vehicle to communicate this victory to Caesar, thereby transforming his suicide itself into a communicative act. Thus, Brower rightly acknowledges the possibility of reading Antony's final words as self-indulgent and overly optimistic; "Antony dies, as T. S. Eliot outrageously said of Othello, 'pretty pleased with himself'."[51] This direct reference to Othello is fitting since both figures attempt to gloss over the contradictory messages their suicides may send. Othello, although wronged by society, tries to justify the crime he has committed in order to paint a more favourable picture of himself. Similarly, any audience would probably sense the fractures in Antony's performance of self-proclaimed heroism. Antony's wry commentary on his suicide suggests a more accurate self-awareness, but in both cases, the attempt to deceive both themselves and their audiences creates emotional detachment from rather than empathy with the tragic hero.

In spite of these ostensible incongruences, Antony's suicide achieves various forms of reconciliation, primarily for him and Cleopatra. Directly after he has spoken his last word – their shared line points to her reaction as immediate and impulsive – Cleopatra idealises him again. "The crown o'th'earth doth melt" (4.15.65), she cries out. Moreover, the possible stage tableau invokes the biblical imagery of the *Pietà* with Cleopatra holding the bleeding Antony in her arms like Mary holds Christ after the crucifixion. For anyone who has witnessed Antony's suicide, this analogy may seem displaced. It exaggerates Antony's position and, hence, potentially creates a moment of friction. The first of Antony's several eulogies, too, is provided by Cleopatra. When anticipating her own suicide, she visualises an elaborate, colossus-like resurrection of the man whose "legs bestrid the ocean: his reared arm / Crested the world" (5.2.81–82). Hyperbolic though her words may be, this is the Antony known from another play, the Antony of *Julius Caesar*. Cleopatra's words erase the image of the rather pitiful comic Antony and restore that of the Mars-like warrior. As Craig puts it, "[a]ware of the communicative and symbolic possibilities of the act of suicide, she is able to translate the nature of his ignoble end, thus re-writing the character of Antony."[52] Whereas both Antony and the audience have seen that he has done his work ill, on all the others in the play, it has the desired effect.

Octavius Caesar's eulogy is less vivid than Cleopatra's, yet equally reverential: "The death of Antony / Is not a single doom; in the name lay / A moiety of the world" (5.1.17–19). Never before in the play has he shown more respect and admiration for Antony, and so, like Cleopatra, Caesar wipes out the miserable Antony the audience, but apparently nobody else, has seen. This post-mortal rehabilitation can also be understood in another way, as Vanhoutte points out: "Although his suicide allows him a moment of unfettered sovereignty, it initially feeds the ideological forces he had attempted to defeat. And in that irony lies the 'sorrow of Antony's death'."[53] Throughout the play, Antony opposes these ideological forces Vanhoutte refers to. In fact, the entire conflict is caused by Antony's preference of exotic, sensual, and feminine Egypt over restrained and masculine Rome. Antony's reconciliation with Rome and Roman ideology is ironic but not surprising. The values endorsed by Antony have no place in the patriarchal world of either Rome or tragedy, and so the status quo needs to be restored. In that sense, Antony's exaggerated eulogies are more adequately understood as moves of political propaganda rather than adequate representations of either his character or his suicide.

Reconsidering all previous tragedies in which characters kill themselves, the dramatisation of suicide in *Antony and Cleopatra* finally turns tragic power structures upside down. In the first place, this impression is sustained through the contrastive emotional responses elicited by the two deaths. Whereas his invites laughter, hers communicates dignity and control. The staging confirms this impression: with the exception of Juliet, all other female suicides happen offstage. While this could be taken as tragedy's attempt at silencing female characters, in this play, it is Cleopatra's, not the tragic hero's, suicide that forms the centre of tragic denouement. Her death reaffirms her control over the play, visibly acknowledged through her name in the title. *Antony and Cleopatra*, thus, portrays a 'Romanness' that is not exclusively male and, furthermore, calls into question the male prerogative inherent to tragedy. But also, if with slight mishaps along the way, this play shows how suicide may end in triumph. Whereas in the previous tragedies, both male and female figures identify the effect a suicide may have, more often than not they can only partly profit from this potential. Antony and Cleopatra know how to use the communicative potential of suicide to their benefit. Whereas Antony's suicide ultimately rehabilitates his masculinity and heroic reputation, Cleopatra's suicide not only secures her triumph over Caesar, but also generates her transformation into a goddess-like iconic figure. Here, suicide is well done. How fitting, then, that Cleopatra's is the final suicide in the canon.

Notes

1 See Jacqueline Vanhoutte, "Antony's 'Secret House of Death:' Suicide and Sovereignty in *Antony and Cleopatra*," *Philological Quarterly* 79 (2000): 157–158; David Read discusses the curious nature of Enobarbus's death in

"Disappearing Act: The Role of Enobarbus in *Antony and Cleopatra*," *Studies in Philology* 110.3 (2013): 562–583. Since Enobarbus's death is described as wished-for yet not self-inflicted, I do not include him in my analysis.

2 Barbara Hodgdon, "*Antony and Cleopatra* in the Theatre," in *The Cambridge Companion to Shakespearean Tragedy*, ed. Claire McEachern (Cambridge: Cambridge University Press, 2002), 258.

3 See, for instance, Janet Adelman, *The Common Liar, An Essay on Antony and Cleopatra* (New Haven, CT: Yale University Press, 1973), 50–52; Martha Tuck Rozett, "The Comic Structures of Tragic Endings: The Suicide Scenes in *Romeo and Juliet* and *Antony and Cleopatra*," *Shakespeare Quarterly* 36.2 (1985): 158–164.

4 Coppélia Kahn, *Roman Shakespeare: Warriors, Wounds, and Women* (London and New York: Routledge, 1997), 110.

5 Amy Delynne Craig, "Getting the Last Word: Suicide and the 'Feminine' Voice in the Renaissance" (PhD diss., Princeton University, 2002), 179.

6 Robert Wilcher, "Dying for Love: The Tragicomedy of Shakespeare's Cleopatra," in *Eroticism and Death in Theatre and Performance*, ed. Karoline Gritzner (Hatfield: University of Hertfordshire Press, 2010), 36.

7 Juliet Dusinberre, "Squeaking Cleopatras: Gender and Performance in *Antony and Cleopatra*," in *Shakespeare, Theory, and Performance*, ed. James C. Bulman (London: Routledge, 1996), 46.

8 Dympna Callaghan, *Shakespeare without Women: Representing Gender and Race on the Renaissance Stage* (London and New York: Routledge, 2000), 13.

9 Phyllis Rackin, "Shakespeare's Boy Cleopatra, the Decorum of Nature, and the Golden World of Poetry," *PMLA* 87.2 (1972): 208.

10 Marga Munkelt, "Shakespeare's Cleopatra: Aspects of Queenship and Authority" (Lecture at the University of Münster, Germany, January 24, 2011).

11 Hodgdon, "*Antony and Cleopatra* in the Theatre," 260–261. On the performance history of Cleopatra's suicide see also Dorothea Kehler, "Cleopatra's *Sati*: Old Ideologies and Modern Stagings," in *Antony and Cleopatra: New Critical Essays*, ed. Sara Munson Deats (London and New York: Routledge, 2005), 137–152.

12 Rowland Wymer, *Suicide and Despair in the Jacobean Drama* (Brighton: Harvester, 1986), 131.

13 Plutarch, *Shakespeare's Plutarch*, trans. Thomas North, ed. C. F. Tucker Brooke, vol. II containing the main sources of *Anthony and Cleopatra and of Coriolanus* (New York: Duffield and Company, 1909), 134. Shakespeare does, however, retain the information that Cleopatra experiments with various forms of poison. In his concluding speech, Caesar says that "her physicians tell me that / pursued conclusions infinite / of easy ways to die" (5.2.353–355). See also *Antony and Cleopatra*, ed. John Wilders, The Arden Shakespeare Third Series (London: Arden Shakespeare, 1995), note to 5.2.242–278.

14 Lisa S. Starks, "'Immortal Longings:' The Erotics of Death in *Antony and Cleopatra*," in *Antony and Cleopatra: New Critical Essays*, ed. Sara Munson Deats (London and New York: Routledge, 2005), 252.

15 E. A. J. Honigmann, *Shakespeare: Seven Tragedies: A Dramatist's Manipulation of Response* (London: Macmillan, 1976), 167.

16 Ibid., 169.

17 Lorraine Helms, "'The High Roman Fashion:' Sacrifice, Suicide, and the Shakespearean Stage," *PMLA* 107.3 (1992): 555.

18 Rozett offers a comprehensive and insightful discussion of the scene's comic elements, both generically and tonally and furthermore in comparison with *Romeo and Juliet*, in "The Comic Structures of Tragic Endings," 158–164.

19 Jonathan Bate, *The Genius of Shakespeare* (London: Picador, 1997), 175.

20 John Wilders, Introduction to *Antony and Cleopatra*, by William Shakespeare, ed. John Wilders, The Arden Shakespeare Third Series (London: Arden Shakespeare, 1995), 47.

21 As Wilders's note to 5.2.365 in the Arden Third Series explains, John Dover Wilson (The New Cambridge Shakespeare, 1950) added "*The Soldiers Bearing the Dead Bodies.*"

22 Hodgdon, "*Antony and Cleopatra* in the Theatre," 262.

23 Mary Beth Rose, "Suicide as Profit or Loss," *Shakespeare in Our Time: A Shakespeare Association of America Collection*, ed. Dympna Callaghan and Suzanne Gossett (London and New York: Arden Shakespeare, 2016), 79.

24 Wilders, Introduction to *Antony and Cleopatra*, 45.

25 Michael Neill, introduction to *Antony and Cleopatra*, by William Shakespeare, ed. Michael Neill (Oxford: Oxford University Press, 2008), 76.

26 Reuben A. Brower, *Hero and Saint: Shakespeare and the Graeco-Roman Heroic Tradition* (Oxford: Clarendon, 1971), 346.

27 Vanhoutte, "Antony's 'Secret House of Death'," 162.

28 "Now he had a man of his called Eros, whom he loved and trusted much, and whom he had long before caused to swear unto him, that he should kill him when he did command him: and then he willed him to keep his promise. His man drawing his sword lift it up as though he had meant to have stricken his master: but turning his head at one side he thrust his sword into himself, and fell down dead at his master's foot. Then said Antonius, 'O noble Eros, I thank thee for this, and it is valiantly done of thee, to shew me what I should do to myself, which thou couldst not do for me'. Therewithal he took his sword, and thrust it into his belly, and so fell down upon a little bed. The wound he had killed him not presently, for the blood stinted a little when he was laid: and when he came somewhat to himself again, he prayed them that were about him to despatch him. But they all fled out of the chamber, and left him crying out and tormenting himself: until at last there came a secretary unto him called Diomedes, who was commanded to bring him into the tomb or monument where Cleopatra was." (Plutarch, *Shakespeare's Plutarch*, vol. II, 121–122).

29 Kahn, *Roman Shakespeare*, 123.

30 Bruce Smith, *Shakespeare and Masculinity* (Oxford: Oxford University Press, 2000), 48–49.

31 See Wilders's note to 4.12.43–45 in the Arden Third Series.

32 On the interplay between shame, honour, and the public gaze in ancient Rome see Carlin Barton, "Being in the Eyes: Shame and Sight in Ancient Rome," in *The Roman Gaze. Vision, Power and the Body*, ed. David Fredrick (Baltimore: The Johns Hopkins University Press, 2002), 216–236.

33 Gordon Braden, "Fame, Eternity, and Shakespeare's Romans," in *Shakespeare and Renaissance Ethics*, ed. Patrick Gray and John D. Cox (Cambridge: Cambridge University Press, 2014), 50.

34 Craig, "Getting the Last Word," 189.

35 Kahn, *Roman Shakespeare*, 131.

36 Brower, *Hero and Saint*, 335.

37 Honigmann, *Seven Tragedies*, 150–151.

38 Lois Potter, "Assisted Suicides: *Antony and Cleopatra* and *Coriolanus* in 2006–7," *Shakespeare Quarterly* 58.4 (2007): 509.

39 Rozett, "The Comic Structures of Tragic Endings," 160.
40 Cynthia Marshall, "Man of Steel Done Got the Blues: Melancholic Subversion of Presence in *Antony and Cleopatra*," *Shakespeare Quarterly* 44.4 (1993): 403.
41 Richard Madeleine, *Shakespeare in Production: Antony and Cleopatra* (Cambridge: Cambridge University Press, 1998), 283.
42 Michael Scott, *Antony and Cleopatra: Text and Performance* (London: Macmillan, 1983), 64, quoted in in Madeleine, *Shakespeare in Production*, 283.
43 Potter, "Assisted Suicides," 513–514.
44 Kahn, *Roman Shakespeare*, 133.
45 See Hodgdon, "*Antony and Cleopatra* in the Theatre," 258.
46 Katherine Duncan-Jones, "It Is Well Done," review of *Antony and Cleopatra*, by William Shakespeare, directed by Jonathan Munby, Shakespeare's Globe, London, *TLS*, June 6, 2014, 18.
47 Hodgdon, "*Antony and Cleopatra* in the Theatre," 259.
48 Lisa S. Starks, "'Immortal Longings'," 254.
49 Wilcher, "Dying for Love," 33.
50 Vanhoutte, "Antony's 'Secret House of Death'," 161.
51 Brower, *Hero and Saint*, 335–336.
52 Craig, "Getting the Last Word," 181.
53 Vanhoutte, "Antony's 'Secret House of Death'," 171.

Epilogue

There are things in this comedy of Pyramus and Thisbe that will never please. First, Pyramus must draw a sword to kill himself; which the ladies cannot abide. How answer you that?

(*MND* 3.1.8–11)

I hope to have shown that Shakespeare's suicides matter and that parameters of whether characters kill themselves at all and if so, how and when are crucial. Both weapons and locations are replete with symbolic connotation and together with the often-lengthy final speeches, or the absence thereof, all of these constituents form a complex web of meaning. Throughout the history of ideas, suicide has always been a gendered convention, especially in its Roman context. However, in all of the cases addressed in this study, traditional notions of what are considered masculine or feminine weapons, executions, and justifications are subverted. As I have argued, the dramatisation of Shakespeare's suicides destabilises restrictive and essentialist oppositions of masculinity versus femininity, thus proposing a remarkably modern, performative concept of gender.

The question as to whether suicides should be considered moments of submission or, conversely, acts of self-empowerment is a significant one, in terms of not only my own argument, but also the tragic genre at large. Generic conventions dictate the hero or heroine's eventual death, and, accordingly, several of Shakespeare's characters address the question of whether they are casualties of tragic inevitability. Romeo considers himself a victim of "inauspicious stars," Hamlet quarrels with the task imposed upon him by the revenge tragedy genre, and Othello maintains that he has been manipulated into murdering his wife. All of these tragic heroes die believing they have been defeated by a larger power. By claiming the role of the victim and blaming the fickleness of fortune, they negate any form of agency they might have had.

Debates concerning the potential of mankind, of their agency and creativity, predominated Renaissance philosophical discourses. With its burgeoning secularisation and challenging of hierarchies propagated by the Church, Humanism brought about an increasing interest in the individual. For a long time, Renaissance Italy was credited with the birth of individualism, fostered by Jacob Burckhardt's *The Civilization of the Renaissance in Italy* (1860).[1] More recently, though, scholars have reconsidered this emphasis on human autonomy and the Renaissance individual, as it is now often perceived as what John Jeffries Martin names "the harbinger of the postmodern ego: fragmented, divided, even fictitious."[2] Valerie Traub, M. Lindsay Kaplan, and Dympna Callaghan hold a similar, if less radical view, suggesting that "it is less that the modern subject came into being in the early modern period than that the terms of the subject's intelligibility were reconfigured during two hundred years of economic, political, epistemological, and social upheaval."[3] Rather than following an ontological argument, they believe that "the subject, in both social and psychological terms, is always in the process of emerging," thereby emphasising that a subject's individuality necessarily remains unfinished or incomplete.[4]

In many ways analogous to such socio-historical and philosophical debates, the question of autonomy, of whether human beings are perceived as fortune's fools or whether they are able to form independent decisions, equally defines the tragic genre. Classical tragedy implies an inevitability of fate, which can only be accelerated through protest and defiance. Within this context, the tragic hero's (or heroine's) death is purely functional. In Blair Hoxby's words, it "affirms his ethical superiority to the gods; serves as a sacrifice dedicated to the national community; or by means of its very sublimity produces a glimpse of the divine."[5] Similarly, Aristotle's concept of *hamartia* that necessarily brings about the tragic hero's downfall suggests limited agency. No matter whether this materialises as a tragic flaw or, alternatively, a fatal decision in the manner of Oedipus's unconscious fulfilment of the oracle, either way, the tragic protagonist is doomed.

In Renaissance drama, the conflict of human autonomy is particularly defined. On the one hand, early modern thought envisions mankind as autonomous and responsible, which complicates the idea of divine pre-determinacy. On the other, according to the *rota fortuna*, fate might either strike entirely arbitrarily or, alternatively, as a deserved punishment. The idea of an external force invading and challenging the tragic world leaves only little room for agency on the part of the tragic hero or heroine. Within this context, the small amount of autonomy left is reflected in the way in which they respond to fate, either bowing down submissively or rebelling and fighting for their cause. Their death, however, is inevitable; it can only be either accelerated or prolonged.

When all Shakespearean suicides, male and female, are reviewed in combination, the tragedies posit rather than answer the question of autonomy and freedom of choice.[6] The Roman plays are particularly elusive here, since all of Shakespeare's Roman suicides are pre-determined by historical record. And yet, all characters examined in the present study not only address the question of agency by committing suicide, or else refusing to do so, but also by justifying their decision in a certain way. All of their deaths are responses to the challenges transferred upon them by their respective tragedies; they signal either capitulation or opposition. If death and destruction are certain from the start, the portrayal of a character's death gains importance. Looked at from the position of a playwright, the hero or heroine's death is pre-scripted by genre. But the exact point at which a character exits the play as well as the particular way he or she dies is up for the playwright to decide. For this reason, Shakespeare's suicides should not be dismissed as a necessary and formulaic tragic convention. On the contrary, they have to be treated as prime vehicles of dramatic characterisation.

A chronological approach brings several insights into the genderdness of Shakespeare's suicides, for instance that the nexus between suicide and female self-empowerment emerges more strongly towards the later plays. Clearly, the large number of female suicides alone may not seem extraordinary. As Traub phrases it, often enough, the tragedies appear "to give women speech only to silence them; to make women move only to still them; to represent their bodies on stage only to enclose them; to infuse their bodies with warmth only to coldly 'encorpse' them."[7] A closer look at the precise manner of this 'encorpsing', however, brings to light that Lavinia and Cleopatra are at oppositional ends, not only chronologically, but also in terms of what may be called a scale of agency. Whereas Lavinia is deemed physically unable to kill herself, which epitomises her helplessness, Cleopatra fully capitalises on the potential of self-fashioning inherent in suicide. Thus, conspicuously, both Shakespeare's earliest and latest dramatisation of suicide (or the absence thereof) concerns female characters, which may seem surprising in light of tragedy's assumed gender bias.

Regarding those characters chronologically placed in-between Lavinia and Cleopatra, the most linearly discernable development equally concerns the women: they become increasingly defiant of their submissive role. Whereas Juliet still readily accepts her fate as heroine within a tragedy of love and, hence, kills herself once all other possibilities are exhausted, Portia's brutal suicide is a protest against her confinement into the private sphere. Subsequently, Ophelia's death may at first glance appear a relapse into marginalisation and objectification. Yet, similar to Portia's suicide, Ophelia's death, too, can be read as a revolt against male attempts at silencing her – a wilful exit out of a world that does not grant her a voice of her own. Probably the most peculiar of all deaths discussed in this book, Desdemona re-defines her murder as suicide, thereby rejecting the role of the victim and raising her voice against those who try to speak for her. Goneril, an earlier and less complex version of Lady Macbeth, struggles for dominance in a world entirely controlled by men. She only kills herself once she realises that she has struggled in vain, just in time to exit the play with her head held high rather than once again be subjected to male rule. Lady Macbeth, although by way of scheming and manipulation, initially seems to fulfil her ambition and succeed in her fight for dominance. She eventually loses the battle against the genre, but like Goneril, she exits the play on a dignified note, as a queen rather than a war trophy paraded around.

Another pattern that can be identified within the spectrum of female suicides concerns the question of why so many women die offstage. The suicides of Portia, Ophelia, Goneril, and Lady Macbeth are reported only, hidden away from dramatic attention. Simultaneously, all except for Goneril are declared mad, if not by the authority of a doctor then at least by other, male characters who struggle to find an explanation for the women's unruly and strange behaviour. Even though Goneril is not explicitly described as mad, her portrayal as an 'unnatural' woman – an incarnation of evil – allows for her to be discussed along similar lines. It is telling that those characters fall victim to what Elaine Showalter has identified as a "female malady" before they conveniently die a death that seems to be reserved for females only. As outlined by Michel Foucault, the cultural construct of madness functions as a tool of oppression, a way of coercing insubordinate voices into docility. The label 'mad' not only denies the women characters any agency as long as they are alive, but also devalues their suicides as accidents rather than wilful decisions. By pushing female suicides off the stage and furthermore re-writing them as acts of madness, the tragedies seem to defend their male hegemony against female resistance.

As I have suggested, however, when taking a closer look at the dramatisation of these offstage suicides, such a defeatist notion – as far as female agency is concerned – does not hold true. A striking contrast to Hamlet's mere talking about suicide, Ophelia's suicide highlights the tragic hero's inaction even further, and though not staged, her death is one of the most visually powerful moments of the play. Portia's suicide transcends the offstage space through its drastic nature, making the play's male, Roman gestures turn pale by comparison. Goneril's suicide is preceded by another dramatically decisive act of violence – the murder of her sister – and the two bodies are deemed sufficiently important to be dragged back onto the stage again. And finally, Lady Macbeth's offstage death leaves audiences craving for further information as to what exactly has happened. In none of these plays does 'offstage' coincide with 'uninteresting' or, to quote Judith Butler again, "ungrievable."[8] Rather, dramaturgical matters subtly but effectively interrogate gendered categories such as 'Roman', 'heroic', and 'agency'.

Even though it is more difficult to identify a similarly linear development from the earliest play to the latest among the men, what all their suicides have in common is that they exhibit a performative notion of masculinity. Through the choice of weapons, locations, and final speeches, the heroes seek to reinforce their masculinity, but more often than not constructions of masculinity are undercut and destabilised. Brutus and Antony, for example, initially shy away from killing themselves, thus subverting notions of heroic Roman manliness. Since clearcut dichotomies of masculine/feminine, strong/weak, and active/passive are equally rendered performative by the various female suicides, male dominance in the tragedies is, at least tentatively, called into question.

Analogous to Cleopatra's death as a synthesis of all female suicidal predecessors, Antony's suicide conjoins several of the qualities found in the earlier tragic heroes: Romeo's seeming delight in the role of the star-crossed lover, Brutus's and Cassius's preoccupation with 'Romanness', and Othello's insistence that he has been tricked. Thus, in many ways, *Antony and Cleopatra* is the epitome of Shakespeare's manifold portrayals of suicide. In this respect, it is fitting that this play presents a meta-comment on suicide as a (Roman) convention. Both Antony and Cleopatra exhibit an acute awareness of the communicative power a suicide may have – the potential to fashion a lasting image by which to be remembered. They know that their suicides are performances staged for an audience, both within and outside the realm of the play.

In addition to providing Shakespeare's definitive dramatisation of suicide, as it were, *Antony and Cleopatra* challenges the generic boundaries of tragedy itself. Even though all plays taken into consideration so far are tragedies, in many of the suicides, comedy, both tonally and structurally, is implied. Not only Antony's suicide, but also the deaths of Romeo and Juliet, Brutus, Hamlet, and Gloucester are pervaded by slightly grotesque undercurrents. As follows, suspicion arises that suicide is not an altogether tragic phenomenon. In fact, several comedies and romances offer surprisingly close parallels to the contexts in which suicide is addressed in the tragedies. As the first example shows, this may only be in the form of employing a similar line of argument. Regarding both wording and implications, Titus's and Marcus's conviction that the shamed Lavinia needs to be killed closely resembles Hero's fate in *Much Ado About Nothing*. When Claudio suspects Hero to have been unfaithful and as a consequence publicly humiliates her at the altar, Leonato's instinctive reaction to his daughter's alleged crime is that "Death is the fairest cover for her shame / That may be wish'd for" (*Ado* 4.1.115–116). As both the Friar and Beatrice are confused by his drastic outburst, Leonato elaborates on his reasoning:

LEONATO: Wherefore? Why, doth not every earthly thing
           Cry shame upon her? Could she here deny
           The story that is printed in her blood?
           Do not live, Hero; do not ope thine eyes;
           For did I think thou wouldst not quickly die,
           Thought I thy spirits were stronger than thy shames,
           Myself would on the rearward of reproaches

> Strike at thy life. Griev'd I, I had but one?
> Chid I for that at frugal Nature's frame?
> O, one too much by thee! Why had I one?
>
> (*Ado* 4.1.119–128)

He continues for another thirteen lines, but this extract is sufficient to highlight the parallels to Titus's belief that he is obliged to kill Lavinia and, thus, take from her the burden of shame. As its titular pun suggests, *Much Ado* is equally obsessed with female chastity; as commonly known in early modern English, 'nothing' was used as slang for female genitalia. The only difference between the two women is that, whereas Hero is unjustly accused, in Lavinia's case, the "story that is printed in her blood" – the rape – has actually taken place. Within the realm of the play, the fact that it has happened against Lavinia's will makes little to no difference. Like Titus, Leonato constructs Hero's shame as his own, which makes him launch into extended self-loathing. Also like Titus, he addresses his moral obligation to kill Hero, thereby ending her, but primarily his own, suffering.

Whereas Lavinia no longer has a voice to speak up, Hero's voice is ignored, and the interpretative authority over this situation is taken over by men. Against this backdrop, the subsequent stratagem – Hero's mock funeral to make Claudio realise his error of judgement – is particularly uncomfortable to watch.[9] Claudio's love for Hero, the equivalent of the Andronici's family honour, is restored as soon as Hero has "died" and is, thus, cleared from her guilt. Thus, as Kasey Evans points out, "Hero is granted the right to control her bodily signification only in the negative; her 'blood' can speak of her innocence only when it has been taken from her by someone else."[10] *Much Ado*'s generic framework alone predicts that danger can be averted. And yet, Leonato's speech exposes a latent misogynist viewpoint that anticipates the deaths of Ophelia and Desdemona: women who cannot secure their chastity have to die for it.

In *Cymbeline*, Imogen makes a reference to religious impediments against suicide, which is remarkably similar to Hamlet's "Too solid flesh" speech. When Posthumus orders his servant Pisanio to murder Imogen, Pisanio believes in Imogen's innocence and, so, refuses to kill her. Yet Imogen encourages him to kill her in spite of his doubts, telling him "Do his bidding, strike. / Thou mayst be valiant in a better cause; / But now thou seem'st a coward" (*Cym.* 3.4.70–72). Since Pisanio's "valiant" disobedience traditionally signals unmanly cowardice, she continues:

IMOGEN: Why, I must die:
> And if I do not by thy hand, thou art
> No servant of thy master's. Against self-slaughter
> There is a prohibition so divine
> That cravens my weak hand.
>
> (*Cym.* 3.4.73 –77)

Within comic convention, committing suicide is not an option for Imogen, but then again, Cymbeline is not a 'pure' comedy. Yet, even if the play's generic hybridity allowed for a serious discussion of the pros and cons of suicide à la Hamlet, at closer scrutiny, this is not so much a speech about religious impediments against self-killing as an argument about gender. Imogen cross-dresses at the end of 3.4, yet – unlike Shakespeare's other cross-dressing heroines – she appears more dominant before she dresses as a boy. The above dialogue precedes her male disguise and marks the high point of her assertive presence. The debate of whether to kill herself seems merely theoretical, a means to test Pisanio's loyalty and simultaneously assert her own strength. Even though she is a woman, she is far more courageous than he is. Her readiness is all, which at least rhetorically subverts the notion of suicide as a manly, heroic deed.

A case that is even more striking than the parallels to *Much Ado* and *Cymbeline* re-visits the suicide of Ophelia. Ophelia's theatrical afterlife saw a number of Jacobean and Caroline imitations, many of which are undoubtedly parodic.[11] The most obvious and telling of such imitations can be found within Shakespeare's oeuvre itself. While the prologue of *The Two Noble Kinsmen* openly acknowledges Chaucer's *The Knights Tale* as its hypotext, the subplot relies on *Hamlet*. The otherwise nameless Jailer's Daughter and Ophelia follow a similar trajectory: both suffer from unrequited love, both lose their fathers – with the crucial difference being that the Jailer's Daughter is responsible for her father's execution – and both descend into madness. Like Ophelia's, the Daughter's madness is characterised by seemingly incoherent speeches and songs, but her mad language is much more direct and bawdy, which can be explained by dramatic convention regarding the representation of lower-class characters.[12] Yet, the most important parallel is that both attempt to drown themselves – only in the case of the Jailer's Daughter, someone jumps to her rescue.

The Two Noble Kinsmen is commonly attributed to both Shakespeare and John Fletcher, but the exact nature of their collaboration remains contested. There is a scholarly consensus that Shakespeare's main contributions are to the first and final acts, and so, in all probability, the Daughter's suicide attempt was devised by Fletcher.[13] The respective passage, however, immediately conjures up the corresponding lines from *Hamlet*:

WOOER: The place
          Was knee-deep where she sat; her careless tresses
          A wreath of bullrush rounded; about her stuck
          Thousand fresh water-flowers of several colours,
          That methought she appeared like the fair nymph
          That feeds the lake with waters, or as Iris

> Newly dropped down from heaven. Rings she made
> Of rushes that grew by and to 'em spoke
> The prettiest posies: 'Thus our true love's tied',‛
> 'This you may loose, not me,' and many a one.
> And then she wept, and sung again, and sighed,
> And with the same breath smiled and kissed her hand.
>
> (*TNK* 4.1.82–93)

This scene, which – like Ophelia's death – is not staged but merely narrated, captures the Jailer's Daughter in exactly the same pose as Ophelia before she falls into the river. The two women are aligned through flower imagery, and the Daughter is described as a nymph to Ophelia's mermaid. As the Wooer's account continues, it is difficult not to acknowledge that Fletcher parodies Shakespeare:

> WOOER: She saw me, and straight sought the flood; I saved her,
> And set her safe to land, when presently
> She slipped away and to the city made,
> With such a cry and swiftness that, believe me,
> She left me far behind her.
>
> (*TNK* 4.1.95–99)

Just as the Jailer's Daughter assumes Ophelia's pose in *Hamlet*, the Wooer steps in to rescue her, entirely missing that she intends to kill herself the minute she sees him. His potentially chivalric gesture is further undermined by her immediate flight. Quite literally, this is an attempt to escape the arm of male control.

Lois Potter discusses the play's generic fluidity and illustrates how the tragic plot lines are constantly interrupted. In this context, she poignantly describes the passage as the Daughter's "offstage attempt to create a tragic ending for herself."[14] Although intended as a heroic rescue, the Wooer's intervention undermines the sense of a happy or generically comic ending. The play provides a solution that is as suggestive as it is absurd: a stratagem in which the Wooer disguises himself as Palamon in order to win the Daughter's hand, even though it is left open whether she is aware of the deception. As Maurice and Hanna Charney comment, "she can be restored to her wits only by the generous sexual activity denied her by Palamon but supplied without stinting by the anonymous gentleman called simply Wooer."[15] Compared to Ophelia's tragic, yet self-determined suicide, this is a dubious reward.

The most obvious and, hence, a commonly referenced example of suicide within comedy is the mechanical's staging of "Pyramus and Thisbe" in *A Midsummer Night's Dream*. There are strong resemblances between *A Midsummer Night's Dream* and *Romeo and Juliet*, presumably written in the same year: the families are divided by a feud, the lovers meet secretly, and the hero mistakenly assumes his beloved to be dead and kills himself, which in turn is followed by the heroine's own suicide.[16] In light of these parallels, Réne Weis remarks, the term "*diptych* has been applied to them, as if they formed different sides of the same coin, tragedy and comedy, Romeo and Juliet/Pyramus and Thisbe as burlesque first cousins."[17] By extension, the mechanicals' staging also anticipates the suicides of Antony and Cleopatra, who are a more mature version of Romeo and Juliet. Like most of Ovid's *Metamorphoses*, "Pyramus and Thisbe" gives a mythical explanation to a natural phenomenon, in this case, the mulberry tree and its reddish-coloured fruit. At the same time, Ovid's myth deals with the dangerous excess of young love, and for this reason, its primary function within *A Midsummer Night's Dream* is a commentary on the main plot. In itself, though, "Pyramus and Thisbe" is a story centring around two suicides.

As far as possible sources for this episode in the play are concerned, Shakespeare resorts to Ovid's original text, possibly also to its various contemporary English and French translations or spin-offs that were popular at the time.[18] Although many critics acknowledge a strong and underrated sense of irony in Ovid's text, it is, of course, not a comic story *per se*. Yet, Shakespeare is not the first to translate the myth to a comic context; during the Middle Ages and the Renaissance, it was not always considered a tragedy.[19] As Brian Crockett argues, the sense of the burlesque is already present in Ovid's text, which makes it difficult to untangle whose version in particular – Ovid's or other contemporary versions – Shakespeare parodies.[20]

Within *A Midsummer Night's Dream*, generic demarcations are clear: this is a tragedy turned farce. The actors are neither able to remember the lines correctly nor do they react on their respective cues, and the roles of both the lioness and the wall are unnecessarily transformed into speech parts. Furthermore, the mechanicals decide that it might be safer to make clear that Pyramus does not actually kill himself so as to "put [the ladies] out of fear" (*MND* 3.1.20–21). The ludicrous reaches its peak with Bottom/Pyramus's suicide:

PROLOGUE: Anon comes Pyramus, sweet youth and tall,
                And finds his trusty Thisbe's mantle slain;
                Whereat with blade, with bloody blameful blade,
                He bravely broach'd his boiling bloody breast;
                And Thisbe, tarrying in mulberry shade,
                His dagger drew, and died.

                                      (*MND* 5.1.143–148)

The content of what is narrated here clashes with the prologue's chipper tone. Through the excessive use of misplaced alliteration, the prelude to Pyramus's suicide is meant to create dramatic tension and convey the severity of the action. Of course, the complete opposite is achieved. This is as much a description of Pyramus as of Romeo, with the significant difference being that the latter is deceived by a seemingly dead body. In order to emphasise Pyramus's haste even more strongly, Thisbe's allegedly blood-stained coat alone suffices for him to kill himself. As indicated by the almost slapstick-like timing in their joint suicides, Romeo and Juliet miss farce by a hair's breadth only.

Similar to the prologue of *Romeo and Juliet*, but less successfully, the mechanical's prologue forecloses the following action. Thus, after the above description of Pyramus's death, his suicide is additionally acted out by Bottom:

> Come tears, confound!
> Out sword, and wound
> The pap or Pyramus;
> Ay, that left pap,
> Where heart doth hop: [*Stabs himself.*]
> Thus die I, thus, thus, thus!
> Now am I dead,
> Now am I fled,
> My soul is in the sky.
> Tongue, lose thy light;
> Moon, take thy flight!
> > *Exit Moonshine.*
> Now die, die, die, die, die. [*Dies.*]
>
> > (*MND* 5.1.289–300)

This entirely histrionic and farcical speech caricatures the theatrical convention of verbalising an action seen onstage. Not only Romeo, but Hamlet and Antony too, repeatedly comment on the fact that they are dying. Pyramus takes this one step further by claiming that he is already dead – that his soul has started its ascension to heaven. And yet, he continues talking for a few more lines. In Michael Hoffman's film adaptation (1999) starring Kevin Kline as Bottom, appropriately dressed in Roman armour, this absurdity is taken to the extreme. After Bottom has stabbed himself, the audience erupt into applause. To everyone's confusion, the dead Bottom continues to speak, rises again, and acts out his final lines. Not even the stage manager can silence him, and so Bottom stabs himself a second time. Bottom's performance, thus, not only foregrounds the inherent comic potential of Roman suicide, but also comments on suicide as a theatrical convention, equally likely to make audiences chuckle uncomfortably.

Thisbe's final lines are rather different from Pyramus's. After a lengthy contemplation of her lover's dead body, she wraps it up quickly:

Tongue, not a word:
Come, trusty sword,
Come, blade, my breast imbrue! [*Stabs herself.*]
And farewell, friends;
Thus Thisbe ends:
Adieu, adieu, adieu! [*Dies.*]

(*MND* 5.1.337–342)

Like Bottom's soliloquy, these first lines equally address the convention of stage suicide. As if to say "this is not a time for lengthy speeches," Thisbe reverts to plain action. Again, the parallel to Juliet's suicide, not only in terms of weapon, but also her conventionally masculine resolution, is noteworthy.

In James Spisak's view, "the mechanicals are excellent actors in the Brechtian sense" because their amateurish performance makes any un-alienated, emotional involvement on the part of the audience impossible. For Spisak, this alienation identifies the young lovers in the inner-play audience as the target of parody. They laugh at Pyramus and Thisbe without noticing that the laughter goes at their own expense.[21] Simultaneously, the Brechtian effect works with regard to suicide. Suicide is exposed as a performance – a dramatic convention that proceeds according to a certain formula. The resemblances between suicide in *Romeo and Juliet* and *A Midsummer Night's Dream* illustrate, as Tom McAlindon puts it, "that in real life the comic is always on the verge of the tragic, and vice versa, and that comedy and tragedy must acknowledge that fact by the controlled inclusion of their generic opposite."[22] The mechanicals' staging and above all Bottom's performance, therefore, foreground the fine line between tragedy and farce; tragedy is revealed to be comedy *manqué*.

As I have suggested, Shakespeare's suicides challenge conventional power structures underlying the preconceived tragic notion of male dominance as opposed to female subordination. Of course negotiations of gender are not exclusive to the tragedies. Although with a slightly more even division of power, the comedies, too, investigate gender roles. By extension, it is not surprising that *Much Ado About Nothing*, *A Midsummer Night's Dream*, *Cymbeline*, and *The Two Noble Kinsmen* also feature debates on suicide, especially since the latter two are romances. In Shakespeare's later plays, matters of life and death sit side by side much more easily, which, of course, is one of the reasons for their slippery generic status. What these brief excursions into the comic terrain are supposed to show, then, is that in Shakespeare's plays, suicides are not necessarily always tragic. But in the comedies, as elsewhere in his dramatic oeuvre, they are always gendered.

Notes

1 See John Jeffries Martin, *Myths of Renaissance Individualism* (Basingstoke and New York: Palgrave, 2004), 1–20.

2 Martin, *Myths of Renaissance Individualism*, 5. Stephen Greenblatt postulates similar concepts of identity and individuality: "It seemed to me the very hallmark of the Renaissance that middle-class and aristocratic males began to feel that they possessed such shaping power over their lives, and I saw this power and the freedom it implied as an important element in my own sense of myself. But as my work progressed, I perceived that fashioning oneself and being fashioned by cultural institutions – family, religion, state – were inseparably intertwined. In all my texts and documents, there were, so far as I could tell, no moments of pure, unfettered subjectivity; indeed, the human subject itself began to seem remarkably unfree, the ideological product of the relations of power in a particular society." *Renaissance Self-Fashioning* (Chicago and London: The University of Chicago Press, 2005), 256.

3 Valerie Traub, M. Lindsay Kaplan, and Dympna Callaghan, Introduction to *Feminist Readings of Early Modern Culture: Emerging Subjects*, ed. Valerie Traub et al. (Cambridge: Cambridge University Press, 1996), 2.

4 Ibid.

5 Blair Hoxby, *What Was Tragedy? Theory and the Early Modern Canon* (Oxford: Oxford University Press, 2015), 4.

6 See also David Scott Kastan, "'A Rarity Most Beloved': Shakespeare and the Idea of Tragedy," in *A Companion to Shakespeare's Works: The Tragedies*, ed. Richard Dutton and Jean E. Howard (Oxford: Blackwell, 2003), 8. Kastan pinpoints several "unanswered (perhaps unanswerable) questions of the tragic world. Are there reasons for the intolerable suffering? Is the tragic motor human error or capricious fate? Is the catastrophe a just, if appalling, retribution, or an arbitrary destiny reflecting the indifference, or, worse, the malignity of the heavens?" and similarly arrives at the conclusion that, ultimately, "the uncertainty is the point." (8).

7 Valerie Traub, *Desire and Anxiety: Circulations of Sexuality in Shakespearean Drama* (London and New York: Routledge, 1992), 26.

8 Judith Butler, *Precarious Life: The Powers of Mourning and Violence* (London and New York: Verso, 2004), xiv.

9 On this scene's elements of parody and its politics, both in terms of the play and the socio-cultural context, see Tobias Döring, *Performances of Mourning in Shakespearean Theatre and Early Modern Culture* (New York: Palgrave, 2006), 157–166.

10 Kasey Evans, "Misreadings and Misogyny: Ariosto, Spenser, and Shakespeare," *Renaissance Drama* 36/37 (2010): 281.

11 Lois Potter, "Ophelia and Some Theatrical Successors," in *The Afterlife of Ophelia*, ed. Kaara L. Peterson and Deanne Williams (New York: Palgrave, 2012), 154. Potter discusses Lucibella in Henry Chettles' *Hoffman, or Revenge for a Father*, Aspatia in Beaumont and Fletcher's *The Maid's Tragedy*, the two Constances in Richard Brome's *The Northern Lass* as well as Penthea in John Ford's *The Broken Heart*.

12 On other inspirations for the character, see Lois Potter, Introduction to *The Two Noble Kinsmen*, by William Shakespeare, ed. Lois Potter The Arden Shakespeare Third Series (London: Arden Shakespeare, 1997), 47–53. On a comparison between Ophelia's and the Daughter's language of madness, see Douglas Bruster, "The Jailer's Daughter and the Politics of Madwomen's Language," *Shakespeare Quarterly* 46.3 (1995): 280–282; Carol Thomas

Neely, *Distracted Subjects: Madness and Gender in Shakespeare and Early Modern Culture* (New York: Cornell University Press, 2004), 69–98.

13 Suzanne Gossett lists the following scenes as (presumably) written by Shakespeare: Act 1 (possibly with the exception of 1.5), 2.1, 3.1, 3.2, 4.3, 5.1, 5.3, and 5.4. "*The Two Noble Kinsmen* and *Henry VIII*: The Last Last Plays," in *The Cambridge Companion to Shakespeare's Last Plays*, ed. Catherine M. S. Alexander (Cambridge: Cambridge University Press, 2009), 190. On the debate surrounding the play's authorship and collaborative composition see also Potter, Introduction to *The Two Noble Kinsmen*, 16–35; Jonathan Hope, *The Authorship of Shakespeare's Plays: A Socio-Linguistic Study* (Cambridge: Cambridge University Press, 1994) 83–89; Kenneth Muir, *Shakespeare as Collaborator* (London: Methuen, 1960), 98–147.

14 Potter, Introduction to *The Two Noble Kinsmen*, 4. On the debate surrounding the play's genre see pp. 4–6 as well as Gossett, "*The Two Noble Kinsmen* and *Henry VIII*," 192–196.

15 Maurice Charney, and Hanna Charney, "The Language of Madwomen in Shakespeare and His Fellow Dramatists," *Signs* 3.2 (1977): 457.

16 According to Stanley Wells and Gary Taylor, *William Shakespeare: A Textual Companion* (Oxford: Clarendon, 1987), 118.

17 René Weis, Introduction to *Romeo and Juliet*, by William Shakespeare, ed. René Weis, The Arden Shakespeare Third Series (London: Arden Shakespeare, 2012), 41.

18 On the play's sources, see Kenneth Muir, "Pyramus and Thisbe: A Study in Shakespeare's Method," *Shakespeare Quarterly* 5.2 (1954): 141–153; A. H. Diverres, "The Pyramus and Thisbe Story and its Contributions to the Romeo and Juliet Legend," in *The Classical Tradition in French Literature*, ed. H. T Barnwell et al. (London: Grant & Cutler, 1977), 9–22. Muir in particular offers a detailed discussion of which intertextual references are traceable in the text of *MND*. James W. Spisak traces "verbal echoes of Golding's Ovid, of Thomson's poem in Robinson's *Handful of Pleasant Delites*, of *The Gorgeous Gallery of Gallant Inventions*, of Dunstan Gale's *Pyramus and Thisbe*, which was written in heroic couplets, of Chaucer's *Legend of Good Women*, perhaps of Thomas Mouffet's poem, *The Silkewormes and their Flies*, and even, perhaps and alas, of Gower's *Confessio Amantis*." "Pyramus and Thisbe in Chaucer and Shakespeare," in *Chaucerian Shakespeare: Adaptation and Transformation*, ed. E. Talbot and Judith J. Kollmann (Detroit: Marygrove College, 1983), 88.

19 Brian Crockett, "'The Wittiest Partition': Pyramus and Thisbe in Ovid and Shakespeare," *Classical and Modern Literature* 12.1 (1991): 50.

20 Crockett, "'The Wittiest Partition'," 51.

21 Spisak, "Pyramus and Thisbe in Chaucer and Shakespeare," 94.

22 Tom McAlindon, "What is a Shakespearean Tragedy?" in *The Cambridge Companion to Shakespearean Tragedy*, ed. Claire McEachern (Cambridge: Cambridge University Press, 2002), 5.

Bibliography

Primary Literature

Brooke, Arthur. "Romeus and Juliet." In *Romeo and Juliet*, edited by G. Blakemore Evans, 229–263. Cambridge: Cambridge University Press, 2003.

Burton, Robert. *The Anatomy of Melancholy*. New York: New York Review Books, 2001.

Donne, John. *Biathanatos*. Edited by Ernest W. Sullivan II. Newark: University of Delaware Press, 1984.

Kyd, Thomas. *The Spanish Tragedy*. In *Four Revenge Tragedies*, edited by Katharine Eisaman Maus, 3–91. Oxford: Oxford University Press, 1995.

Ovid. *Metamorphoses*. London: Penguin, 2004.

Plutarch. *Shakespeare's Plutarch*. Translated by Thomas North and edited by C. F. Tucker Brooke. Vol. I, containing the main sources of *Julius Caesar*. New York: Duffield and Company, 1909.

Plutarch. *Shakespeare's Plutarch*. Translated by Thomas North and edited by C. F. Tucker Brooke. Vol. II, containing the main sources of *Anthony and Cleopatra* and of *Coriolanus*. New York: Duffield and Company, 1909.

Shakespeare, William. *Antony and Cleopatra*. Edited by John Wilders. The Arden Shakespeare Third Series. London: Arden Shakespeare, 1995.

————. *Hamlet*. Edited by Philip Edwards. The New Cambridge Shakespeare. Cambridge: Cambridge University Press, 2003.

————. *Hamlet*. Edited by Ann Thompson and Neil Taylor. The Arden Shakespeare Third Series. London: Arden Shakespeare, 2006.

————. *Hamlet. The Texts of 1603 and 1623*. Edited by Ann Thompson and Neil Taylor. The Arden Shakespeare Third Series. London: Arden Shakespeare, 2006.

————. *Julius Caesar*. Edited by David Daniell. The Arden Shakespeare Third Series. London: Arden Shakespeare, 1998.

————. *King Lear*. Edited by R. A. Foakes. The Arden Shakespeare Third Series. London: Arden Shakespeare, 1997.

————. *Macbeth*. Edited by Sandra Clark and Pamela Mason. The Arden Shakespeare Third Series. London: Arden Shakespeare, 2015.

————. *Othello*. Edited by M. R. Ridley. The Arden Shakespeare. London: Arden Shakespeare, 1958.

————. *Othello*. Edited by E. A. J. Honigmann. The Arden Shakespeare Third Series. London: Arden Shakespeare, 1997.

————. *Othello*. Edited by Michael Neill. The Oxford Shakespeare. Oxford: Clarendon, 2006.

————. *Othello.* Edited by Norman Sanders. The New Cambridge Shakespeare. Cambridge: Cambridge University Press, 2003.

————. *Romeo and Juliet.* Edited by Jill L. Levenson. The Oxford Shakespeare. Oxford: Oxford University Press, 2000.

————. *Romeo and Juliet.* Edited by René Weis. The Arden Shakespeare Third Series. London: Arden Shakespeare, 2012.

————. *Titus Andronicus.* Edited by Jonathan Bate. The Arden Shakespeare Third Series. London: Arden Shakespeare, 1995.

————. *William Shakespeare: Complete Works.* Edited by Jonathan Bate and Eric Rasmussen. London: Palgrave Macmillan, 2008.

Sidney, Sir Philip. *The Countess of Pembroke's Arcadia (The New Arcadia).* Edited by Victor Skretkowicz. Oxford: Clarendon, 1987.

Performances & Adaptations

Antony and Cleopatra. By William Shakespeare. Directed by Michael Benthall. St. James's Theatre, London, 1951.

————. By William Shakespeare. Directed by Trevor Nunn. RSC, Stratford-upon-Avon, 1972.

————. By William Shakespeare. Directed by Jon Scoffield. ITV, 1974.

————. By William Shakespeare. Directed by Peter Hall. Aldwich and Olivier Theatres, London, 1987.

————. By William Shakespeare. Directed by Steven Pimlott. RSC, Stratford-upon-Avon, 1999.

————. By William Shakespeare. Directed by Giles Block. Shakespeare's Globe, London, 1999.

————. By William Shakespeare. Directed by Dominic Dromgoole. Shakespeare's Globe, London, 2006.

————. By William Shakespeare. Directed by Jonathan Munby. Shakespeare's Globe, London, 2014.

Coriolanus. By William Shakespeare. Directed Dominic Dromgoole. Shakespeare's Globe, London, 2006.

————. By William Shakespeare. Directed by Gregory Doran. RSC, Stratford-upon-Avon, 2007.

————. William Shakespeare. Directed by Ralph Fiennes. The Weinstein Company, 2011.

Hamlet. By William Shakespeare. Directed by Laurence Olivier. Universal International, 1948.

————. By William Shakespeare. Directed by Robert Walker. Half Moon Theatre, London, 1979.

————. By William Shakespeare. Directed by Franco Zeffirelli. Universal Pictures, 1990.

————. By William Shakespeare. Directed by Kenneth Branagh. Columbia Pictures, 1996.

————. By William Shakespeare. Directed by Peter Zadek. Volkstheater, Wien, 1999.

————. By William Shakespeare. Directed by Sarah Frankcom. Royal Exchange, Manchester, 2014.

Julius Caesar. By William Shakespeare. Directed by Herbert Wise. BBC, 1979.

King Lear. Directed by John Gielgud and Anthony Quayle. RSC, Stratford-upon-Avon, 1950.

————. Directed by Peter Brook. RSC, Straford-upon-Avon, 1962.

————. Directed by Jonathan Miller. BBC, 1982.

————. Directed by Nicholas Hytner. RSC, Stratford-upon-Avon, 1990.

————. Directed by Adrian Noble. RSC, Stratford-upon-Avon, 1993.

————. Directed by Richard Eyre. National Theatre, London, 1997.

————. Directed by Sam Mendes. National Theatre, London, 2014.

————. Directed by Gregory Doran. RSC, Straford-upon-Avon, 2016.

Macbeth. By William Shakespeare. Directed by Roman Polanski. Columbia Pictures, 1971.

————. By William Shakespeare. Directed by Adrian Noble. RSC, Stratford-upon-Avon, 1993.

————. By William Shakespeare. Directed by Dominic Cooke. RSC, Stratford-upon-Avon, 2004.

————. By William Shakespeare. Directed by John Caird. Almeida, London, 2005.

————. By William Shakespeare. Directed by Declan Donnellan. Barbican, London, 2010.

————. By William Shakespeare. Directed by Lucy Bailey. Shakespeare's Globe, London, 2010.

————. By William Shakespeare. Directed by Justin Kurzel. The Weinstein Company, 2015.

A Midsummer Night's Dream. Directed by Michael Hoffman. Fox Searchlight Pictures, 1999.

"*O*." Directed by Tim Blake Nelson. Lionsgate, 2001.

Othello. Directed by Stuart Burge. Eagle-Lion Films, 1965.

————. Directed by Oliver Parker. Columbia Pictures, 1995.

————. Directed by Michael Kahn. The Shakespeare Theatre, Washington, DC, 1997.

————. Directed by Geoffrey Sax. ITV, 2011.

————. Directed by Jette Steckel. Deutsches Theater, Berlin, 2011.

————. Directed by Nicholas Hytner. The National Theatre, London, 2013.

Shakespeare in Love. Directed by John Madden. Universal Pictures, 1998.

Titus. Directed by Julie Taymor. Fox Searchlight Pictures, 1999.

Titus Andronicus. By William Shakespeare. Directed by Peter Brook. RSC, Stratford-upon-Avon, 1955/57.

————. By William Shakespeare. Directed by Deborah Warner. RSC, Stratford-upon-Avon, 1987–88.

————. By William Shakespeare. Directed by Lucy Bailey. Shakespeare's Globe, London, 2006/2014.

William Shakespeare's Romeo + Juliet. By William Shakespeare. Directed by Baz Luhrmann. Twentieth Century Fox, 1996.

Secondary Literature

Adelman, Janet. *The Common Liar: An Essay on Antony and Cleopatra*. New Haven: Yale University Press, 1973.

————. *Suffocating Mothers: Fantasies of Maternal Origin in Shakespeare's Plays, Hamlet to The Tempest*. New York: Routledge, 1992.

Aebischer, Pascale. *Shakespeare's Violated Bodies: Stage and Screen Performance*. Cambridge: Cambridge University Press, 2004.

Alfar León, Cristina. *Fantasies of Female Evil: The Dynamics of Gender and Power in Shakespearean Tragedy*. Newark: University of Delaware Press, 2003.

Alvarez, Al. *The Savage God: A Study of Suicide*. London: Bloomsbury, 2002.

Auden, W. H. *Lectures on Shakespeare*. Edited by Arthur Kirsch. Princeton: Princeton University Press, 2000.

Bailey, Amanda. "Occupy Macbeth: Masculinity and Political Masochism in *Macbeth*." In *Violent Masculinities: Male Aggression in Early Modern Texts and Culture*, edited by Jennifer Feather and Catherine E. Thomas, 191–212. New York and Basingstoke: Palgrave, 2013.

Bamber, Linda. *Comic Women, Tragic Men: A Study of Gender and Genre in Shakespeare*. Stanford: Stanford University Press, 1982.

Barber, Charles Laurence. *The Idea of Honour in the English Drama 1591–1700*. Stockholm: Almqvist and Wiksell, 1957.

Bartels, Emily. "Strategies of Submission: Desdemona, the Duchess, and the Assertion of Desire." *SEL* 36.2 (1996): 417–433.

Bate, Jonathan. Introduction to *Titus Andronicus*, by William Shakespeare, edited by Jonathan Bate, 1–121. The Arden Shakespeare Third Series. London: Arden Shakespeare, 1995.

————. *The Genius of Shakespeare*. London: Picador, 1997.

Belsey, Catherine. "Gender and Family." In *The Cambridge Companion to Shakespearean Tragedy*, edited by Claire McEachern, 123–141. Cambridge: Cambridge University Press, 2002.

Benton, Michael, and Sally Butcher. "Painting Shakespeare." *Journal of Aesthetic Education* 32.3 (1998): 53–66.

Bialo, Caralyn. "Popular Performance, the Broadside Ballad, and Ophelia's Madness." *SEL* 53.2 (2013): 293–309.

Blits, Jan H. "Manliness and Friendship in *Julius Caesar*." In *William Shakespeare's Julius Caesar*, edited and introduced by Harold Bloom, 31–46. New York: Infobase, 2010.

Bloom, Harold. *Shakespeare: The Invention of the Human*. London: Fourth Estate, 1999.

Book of Common Prayer. Oxford: Oxford University Press, 1965.

Boswell-Stone, W. G. *Shakespeare's Holinshed: The Chronicle and the Plays Compared*. New York: Dover, 1968.

Braden, Gordon. "Fame, Eternity, and Shakespeare's Romans." In *Shakespeare and Renaissance Ethics*, edited by Patrick Gray and John D. Cox, 37–55. Cambridge: Cambridge University Press, 2014.

Bradley, A. C. *Shakespearean Tragedy*. 1904. Reprint, London: Penguin, 1991.

Branam, George C. "The Genesis of David Garrick's *Romeo and Juliet*." *Shakespeare Quarterly* 35 (1984): 170–179.

Breitenberg, Mark. *Anxious Masculinity in Early Modern England*. Cambridge: Cambridge University Press, 1996.

Bronfen, Elisabeth. *Over Her Dead Body: Death Femininity and the Aesthetic*. Manchester: Manchester University Press, 1992.

Brower, Reuben A. *Hero and Saint: Shakespeare and the Graeco-Roman Heroic Tradition.* Oxford: Clarendon, 1971.

Brucher, Richard T. "'Tragedy, Laugh On': Comic Violence in *Titus Andronicus.*" *Renaissance Drama* 10.1 (1979): 71–91.

Bruster, Douglas. "The Jailer's Daughter and the Politics of Madwomen's Language." *Shakespeare Quarterly* 46.3 (1995): 277–300.

Burnett, Mark Thornton. "The 'Fiend-Like Queen': Rewriting Lady Macbeth." *Parergon* 11.1 (1993): 1–19.

Burton, Robert. *The Anatomy of Melancholy.* 1621. Reprint, New York: The New York Review of Books Classics, 2001.

Butler, Judith. *Bodies That Matter: On the Discursive Limits of 'Sex.'* London and New York: Routledge, 1993.

————. *Gender Trouble: Feminism and the Subversion of Identity.* London and New York: Routledge, 1990.

————. *Precarious Life: The Powers of Mourning and Violence.* London and New York: Verso, 2004.

Callaghan, Dympna. *Shakespeare without Women: Representing Gender and Race on the Renaissance Stage.* London and New York: Routledge, 2000.

————. "Wicked Women in *Macbeth*: A Study of Power, Ideology, and the Production of Motherhood." In *Reconsidering the Renaissance: Papers from the Twenty-First Annual Conference*, edited by Mario Di Cesare, 355–369. Binghamton, NY: Medieval & Renaissance Texts & Studies, 1992.

————. *Woman and Gender in Renaissance Tragedy: A Study of King Lear, Othello, The Duchess of Malfi and The White Devil.* New York: Harvester Wheatsheaf, 1989.

Camus, Albert. *The Myth of Sisyphus.* Translated by Justin O'Brien. Harmondsworth: Penguin, 1975.

Chamberlain, Stephanie. "Fantasizing Infanticide: Lady Macbeth and the Murdering Mother in Early Modern England." *College Literature* 32.3 (2005): 72–91.

Charney, Maurice. *Titus Andronicus.* London: Harvester Wheatsheaf, 1990.

Charney, Maurice, and Hanna Charney. "The Language of Madwomen in Shakespeare and His Fellow Dramatists." *Signs* 3.2 (1977): 451–460.

Clark, Sandra, and Pamela Mason. Introduction to *Macbeth*, by William Shakespeare, edited by Sandra Clark and Pamela Mason, 1–124. The Arden Shakespeare Third Series. London: Arden Shakespeare, 2015.

Clayton, Thomas. "'Should Brutus Never Taste of Portia's Death but Once?' Text and Performance in *Julius Caesar.*" *SEL* 23.2 (1983): 237–255.

Cohen, Derek. "Othello's Suicide." *University of Toronto Quarterly* 62.3 (1993): 323–333.

————. *Searching Shakespeare: Studies in Culture and Authority.* Toronto: University of Toronto Press, 2003.

————. *Shakespeare's Culture of Violence.* Ipswich and New York: St. Martin's, 1993.

————. *The Politics of Shakespeare.* New York: St. Martin's, 1993.

Couche, Christine. "A Mind Diseased: Reading Lady Macbeth's Madness." In *Word and Self Estranged in English Texts, 1550–1660*, edited by Philippa Kelly and L. E. Semler, 135–148. Farnham: Ashgate, 2010.

Craig, Amy Delynne. "Getting the Last Word: Suicide and the 'Feminine' Voice in the Renaissance." PhD diss., Princeton University, 2002.

Croall, Jonathan. *Performing King Lear. Gielgud to Russell Beale*. London and New Yok: Arden Shakespeare, 2015.

Crockett, Brian. "'The Wittiest Partition': Pyramus and Thisbe in Ovid and Shakespeare." *Classical and Modern Literature* 12.1 (1991): 49–58.

Cummings, Brian. *Mortal Thoughts: Religion, Secularity and Identity in Shakespeare and Early Modern Culture*. Oxford: Oxford University Press, 2013.

Cunico, Juliette Marie. "Audience Attitudes toward Suicide in Shakespeare's Tragedies." PhD diss., University of New Mexico, 1991.

Cusack, Sinead. "Lady Macbeth's Barren Sceptre." In *Clamorous Voices: Shakespeare's Women Today*, edited by Carol Rutter, 53–72. London: The Women's Press, 1988.

Dane, Gabrielle. "Reading Ophelia's Madness." *Exemplaria: A Journal of Theory in Medieval and Renaissance Studies* 10.2 (1998): 405–423.

Daniell, David. Introduction to *Julius Caesar*, by William Shakespeare, edited by David Daniell, 1–147. The Arden Shakespeare Third Series. London: Arden Shakespeare, 1998.

Davis, Lloyd. "Embodied Masculinity in Shakespeare's *Julius Caesar*." *Entertext* 3.1 (2003): 161–182. Accessed April 12, 2017. www.brunel.ac.uk/__data/assets/pdf_file/0008/111023/Lloyd-Davis,-Embodied-Masculinity-in-Shakespeares-Julius-Caesar.pdf

Davis, J. Madison, and A. Daniel Frankforter. *The Shakespeare Name Dictionary*. Abingdon and New York: Routledge, 1995.

de Grazia, Margreta. *Hamlet without Hamlet*. Cambridge: Cambridge University Press, 2007.

de Montaigne, Michel. "A Custom of The Isle of Cea." In *The Complete Essays*, translated and edited by M. A. Screech, 392–407. London: Penguin, 2012.

DeNeef, A. Leigh. "Poetics, Elizabethan." In *The Spenser Encyclopedia*, edited by Albert Charles Hamilton, 551–553. Toronto et al.: Toronto University Press, 1990.

Dessen, Alan C. *Shakespeare in Performance: Titus Andronicus*. Manchester: Manchester University Press, 1989.

Detmer-Goebel, Emily. "The Need for Lavinia's Voice: *Titus Andronicus* and the Telling of Rape." *Shakespeare Studies* 29 (2001): 75–92.

Distiller, Natasha. *Desire and Gender in the Sonnet Tradition*. Basingstoke and New York: Palgrave, 2008.

Diverres, A. H. "The Pyramus and Thisbe Story and its Contributions to the Romeo and Juliet Legend." In *The Classical Tradition in French Literature*, edited by H. T. Barnwell, A. H. Diverres, and G. F. Evans, 9–22. London: Grant & Cutler, 1977.

Dollimore, Jonathan. *Death, Desire and Loss in Western Culture*. New York: Taylor & Francis, 2001.

————. *Radical Tragedy: Religion, Ideology and Power in the Drama of Shakespeare and his Contemporaries*. Brighton: Harvester, 1984.

Döring, Tobias. *Performances of Mourning in Shakespearean Theatre and Early Modern Culture*. New York: Palgrave, 2006.

Draper, John. *The Hamlet of Shakespeare's Audience*. 1939. Reprint, London: Frank Cass & Co. Ltd, 1966.

Drew, Daniel. "'I Am More an Antique Roman than a Dane': Suicide, Masculinity and National Identity in *Hamlet*." In *Identity, Otherness and Empire in Shakespeare's Rome*, edited by Maria del Sapio Garbero, 75–87. Farnham and Burlington: Ashgate, 2009.

Duncan-Jones, Katherine. "It Is Well Done." Review of *Antony and Cleopatra*, by William Shakespeare, 17–18. Directed by Jonathan Munby. Shakespeare's Globe, London. *TLS*, June 6, 2014.

————. "'O Happy Dagger:' The Autonomy of Shakespeare's Juliet." *Notes and Queries* 45.3 (1998): 314–316.

Dunn, Leslie C. "Ophelia's Song in *Hamlet*: Music, Madness, and the Feminine." In *Embodied Voices: Representing Female Vocality in Western Culture*, edited by Leslie C. Dunn and Nancy A. Jones, 50–64. Cambridge: Cambridge University Press, 1994.

Durkheim, Émile. *On Suicide*. Translated by Robin Buss. 1897. Reprint, London: Penguin, 2006.

Dusinberre, Juliet. *Shakespeare and the Nature of Women*. London and Basingstoke: Macmillan, 1975.

————. "Squeaking Cleopatras: Gender and Performance in *Antony and Cleopatra*." In *Shakespeare, Theory, and Performance*, edited by James C. Bulman, 46–67. London and New York: Routledge, 1996.

Edwards, Catharine. *Death in Ancient Rome*. New Haven: Yale University Press, 2007.

Eliot, T. S. *Selected Essays 1917–1932*. New York: Harcourt, 1932.

Ellis, John. "The Gulling of Gloucester: Credibility in the Subplot of *King Lear*." *SEL* 12.2 (1972): 275–289.

Engle, Lars. "How is Horatio Just?: How Just Is Horatio?" *Shakespeare Quarterly* 62.2 (2011): 256–262.

Engler, Balz. "Othello's Great Heart." *English Studies* 68 (1987): 129–136.

Erickson, Peter, and Kim F. Hall. "'A New Scholarly Song': Rereading Early Modern Race." *Shakespeare Quarterly* 67.1 (2016): 1–13.

Evans, Kasey. "Misreadings and Misogyny: Ariosto, Spenser, and Shakespeare." *Renaissance Drama* 36/37 (2010): 261–292.

Faber, Melvyn Donald. "Lord Brutus' Wife: A Modern View." *Psychoanalytic Review* 52.4 (1965): 109–115.

————. "Ophelia's Doubtful Death." *Literature and Psychology* 16 (1966): 103–108.

————. "Some Remarks on the Suicide of King Lear's Eldest Daughter." *University Review* 33 (1967): 313–317.

————. "Suicide in Shakespeare." PhD diss., University of California, 1963.

Fawcett, Mary Laughlin. "Arms/Words/Tears: Language and the Body in *Titus Andronicus*." *ELH* 50.2 (1983): 261–277.

Ferngren, Gary B. "The Ethics of Suicide in the Renaissance and Reformation." In *Suicide and Euthanasia*, edited by Baruch A. Brody, 155–181. Dordrecht: Springer Netherlands, 1989.

Ferrell, Lori Anne. "New Directions: Promised End? *King Lear* and the Suicide Trick." In *King Lear: A Critical Guide*, edited by Andrew Hiscock and Lisa Hopkins, 99–117. London: Continuum, 2011.

Findlay, Alison. *Women in Shakespeare: A Dictionary*. London and New York: Continuum, 2010.

Fly, Richard. *Shakespeare's Mediated World*. Amherst: University of Massachusetts Press, 1976.

Foakes, R. A. "An Approach to *Julius Caesar.*" *Shakespeare Quarterly* 5.3 (1954): 259–270.

————. Introduction to *King Lear*, by William Shakespeare, edited by R. A. Foakes, 1–151. The Arden Shakespeare Third Series. London: Arden Shakespeare, 1997.

————. *Shakespeare and Violence*. Cambridge: Cambridge University Press, 2003.

Foucault, Michel. *Madness and Civilization: A History of Insanity in the Age of Reason.* 1964. Reprint, New York: Vintage, 1988.

Fox, Alice. "Obstetrics and Gynecology in *Macbeth.*" *Shakespeare Studies* 12 (1979): 127–141.

Fox-Good, Jacquelyn A. "Ophelia's Mad Songs: Music, Gender, Power." In *Subjects on the World's Stage: Essays on British Literature of the Middle Ages and the Renaissance*, edited by David C. Allen and Robert A. White, 217–238. Newark: University of Delaware Press, 1995.

Freud, Sigmund. *Beyond the Pleasure Principle and Other Writings.* 1920. Reprint, London: Penguin, 2003.

————. *Totem and Taboo: Some Points of Agreement between the Mental Lives of Savages and Neurotics.* 1913. Reprint, London: Routledge, 2001.

Frye, Roland Mushat. "Macbeth's Usurping Wife." *Renaissance News* 8.2 (1955): 102–105.

————. *The Renaissance Hamlet: Issues and Responses in 1600.* Princeton: Princeton University Press, 1984.

Gibinska, Marta. "Villains on the Throne. Some Remarks on the Dramatic Craft of *Richard III* and *Macbeth.*" In *Word and Action in Drama*, edited by Günter Ahrends, Stephan Kohl, Joachim Kornelius, and Gerd Stratmann, 8–1. Trier: WVT, 1994.

Goldberg, Jonathan. "Speculations: *Macbeth* and Source." In *Shakespeare Reproduced: The Text in History and Ideology*, edited and introduced by Jean E. Howard and Marion F. O'Connor, 242–264. New York: Methuen, 1987.

Gossett, Suzanne. "*The Two Noble Kinsmen* and *Henry VIII*: The Last Last Plays." In *The Cambridge Companion to Shakespeare's Last Plays*, edited by Catherine M. S. Alexander, 185–202. Cambridge: Cambridge University Press, 2009.

Gowing, Laura. *Gender Relations in Early Modern England*. London and New York: Routledge, 2014.

Gray, Patrick. "The Compassionate Stoic: Brutus as Accidental Hero." *Shakespeare Jahrbuch* 152 (2016): 30–44.

Greenblatt, Stephen. *Hamlet in Purgatory.* 2001. Reprint, Princeton: Princeton University Press, 2013.

————. *Renaissance Self-Fashioning.* Chicago and London: University of Chicago Press, 2005.

————. *Shakespearean Negotiations: The Circulation of Social Energy in Renaissance England.* Oxford: Clarendon, 1988.

Griffin, Miriam. "Philosophy, Cato, and Roman Suicide: I." *Greece & Rome* 33.1 (1986): 64–77.

Gunderson, Erik. *Staging Masculinity: The Rhetoric of Performance in the Roman World*. Ann Arbor: University of Michigan Press, 2000.

Halio, Jay L. "The Promised Endings of *King Lear*." In *The Work of Dissimilitude: Essays from the Sixth Citadel Conference on Medieval and Renaissance Literature*, edited by David G. Allen and Robert A. White, 235–242. Newark/London: University of Delaware Press/Associated University Press, 1992.

Hall, Kim F. *Things of Darkness: Economies of Race and Gender in Early Modern England*. Ithaca and London: Cornell University Press, 1995.

Halter, Peter. "The Endings of *King Lear*." In *On Strangeness*, edited by Margaret Bridges, 85–98. Tübingen: Narr, 1990.

Hankins, John Erskine. "Suicide in Shakespeare." In *The Character of Hamlet and other Essays*, edited by John Erskine Hankins, 222–239. Chapel Hill: University of North Carolina Press, 1941.

Hart, Evalee. "A Comparative Study: *Macbeth* and *Richard III*." *The English Journal* 61.6 (1972): 824–830.

Hartley, Andrew James. *Julius Caesar in Performance*. Manchester: Manchester University Press, 2014.

Hazlitt, William. *Characters of Shakespeare's Plays*. Edited by F. J. S. London: Dent, 1906.

Heavey, Katherine. *The Early Modern Medea. Medea in English Literature, 1558–1688*. Basingstoke and New York: Palgrave, 2015.

Helms, Lorraine. "'The High Roman Fashion:' Sacrifice, Suicide, and the Shakespearean Stage." *PMLA* 107.3 (1992): 554–565.

Henry, Patrick. "The Dialectic of Suicide in Montaigne's 'Coustume de l'Isle de Cea.'" *The Modern Language Review* 79.2 (1984): 278–289.

Higonnet, Margaret. "Speaking Silences: Women's Suicide." In *The Female Body in Western Culture: Contemporary Perspectives*, edited by Susan Rubin Suleiman, 68–83. Cambridge, MA and London: Harvard University Press, 1985.

Hodgdon, Barbara. "Absent Bodies, Present Voices: Performance Work and the Close of *Romeo and Juliet*'s Golden Story." *Theatre Journal* 41.3 (1989): 341–359.

———. "*Antony and Cleopatra* in the Theatre." In *The Cambridge Companion to Shakespearean Tragedy*, edited by Claire McEachern, 241–263. Cambridge: Cambridge University Press, 2002.

———. "Race-ing *Othello*: Re-Engendering White-Out." In *Shakespeare, the Movie: Popularizing the Plays on Film, TV and Video*, edited by Lynda E. Boose and Richard Burt, 23–44. London: Routledge, 1997.

Holmer, Joan Ozark. "Desdemona, Woman Warrior: 'O, These Men, These Men!' (4.3.59)" *Medieval and Renaissance Drama in England* 17 (2005): 132–164.

Honigmann, E. A. J. Introduction to *Othello*, by William Shakespeare, edited by E. A. J. Honigmann, 1–111. The Arden Shakespeare Third Series. London: Arden Shakespeare, 1997.

———. *Shakespeare: Seven Tragedies: A Dramatist's Manipulation of Response*. London: Macmillan, 1976.

———. *The Texts of Othello and Shakespearean Revision*. London and New York: Routledge, 1996.

————. "*Timon of Athens.*" *Shakespeare Quarterly* 12.1 (1961): 3–20.

Hoover, Claudette. "Goneril and Regan: 'So Horrid as in Woman.'" *San Jose Studies* 10.3 (1984): 49–65.

Hope, Jonathan. *The Authorship of Shakespeare's Plays: A Socio-Linguistic Study.* Cambridge: Cambridge University Press, 1994.

Hope, Valerie M. *Roman Death: The Dying and the Dead in Ancient Rome.* London: Continuum, 2009.

Hotine, Margaret. "*Richard III* and *Macbeth* – Studies in Tudor Tyranny?" *Notes and Queries* 38.4 (1991): 480–486.

Houston, R. A. *Punishing the Dead? Suicide, Lordship, and Community in Britain, 1500–1830.* Oxford: Oxford University Press, 2010.

Howard, Tony. *Women as Hamlet: Performance and Interpretation in Theatre, Film and Fiction.* Cambridge: Cambridge University Press, 2007.

Hoxby, Blair. *What Was Tragedy? Theory and the Early Modern Canon.* Oxford: Oxford University Press, 2015.

Hughes, Alan. "Lady Macbeth: A Fiend Indeed?" *Southern Review* 11 (1978): 107–112.

Hughes, Daniel E. "The 'Worm of Conscience' in *Richard III* and *Macbeth.*" *The English Journal* 55.7 (1966): 845–852.

Ichikawa, Mariko. *The Shakespearean Stage Space.* Cambridge: Cambridge University Press, 2013.

Imbracsio, Nicola M. "Stage Hands: *Titus Andronicus* and the Agency of the Disabled Body in Text and Performance." In *Titus out of Joint: Reading the Fragmented Titus Andronicus*, edited by Liberty Stavanage and Paxton Hehmeyer, 113–124. Cambridge: Cambridge Scholars, 2012.

Jacobi, Derek. "Macbeth." In *Players of Shakespeare 4: Further Essays in Shakespearian Performance by Players with the Royal Shakespeare Company*, edited by Robert Smallwood, 193–210. Cambridge: Cambridge University Press, 1998.

James, Heather. "Cultural Disintegration in *Titus Andronicus*: Mutilating Titus, Vergil, and Rome." *Violence in Drama, Themes in Drama* 13 (1991): 123–140.

James, Mervyn. *Society, Politics and Culture: Studies in Early Modern England.* Cambridge: Cambridge University Press, 1986.

Jardine, Lisa. *Still Harping on Daughters: Women and Drama in the Age of Shakespeare.* Brighton: Harvester, 1983.

Jenkins, Harold. Introduction to *Hamlet*, by William Shakespeare, edited by Harold Jenkins, 1–159. The Arden Shakespeare Second Series. London: Arden Shakespeare, 1982.

————. "'To Be, Or Not to Be': Hamlet's Dilemma." *Hamlet Studies* 13.1/2 (1991): 8–24.

Johnson, Christopher. "Appropriating Troy: Ekphrasis in Shakespeare's 'The Rape of Lucrece.'" In *Fantasies of Troy: Classical Tales and the Social Imaginary in Medieval and Early Modern Europe*, edited by Alan Shepard and Stephen D. Powell, 193–214. Toronto: CRRS, 2004.

Kahn, Coppélia. "Afterword: Ophelia Then, Now, Hereafter." In *The Afterlife of Ophelia*, edited by Kaara L. Peterson and Deanne Williams, 231–244. New York: Palgrave, 2012.

————. *Man's Estate: Masculine Identity in Shakespeare*. Berkeley: University of California Press, 1981.

————. *Roman Shakespeare: Warriors, Wounds, and Women*. London and New York: Routledge, 1997.

————. "Shakespeare's Classical Tragedies." In *The Cambridge Companion to Shakespearean Tragedy*, edited by Claire McEachern, 204–223. Cambridge: Cambridge University Press, 2002.

————. "The Absent Mother in *King Lear*." In *Rewriting the Renaissance: The Discourse of Sexual Difference in Early Modern Europe*, edited by Margaret W. Ferguson, Maureen Quilligan, and Nancy J. Vickers, 33–49. Chicago: University of Chicago Press, 1986.

Kamps, Ivo. "'I Love You Madly, I Love You to Death:' Erotomania and Liebestod in *Romeo and Juliet*." In *Approaches to Teaching Shakespeare's Romeo and Juliet*, edited by Maurice Hunt, 37–46. New York: MLA, 2000.

Karim-Cooper, Farah. *The Hand on the Shakespearean Stage: Gesture, Touch and the Spectacle of Dismemberment*. London and New York: Arden Shakespeare, 2016.

Kastan, David Scott. "'A Rarity Most Beloved': Shakespeare and the Idea of Tragedy." In *A Companion to Shakespeare's Works: The Tragedies*, edited by Richard Dutton and Jean E. Howard, 4–22. Oxford: Blackwell, 2003.

————. *A Will to Believe: Shakespeare and Religion*. Oxford: Oxford University Press, 2014.

Kehler, Dorothea. "Cleopatra's *Sati*: Old Ideologies and Modern Stagings." In *Antony and Cleopatra: New Critical Essays*, edited by Sara Munson Deats, 137–152. London and New York: Routledge, 2005.

————. "*Othello* and Racism." In *Understanding Racial Issues in Shakespeare's Othello: Selected Critical Essays*, edited by Solomon Iyasere and Marla Iyasere, 155–169. New York: Whitston, 2008.

Keppel, Tim. "Goneril's Version: *A Thousand Acres* and *King Lear*." *South Dakota Review* 33.2 (1995): 105–117.

Ker, James. *The Deaths of Seneca*. Oxford: Oxford University Press, 2009.

Kirsch, Arthur. *The Passions of Shakespeare's Tragic Heroes*. Charlottesville: University of Virginia Press, 1990.

Kläger, Florian. *Forgone Nations. Constructions of National Identity in Elizabethan Historiography and Literature: Stanihurst, Spenser, Shakespeare*. Trier: WVT, 2006.

Knight, G. Wilson. *The Wheel of Fire: Interpretations of Shakespearean Tragedy*. 1930. Reprint, London and New York: Routledge, 2001.

Kocher, Paul H. "Lady Macbeth and the Doctor." *Shakespeare Quarterly* 5.4 (1954): 341–349.

Kolesch, Doris. "Wie *Othello* Spielen?" *Shakespeare Jahrbuch* 152 (2016): 87–103.

Kolin, Philip C. "*Titus Andronicus* and the Critical Legacy." In *Titus Andronicus: Critical Essays*, edited by Philip C. Kolin, 3–55. New York and London: Garland, 1995.

Kordecki, Lesley, and Karla Koskinen. *Re-Visioning Lear's Daughters: Testing Feminist Criticism and Theory*. New York: Palgrave, 2010.

Kott, Jan. *Shakespeare our Contemporary*. London: Routledge, 1991.

Kottman, Paul A. "Defying the Stars: Tragic Love as the Struggle for Freedom in *Romeo and Juliet.*" *Shakespeare Quarterly* 63.1 (2012): 1–38.

Kristeva, Julia. *Powers of Horror: An Essay on Abjection.* New York: Columbia University Press, 1982.

La Belle, Jenijoy. "'A Strange Infirmity': Lady Macbeth's Amenorrhea." *Shakespeare Quarterly* 31.3 (1980): 381–386.

Langley, Eric. *Narcissism and Suicide in Shakespeare and His Contemporaries.* Oxford: Oxford University Press, 2009.

Laqueur, Thomas. *Making Sex: Body and Gender from the Greeks to Freud.* Cambridge, MA and London: Harvard University Press, 1992.

Lawrence, Sean. "The Difficulty of Dying in *King Lear.*" *ESC* 31.4 (2005): 35–52.

Leavis, F. R. "Diabolic Intellect and the Noble Hero: A Note on Othello." *Scrutiny* 6 (1937): 259–283.

Leech, Clifford. "The Moral Tragedy of Romeo and Juliet." In *Critical Essays on Shakespeare's Romeo and Juliet,* edited by Joseph A. Porter, 7–22. New York: Hall, 1997.

Leggatt, Alexander. *Shakespeare in Performance: King Lear.* Manchester: Manchester University Press, 1991.

———. *Shakespeare's Political Drama: The History Plays and the Roman Plays.* London and New York: Routledge, 1988.

———. *Shakespeare's Tragedies: Violation and Identity.* Cambridge: Cambridge University Press, 2005.

Lenker, Lagretta T. "Suicide and the Dialectic of Gender in *Hamlet.*" In *Youth Suicide: A Comprehensive Manual for Prevention and Intervention,* edited by Barbara Barrett Hicks, 93–114. Bloomington: National Educational Service, 1989.

Leverenz, David. "The Woman in Hamlet: An Interpersonal View." *Signs* 4.2 (1978): 291–308.

Levin, Joanna. "Lady Macbeth and the Daemonologie of Hysteria." *ELH* 69.1 (2002): 21–55.

Lind, Vera. *Selbstmord in der Frühen Neuzeit. Diskurs, Lebenswelt und Kultureller Wandel.* Göttingen: Vandenhoeck und Ruprecht, 1999.

Loomba, Ania. *Gender, Race, Renaissance Drama.* Manchester and New York: Manchester University Press, 1989.

———. *Shakespeare, Race, and Colonialism.* Oxford and New York: Oxford University Press, 2002.

Loxley, James. *Performativity.* The New Critical Idiom. London and New York: Routledge, 2007.

Lusardi, James P., and June Schlueter. *Reading Shakespeare in Performance: King Lear.* Madison: Fairleigh Dickinson University Press, 1991.

Lyons, Bridget Gellert. "The Iconography of Ophelia." *ELH* 44.1 (1977): 60–74.

MacCallum, Mungo William. *Shakespeare's Roman Plays and Their Background.* 1910. Reprint, London and Melbourne: Macmillan, 1967.

MacDonald, Michael. *Mystical Bedlam: Madness, Anxiety, and Healing in Seventeenth-Century England.* Cambridge: Cambridge University Press, 1981.

———. "Ophelia's Maimèd Rites." *Shakespeare Quarterly* 37.3 (1986): 309–317.

_____. *Sleepless Souls: Suicide in Early Modern England*. Oxford: Clarendon, 1993.

MacKenzie, Clayton G. "Love, Sex and Death in *Romeo and Juliet*." *English Studies* 88.1 (2007): 22–42.

Madeleine, Richard. *Shakespeare in Production: Antony and Cleopatra*. Cambridge: Cambridge University Press, 1998.

Mann, David. *Shakespeare's Women: Performance and Conception*. Cambridge: Cambridge University Press, 2008.

Marshall, Cynthia. "Man of Steel Done Got the Blues: Melancholic Subversion of Presence in *Antony and Cleopatra*." *Shakespeare Quarterly* 44.4 (1993): 385–408.

_____. "Portia's Wound, Calphurnia's Dream: Reading Character in *Julius Caesar*." *English Literary Renaissance* 24.2 (1994): 471–488.

Martin, John Jeffries. *Myths of Renaissance Individualism*. Basingstoke and New York: Palgrave, 2004.

Masten, Jeffrey. "Toward a Queer Address: The Taste of Letters and Early Modern Male Friendship." *GLQ* 10.3 (2004): 367–384.

Maxwell, J. C. Introduction to *Titus Andronicus*, by William Shakespeare, edited by J. C. Maxwell, xi–xlv. The Arden Shakespeare Second Series. London: Arden Shakespeare, 1953.

McAlindon, Thomas. *Shakespeare's Tragic Cosmos*. Cambridge: Cambridge University Press, 1991.

_____. "What is a Shakespearean Tragedy?" In *The Cambridge Companion to Shakespearean Tragedy*, edited by Claire McEachern, 1–22. Cambridge: Cambridge University Press, 2002.

McDonald, Russ. *Look to the Lady: Sarah Siddons, Ellen Terry, and Judi Dench on the Shakespearean Stage*. Athens and London: The University of Georgia Press, 2005.

McGuire, Philip C. "Whose Work Is This: Loading the Bed in *Othello*." In *Shakespearean Illuminations: Essays in Honor of Marvin Rosenberg*, edited by Jay L. Halio and Hugh Richmond, 70–92. Newark: University of Delaware Press, 1998.

McLaughlin, John J. "The Dynamics of Power in *King Lear*: An Adlerian Interpretation." *Shakespeare Quarterly* 29.1 (1978): 37–43.

McLuskie, Kathleen. "The Patriarchal Bard: Feminist Criticism and Shakespeare: *King Lear* and *Measure for Measure*." In *Political Shakespeare*, edited by Jonathan Dollimore and Alan Sinfield, 88–108. Manchester: Manchester University Press, 1985.

Menzer, Paul. *Anecdotal Shakespeare: A New Performance History*. London and New York: Arden Shakespeare, 2015.

Miles, Murray. "Plato on Suicide (*Phaedo* 60C–63C)." *Phoenix* 55.3/4 (2001): 244–258.

Minois, Georges. *History of Suicide: Voluntary Death in Western Culture*. Translated by Lydia G. Cochrane. Baltimore: Johns Hopkins University Press, 1999.

Moisan, Thomas. "Rhetoric and the Rehearsal of Death: The 'Lamentations' Scene in *Romeo and Juliet*." *Shakespeare Quarterly* 34.4 (1983): 389–404.

Muir, Kenneth. Introduction to *Macbeth*, by William Shakespeare, edited by Kenneth Muir, xiii–lxv. The Arden Shakespeare Second Series. 2nd ed. London: Arden Shakespeare, 1997.

_____. "Pyramus and Thisbe: A Study in Shakespeare's Method." *Shakespeare Quarterly* 5.2 (1954): 141–153.

_____. *Shakespeare as Collaborator.* London: Methuen, 1960.

_____. *The Sources of Shakespeare's Plays.* London and New York: Routledge, 1977.

Munkelt, Marga. "Shakespeare's Cleopatra: Aspects of Queenship and Authority." Lecture at the University of Münster, Germany, January 24, 2011.

Murray, Alexander. *Suicide in the Middle Ages: Volume I: The Violent against Themselves.* Oxford: Oxford University Press, 1998.

_____. *Suicide in the Middle Ages: Volume II: The Curse on Self-Murder.* Oxford: Oxford University Press, 2000.

Neely, Carol Thomas. *Distracted Subjects: Madness and Gender in Shakespeare and Early Modern Culture.* New York: Cornell University Press, 2004.

_____. "Documents in Madness: Reading Madness and Gender in Shakespeare's Tragedies and Early Modern Culture." In *Shakespearean Tragedy and Gender*, edited by Shirley Nelson Garner and Madelon Sprengnether, 75–104. Bloomington: Indiana University Press, 1996.

Neill, Michael. "Death and *King Lear*." In *Shakespeare in Our Time: A Shakespeare Association of America Collection*, edited by Dympna Callaghan and Suzanne Gossett, 81–85. London and New York: Arden Shakespeare, 2016.

_____. Introduction to *Antony and Cleopatra*, by William Shakespeare, edited by Michael Neill, 1–130. Oxford: Oxford University Press, 2008.

_____. *Issues of Death: Mortality and Identity in English Renaissance Tragedy.* Oxford: Clarendon, 1997.

_____. "*Othello* and Race." In *Approaches to Teaching Shakespeare's Othello*, edited by Peter Erickson and Maurice Hunt, 37–52. New York: MLA, 2005.

_____. "Unproper Beds: Race, Adultery, and the Hideous in *Othello*." In *Understanding Racial Issues in Shakespeare's Othello: Selected Critical Essays*, edited by Solomon and Marla Iyasere, 15–53. New York: Whitston, 2008.

Nelson, T. G. A., and Charles Haines. "Othello's Unconsummated Marriage." *Essays in Criticism* 33.1 (1983): 1–18.

Nevo, Ruth. "Tragic Form in *Romeo and Juliet*." SEL 9 (1969): 241–258.

Nosworthy, J. M. "The Death of Ophelia." *Shakespeare Quarterly* 15.4 (1964): 345–348.

Novy, Marianne. *Shakespeare and Outsiders.* Oxford: Oxford University Press, 2013.

O'Dair, Sharon. "Social Role and the Making of Identity in *Julius Caesar*." *SEL* 33.2 (1993): 289–307.

Oates, Joyce Carol. "'Is This the Promised End?': The Tragedy of *King Lear*." *The Journal of Aesthetics and Art Criticism* 33.1 (1974): 19–32.

Olk, Claudia. "Performing Conscience in *Richard III*." *Anglia* 130.1 (2012): 1–18.

Orgel, Stephen. *Impersonations: The Performance of Gender in Shakespeare's England.* Cambridge: Cambridge University Press, 1996.

Orkin, Martin. "Othello and the 'Plain Face' of Racism." *Shakespeare Quarterly* 38.2 (1987): 166–188.

Packard, Bethany. "Lavinia as Coauthor of Shakespeare's *Titus Andronicus*." *SEL* 50.2 (2010): 281–300.

Pao, Angela C. "Ocular Revisions: Re-Casting *Othello* in Text and Performance." In *Colorblind Shakespeare: New Perspectives on Race and Performance*, edited by Ayanna Thompson, 27–45. New York and Abingdon: Routledge, 2006.

Paolucci, Anne. "The Tragic Hero in *Julius Caesar*." *Shakespeare Quarterly* 11.3 (1960): 329–333.

Paster, Gail Kern. "'In the Spirit of Men There Is No Blood': Blood as Trope of Gender in *Julius Caesar*." *Shakespeare Quarterly* 40.3 (1989): 284–298.

Peterson, Kaara. "Framing Ophelia: Representation and the Pictorial Tradition." *Mosaic* 31.3 (1998): 1–24.

Peterson, Kaara, and Deanne Williams. "Introduction: The Afterlives of Ophelia." In *The Afterlife of Ophelia*, edited by Kaara L. Peterson and Deanne Williams, 1–10. New York: Palgrave, 2012.

Petronella, Vincent F. "Hamlet's 'To Be Or Not To Be' Soliloquy: Once More unto the Breach." *Studies in Philology* 71.1 (1974): 72–88.

Philip, Ranjini. "The Shattered Glass: The Story of (O)phelia." *Hamlet Studies* 13.1/2 (1991): 73–84.

Phillips, Chelsea. "'Unsex Me Here': Bodies and Femininity in the Performance History of Lady Macbeth." *Testi e Linguaggi* 7 (2013): 353–361.

Pitt, Angela. *Shakespeare's Women*. Newton Abbot: David & Charles, 1981.

Pollard, Tanya. "'A Thing Like Death:' Sleeping Potions and Poisons in *Romeo and Juliet* and *Antony and Cleopatra*." *Renaissance Drama* 32 (2003): 95–121.

Pollin, Burton R. "Hamlet, A Successful Suicide." *Shakespeare Studies* 1 (1965): 240–260.

Potter, Lois. "Assisted Suicides: *Antony and Cleopatra* and *Coriolanus* in 2006–7." *Shakespeare Quarterly* 58.4 (2007): 509–529.

———. Introduction to *The Two Noble Kinsmen*, by William Shakespeare, edited by Lois Potter, 1–129. The Arden Shakespeare Third Series. London: Arden Shakespeare, 1997.

———. "Ophelia and Some Theatrical Successors." In *The Afterlife of Ophelia*, edited by Kaara L. Peterson and Deanne Williams, 153–168. New York: Palgrave, 2012.

———. *Othello in Performance*. Manchester: Manchester University Press, 2002.

Quabeck, Franziska. *Just and Unjust Wars in Shakespeare*. Berlin: de Gruyter, 2013.

Quarmby, Kevin A. "Sexing Up Goneril: Feminism and Fetishization in Contemporary *King Lear* Performance." In *Women Making Shakespeare: Text, Reception and Performance*, edited by Gordon McMullan, Lena Cowen Orlin, and Virginia Mason Vaughan, 323–333. London and New York: Arden Shakespeare, 2014.

Rackin, Phyllis. *Shakespeare and Women*. Oxford: Oxford University Press, 2005.

———. "Shakespeare's Boy Cleopatra, the Decorum of Nature, and the Golden World of Poetry." *PMLA* 87.2 (1972): 201–212.

_____. "Staging the Female Body: Maternal Breastfeeding and Lady Macbeth's 'Unsex Me Here.'" In *Corps/Décors: Femmes, Orgie, Parodie*, edited and introduced by Catherine Nesci, Gretchen Van Slyke, and Gerald Prince, 17–29. Amsterdam: Rodopi, 1999.

Ramsey, Jarold. "The Perversion of Manliness in *Macbeth*." *SEL* 13.2 (1973): 285–300.

Ratcliffe, Stephen. *Reading the Unseen: (Offstage) Hamlet*. Denver: Counterpath, 2010.

Read, David. "Disappearing Act: The Role of Enobarbus in *Antony and Cleopatra*." *Studies in Philology* 110.3 (2013): 562–583.

Reid, Stephen. "In Defense of Goneril and Regan." *American Imago* 27 (1970): 226–244.

Ribner, Irving. *Patterns in Shakespearian Tragedy*. 1960. Reprint, London and New York: Routledge, 2005.

Riccomini, Donald R. "Warrior Ethic in *Macbeth* and *Henry V*." *The Upstart Crow* 30 (2011): 42–66.

Rice, Julian C. "Hamlet and the Dream of Something after Death." *Hartford Studies in Literature* 6 (1974): 109–116.

Rist, J. M. *Stoic Philosophy*. Cambridge: Cambridge University Press, 1969.

Roberts, Joanne Addison. "Sex and the Female Tragic Hero." In *The Female Tragic Hero in English Renaissance Drama*, edited by Naomi Conn Liebler, 199–215. New York and Basingstoke: Palgrave, 2002.

Roe, John. "'Character' in Plutarch and Shakespeare: Brutus, Julius Caesar, and Mark Antony." In *Shakespeare and the Classics*, edited by Charles Martindale and A. B. Taylor, 173–178. Cambridge: Cambridge University Press, 2004.

Ronk, Martha. "Desdemona's Self-Presentation." *English Literary Renaissance* 35.1 (2005): 52–72.

_____. "Representations of Ophelia." *Criticism* 36.1 (1994): 21–43.

Rose, Mary Beth. "Suicide as Profit or Loss." In *Shakespeare in Our Time: A Shakespeare Association of America Collection*, edited by Dympna Callaghan and Suzanne Gossett, 73–80. London and New York: Arden Shakespeare, 2016.

Rowe, Katherine A. "Dismembering and Forgetting in *Titus Andronicus*." *Shakespeare Quarterly* 45.3 (1994): 279–303.

Rozett, Martha Tuck. "The Comic Structures of Tragic Endings: The Suicide Scenes in *Romeo and Juliet* and *Antony and Cleopatra*." *Shakespeare Quarterly* 36.2 (1985): 152–164.

Rubinstein, Frankie. "Speculating on Mysteries: Religion and Politics in *King Lear*." *Renaissance Studies* 16.2 (2002): 234–262.

Rudnytsky, Peter L. "'The Darke and Vicious Place': The Dread of the Vagina in *King Lear*." *Modern Philology* 96.3 (1999): 291–311.

Russell Beale, Simon. "Macbeth." In *Performing Shakespeare's Tragedies Today: The Actor's Perspective*, edited by Michael Dobson, 107–118. Cambridge: Cambridge University Press, 2006.

Rutter, Carol Chillington. *Enter the Body: Women and Representation on Shakespeare's Stage*. London and New York: Routledge, 2001.

Rymer, Thomas. "From *A Short View of Tragedy* (1693)." In *Shakespeare: Othello: A Casebook*, edited by John Wain, 39–49. Basingstoke and London: Macmillan, 1994.

Sacharoff, Mark. "Suicide and Brutus' Philosophy in *Julius Caesar*." *Journal of the History of Ideas* 33.1 (1972): 115–122.

Sanderson, Richard K. "Suicide as Message and Metadrama in English Renaissance Tragedy." *Comparative Drama* 26.3 (1992): 199–217.

Schoff, Francis G. "Horatio: A Shakespearean Confidant." *Shakespeare Quarterly* 7.1 (1956): 53–57.

Schücking, Levin L. *The Meaning of Hamlet*. Oxford: Oxford University Press, 1937.

Shalvi, Alice. "'Honor' in *Troilus* and *Cressida*." *SEL* 5.2 (1965): 283–302.

Shannon, Laurie. *Sovereign Amity: Figures of Friendship in Shakespearean Contexts*. Chicago: University of Chicago Press, 2002.

Sharrock, Alison. "Gender and Sexuality." In *The Cambridge Companion to Ovid*, edited by Philip Hardie, 95–107. Cambridge: Cambridge University Press, 2002.

Shell, Alison. *Shakespeare and Religion*. London and New York: Arden Shakespeare, 2010.

Shneidman, Edwin S. *Definition of Suicide*. Northvale: Jason Aronson, 1985.

Showalter, Elaine. "Representing Ophelia: Women, Madness, and the Responsibilities of Feminist Criticism." In *Shakespeare and the Question of Theory*, edited by Geoffrey H. Hartman and Patricia Parker, 77–94. London and New York: Routledge, 1985.

———. *The Female Malady: Women, Madness, and English Culture, 1830–1980*. London: Virago, 1987.

Sillars, Stuart. *Painting Shakespeare: The Artist as Critic, 1720–1820*. Cambridge: Cambridge University Press, 2006.

Slights, Camille. "Murder, Suicide and Conscience: The Case of Brutus and Hamlet." In *Familiar Colloquy: Essays Presented to Arthur Edward Barker*, edited by Patricia Bruckmann and Jane Couchman, 113–131. Ottawa: Oberon, 1978.

Smith, Barbara. "Neither Accident nor Intent: Contextualizing the Suicide of Ophelia." *South Atlantic Review* 73.2 (2008): 96–112.

Smith, Bruce R. *Shakespeare and Masculinity*. Oxford: Oxford University Press, 2000.

Smith, Emma. "*Romeo and Juliet*." *University of Oxford Podcasts: Approaching Shakespeare*, May 5, 2015. Accessed May 3, 2017. https://podcasts.ox.ac.uk/romeo-and-juliet.

Smith, Warren D. "The Duplicate Revelation of Portia's Death." *Shakespeare Quarterly* 4.2 (1953): 153–161.

Snyder, Susan. "*King Lear* and the Psychology of Dying." *Shakespeare Quarterly* 33.4 (1982): 449–460.

———. "*Romeo and Juliet*: Comedy into Tragedy." *Essays in Criticism* 20 (1970): 391–402.

Sontag, Susan. *Regarding the Pain of Others*. London and New York: Penguin, 2003.

Spencer, Charles. "A Dramatic Power that Makes the Stomach Churn and the Hands Sweat." Review of *Titus Andronicus*, by William Shakespeare. Directed by Lucy Bailey. *The Daily Telegraph*, May 2, 2014. Accessed April 27, 2017. www.telegraph.co.uk/culture/theatre/theatre-reviews/10803436/Titus-Andronicus-review-a-dramatic-power-that-makes-the-stomach-churn-and-the-hands-sweat.html.

Spevack, Marvin. "The Art of Dying in Shakespeare." *Jahrbuch Deutsche Shakespeare-Gesellschaft West* (1989): 169–173.

Spisak, James W. "Pyramus and Thisbe in Chaucer and Shakespeare." In *Chaucerian Shakespeare: Adaptation and Transformation*, edited by E. Talbot and Judith J. Kollmann, 81–95. Detroit: Marygrove College, 1983.

Sproule, Albert Frederick. "A Time Scheme for *Othello*." *Shakespeare Quarterly* 7.2 (1956): 217–226.

Stallybrass, Peter. "*Macbeth* and Witchcraft." In *Focus on Macbeth*, edited by John Russell Brown, 189–209. Boston: Routledge, 1982.

Starks, Lisa S. "'Immortal Longings:' The Erotics of Death in *Antony and Cleopatra*." In *Antony and Cleopatra: New Critical Essays*, edited by Sara Munson Deats, 243–258. London and New York: Routledge, 2005.

———. "Transforming Ovid: Images of Violence, Vulnerability, and Sexuality in Shakespeare's *Titus Andronicus*." In *Staging the Blazon in Early Modern English Theatre*, edited by Deborah Uman and Sara Morrison, 53–66. Farnham and Burlington: Ashgate, 2013.

Starks-Estes, Lisa S. *Violence, Trauma, and Virtus in Shakespeare's Roman Poems and Plays: Transforming Ovid*. Basingstoke: Palgrave, 2014.

Stirling, Brents. "Brutus and the Death of Portia." *Shakespeare Quarterly* 10.2 (1959): 211–217.

Streete, Adrian. "'What Bloody Man Is That?': Questioning Biblical Typology in *Macbeth*." *Shakespeare* 5.1 (2009): 1835.

Sullivan, Ernest W. Introduction to *Biathanatos*, by John Donne, edited by Ernest W. Sullivan, ix–lxxi. Newark: University of Delaware Press, 1984.

Tandon, B. G. "Why Does Ophelia Die Offstage?" *The Aligarh Journal of English Studies* 15 (1993): 1–5.

Taylor, A. B. "Animals in 'Manly Shape As Too the Outward Showe': Moralizing and Metamorphosis in *Titus Andronicus*." In *Shakespeare's Ovid: The Metamorphoses in the Plays and Poems*, edited by A. B. Taylor, 66–80. Cambridge: Cambridge University Press, 2000.

Thomas, Sian. "Lady Macbeth." In *Performing Shakespeare's Tragedies Today: The Actor's Perspective*, edited by Michael Dobson, 95–105. Cambridge: Cambridge University Press, 2006.

Thompson, Ann. "Are There Any Women in *King Lear*?" In *The Matter of Difference: Materialist Feminist Criticism of Shakespeare*, edited by Valerie Wayne, 117–128. Ithaca: Cornell University Press, 1991.

Thompson, Ann, and Neil Taylor. Introduction to *Hamlet*, by William Shakespeare, edited by Ann Thompson and Neil Taylor, 1–145. The Arden Shakespeare Third Series. London: Arden Shakespeare, 2006.

Thompson, Ayanna. Introduction to *Othello*, by William Shakespeare, edited by E. A. J. Honigmann, rev. ed., 1–116. The Arden Shakespeare Third Series. London and New York: Arden Shakespeare, 2016.

Townshend, Dale. "Unsexing *Macbeth*." In *Macbeth: A Critical Reader*, edited by John Drakakis and Dale Townshend, 172–204. London: Arden Shakespeare, 2013.

Traub, Valerie. *Desire and Anxiety: Circulations of Sexuality in Shakespearean Drama*. London and New York: Routledge, 1992.

———. "Gender and Sexuality in Shakespeare." In *The Cambridge Companion to Shakespeare*, edited by Margreta de Grazia and Stanley Wells, 129–146. Cambridge: Cambridge University Press, 2001.

Traub, Valerie, M. Lindsay Kaplan, and Dympna Callaghan. Introduction to *Feminist Readings of Early Modern Culture: Emerging Subjects*, edited by Valerie Traub, M. Lindsay Kaplan, and Dympna Callaghan, 1–15. Cambridge: Cambridge University Press, 1996.

Van Hooff, Anton J. L. *From Autothanasia to Suicide: Self-Killing in Classical Antiquity*. London and New York: Routledge, 1990.

Vanhoutte, Jacqueline. "Antony's 'Secret House of Death:' Suicide and Sovereignty in *Antony and Cleopatra*." *Philological Quarterly* 79 (2000): 153–175.

Vasileiou, Margaret Rice. "Violence, Visual Metaphor, and the 'True' Lucrece." *SEL* 51.1 (2011): 47–63.

Vawter, Marvin L. "'Division 'Tween Our Souls': Shakespeare's Stoic Brutus." *Shakespeare Studies* 7 (1974): 173–195.

Vickers, Brian. *Shakespeare, Co-Author: A Historical Study of Five Collaborative Plays*. Oxford: Oxford University Press, 2002.

Wald, Christina. "'But of Course the Stage Has Certain Limits'? The Adaptation of Ovid's *Metamorphoses* in Shakespeare's Plays." *Anglia* 127.3 (2010): 425–458.

Walen, Denise A. "Unpinning Desdemona." *Shakespeare Quarterly* 58.4 (2007): 487–508.

Waller, Gary. *English Poetry of the Sixteenth Century*. 2nd ed. London and New York: Longman, 1993.

Weis, René. Introduction to *Romeo and Juliet*, by William Shakespeare, edited by René Weis, 1–116. The Arden Shakespeare Third Series. London: Arden Shakespeare, 2012.

Wells, Robin Headlam. "Neo-Petrarchan Kitsch in *Romeo and Juliet*." *Modern Language Review* 93.4 (1998): 913–933.

Wells, Stanley. *Shakespeare, Sex, and Love*. Oxford: Oxford University Press, 2010.

———. "The Integration of Violent Action in *Titus Andronicus*." In *Shakespearean Continuities. Essay in Honour of E. A. J. Honigmann*, edited by John Batchelor, Tom Cain, and Claire Lamont, 206–220. Basingstoke and London: Macmillan, 1997.

Wells, Stanley, and Gary Taylor. *William Shakespeare: A Textual Companion*. Oxford: Clarendon, 1987.

West, Grace Starry. "Going by the Book: Classical Allusions in Shakespeare's *Titus Andronicus*." *Studies in Philology* 79.1 (1982): 62–77.

Wheeler, Roxann. *The Complexion of Race: Categories of Difference in Eighteenth-Century British Culture*. Philadelphia: University of Pennsylvania Press, 2000.

Wilcher, Robert. "Dying for Love: The Tragicomedy of Shakespeare's Cleopatra." In *Eroticism and Death in Theatre and Performance*, edited by Karoline Gritzner, 28–45. Hatfield: University of Hertfordshire Press, 2010.

Wilders, John. Introduction to *Antony and Cleopatra*, by William Shakespeare, edited by John Wilders, 1–84. The Arden Shakespeare Third Series. London: Arden Shakespeare, 1995.

Williams, Carolyn D. "'Silence, Like a Lucrece knife': Shakespeare and the Meaning of Rape." *The Yearbook of English Studies* 23 (1993): 93–110.

Williams, Simon. "Taking Macbeth Out of Himself: Davenant, Garrick, Schiller and Verdi." In *Shakespeare Survey 57: Macbeth and Its Afterlife*, edited by Peter Holland, 54–68. Cambridge: Cambridge University Press, 2004.

Williamson, Marilyn L. "Romeo and Death." *Shakespeare Studies* 14 (1981): 129–137.

Wymer, Rowland. *Suicide and Despair in the Jacobean Drama*. Brighton: Harvester, 1986.

Index